Voices and Visions

Voices and Visions

The Words and Works of Mercè Rodoreda

Edited by
Kathleen McNerney

Selinsgrove: Susquehanna University Press
London: Associated University Presses

Associated University Presses
440 Forsgate Drive
Cranbury, NJ 08512

Associated University Presses
16 Barter Street
London WC1A 2AH, England

Associated University Presses
P.O. Box 338, Port Credit
Mississauga, Ontario
Canada L5G 4L8

The paper used in this publication meets the requirements of the American National Standard for Permanence of Paper for Printed Library Materials Z39.48-1984.

Library of Congress Cataloging-in-Publication Data

Voices and visions : the words and works of Mercè Rodoreda / edited by Kathleen McNerney.
p. cm.
Includes bibliographical references and index.
ISBN 1-57591-018-7 (alk. paper)
1. Rodoreda, Mercè, 1908– —Criticism and interpretation.
I. McNerney, Kathleen.
PC3941.R57Z93 1999
849′.9352—dc21 98-30642
CIP

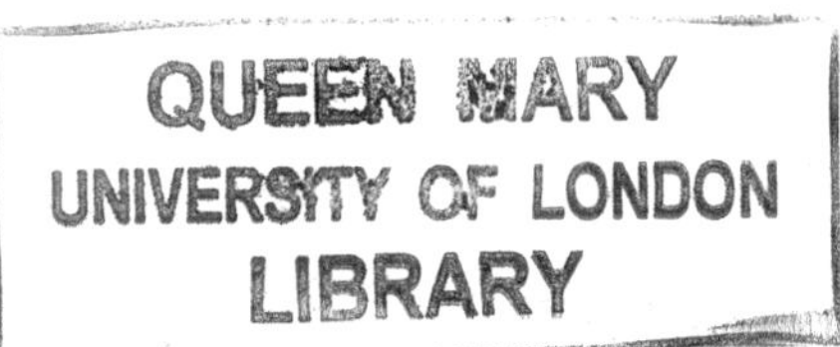

PRINTED IN THE UNITED STATES OF AMERICA

Contents

Voices and Visions

Introduction

Kathleen McNerney

On a number of occasions, Mercè Rodoreda spoke and wrote about her own work. In interviews, letters, and prologues, sometimes with doses of whimsy and fantasy, she was often willing to discuss certain aspects of her fiction; she mentioned her favorite authors and speculated about who might have influenced her writing. She called herself *"una bèstia literària"* (a literary beast),[1] and in fact, despite her limited formal education, she was extremely well read.

As I read and edited the essays that make up this volume, I kept going back to Rodoreda's own words about her literary production. I had long pondered translating some of her comments, particularly the well-known prologue to *Mirall trencat* [Broken mirror], into English. But since the essays included here cover many other works and other aspects of her literary corpus, I decided to use excerpts from various sources that give Rodoreda's words a context within this group of studies. With two caveats, then, I have incorporated many quotations from Rodoreda into this introduction: first, writers are generally not considered to be the most judicious critics of their own work, and second, Rodoreda is complex and at times full of contradictions.

There may be no answer to the question of why writers write, but Rodoreda did have a few ideas on the subject. In 1973, she told Montserrat Roig:

> Escriure em serveix de sedant, d'exitant, és angoixós, és . . . tot a la vegada. Escriure em cansa molt. Ho necessito, perquè una cosa o altra s'ha de fer a la vida. Però el que a mi m'agrada és embaladir-me davant els núvols, o llegir novel.les policíaques, o anar al cinema a veure 'westerns,' que són les pel.licules que més m'agraden.

> [writing is like a sedative to me, it's a stimulant, it produces anxiety, it's . . . everything at once. Writing makes me very tired. I need it, after all one has to do something in life. But what I really

> like is to let the clouds enchant me, or read detective novels, or go to the movies and see a western, that's my favorite kind.][2]

At first glance it seems like a frivolous answer, and yet, as on so many occasions, her words are deceptively simple. While suggesting that she writes in order to escape from boredom, she lets us know that writing is hard work. It's a message she repeats many times, and in fact she was a notoriously careful writer, correcting and revising endlessly. She didn't discount inspiration, and she made a distinction between those chapters that seem to write themselves and those that are a terrible struggle. Rodoreda often began a story or a chapter with a visual image, one of many things she has in common with Gabriel García Márquez,[3] and in her case it is particularly interesting that she was also a painter. The example she gives of this phenomenon is from *Mirall trencat;* the chapter called "Eladi Farriols, de cos present" [Eladi Farriols, lying in wake][4] was the first chapter of the novel originally, before characters had names and plots were developed. But those are the exceptional cases, and she attributes to Valéry the more realistic belief that "la inspiració ve escrivint . . . escrivint o pensant en la cosa que has d'escriure et vas exaltant, i és possible que la inspiració vingui escrivint." (Oller/Arnau, 6); [Inspiration comes as you write . . . writing or thinking about what you're going to write exalts you, and maybe inspiration comes from writing.]

More reflective and introspective when writing a prologue than when giving an interview, she has a somewhat different answer to the unasked question in *Mirall trencat:*

> Escric perquè m'agrada d'escriure. Si no semblés exagerat diria que escric per agradar-me a mi. Si de retop el que escric agrada als altres, millor. Potser és més profund. Potser escric per afirmar-me. Per sentir que sóc . . . I acabo. He parlat de mi i de coses essencials en la meva vida, amb una certa manca de mesura. I la desmesura sempre m'ha fet molta por. (Pròleg, 45)

> I write because I like to write. If it didn't seem exaggerated, I'd say that I write to like myself. If, on top of that, other people like what I write, all the better. Maybe it's deeper. Maybe I write to affirm myself. To feel that I exist . . . That's all. I've spoken about myself and about essential things in my life with a certain lack of moderation. And that has always scared me a lot.]

While these less than candid words cannot answer the unanswerable question either, they do serve as an interesting example of the "escriptura parlada" (spoken writing) Carme Arnau and others have seen in the first-person narration of *La plaça del Diamant* (translated as *The Time of the Doves*).[5] She doesn't mind exaggerating as long as she tells you she's exaggerating; nor does she mind a lack of moderation as long as she tells you that she's being immoderate. Moreover, no one should believe a writer who claims not to care much about pleasing the reader; in Rodoreda's case there is plenty of documentation about her reactions to being passed over for one prize after another.[6] But perhaps the most meaningful quotation on this subject was suggested to her when, as a young writer, she told the director of the periodical *La Rambla* that she wanted to learn how to write through journalism. He said, and she quoted him more than once: "Primer, visqui; després escrigui." (Roig, 170) [Live first, then write.]

Prologue to a Prologue: *Mirall trencat*

Since most of Mercè Rodoreda's writing is in the form of novels, and since she addresses a number of intriguing aspects of her novelistic production at the beginning of this poetic prologue, I believe it worthwhile to first quote, then translate, and finally offer some analysis of her words:

> Una novel.la es fa amb una gran quantitat d'intuïcions, amb una certa quantitat d'imponderables, amb agonies i amb resurreccions de l'ànima, amb exaltacions, amb desenganys, amb reserves de memòria involuntària . . . tota una alquímia. Si jo no he sentit mai cap emoció davant d'una posta de sol, com puc descriure, o, millor dit, suggerir la màgia d'una posta de sol? Els carrers han estat sempre per a mi motiu d'inspiració, com algun tros d'una bona pel.lícula, com un parc en tot l'esclat de la primavera o gebrat i esquelètic a l'hivern, com la bona música sentida en el moment precís, com la cara de certes persones absolutament desconegudes que tot d'una creues, que t'atreuen i que no veuràs mai més. Per això et deixen una recança difícil d'explicar amb paraules. Una mà, en una pintura, et pot donar tot un personatge. Una mirada et pot impressionar més que no pas la bellesa d'uns ulls. Un somriure enigmàtic que de vegades pot ser només la contracció d'uns determinats nervis facials, et roba el cor i necessites fer-lo perdurar. Penses: si pogués descriure aquesta mica de moviment gairebé

imperceptible que canvia tota una expressió . . . Stendhal deia: els detalls és el que hi ha de més important en una novel.la. I Txekhov: s'ha d'intentar l'impossible per dir les coses com no les ha dites mai ningú. Fer una novel.la és difícil. L'estructura, els personatges, l'escenari . . . aquest treball de tria és exaltant perquè t'obliga a vèncer dificultats. Hi ha novel.les que se t'imposen. D'altres les has d'anar traient d'un pou sense fons. Una novel.la són paraules. Voldria fer veure els espasmes lentíssims d'un brot quan surt de la branca, la violència amb què una planta expulsa la llavor, la immobilitat salvatge dels cavalls de Paolo Ucello, l'extrema expressivitat dels somriures andrògins de les Verges de Leonardo da Vinci, o el mirar provocatiu, el mirar més provocatiu del món, d'una dama de Cranach, sense celles, sense pestanyes, embarretada, emplomallada d'estruç, amb els pits fora del gipó. No he arribat a tant. Escriure bé costa. Per escriure bé entenc dir amb la màxima simplicitat les coses essencials. No s'aconsegueix sempre. Donar relleu a cada paraula; les més anodines poden brillar encegadores si les col.loques en el lloc adequat. Quan em surt una frase amb un gir diferent, tinc una petita sensació de victòria. Tota la gràcia de l'escriure radica a encertar el mitjà d'expressió, l'estil. Hi ha escriptors que el troben de seguida, d'altres triguen molt, d'altres no el troben mai. (Pròleg, 13–15)

[A novel is made of a great quantity of intuitions, a certain quantity of imponderables, of agonies and resurrections of the spirit, of exaltations, disappointments, reserves of involuntary memory . . . an entire alchemy. If I'd never felt moved by a sunset, how could I describe, or rather suggest, the magic of a sunset? The streets have always inspired me, like a scene from a good film, like a park in a burst of springtime or frosty and skeletal in winter, like good music heard at a certain moment, like the faces of some completely unknown people whose path you cross, who attract you and you never see again. That's why they leave in you a kind of regret difficult to explain in words. A hand, in a painting, can give you a whole character. A glance can impress you more than the beauty of a pair of eyes. An enigmatic smile that sometimes can just be the contraction of certain facial nerves can steal your heart and you need to make it last. You think: if I could describe that little bit of a movement, almost imperceptible, that changes a whole expression . . . Stendhal said: details are the most important thing in a novel. And Chekhov: you have to attempt the impossible to say things in a way that no one has said them before. It's difficult to make a novel. The structure, the characters, the settng . . . the task of choosing is exalting because it obliges you to overcome difficulties. There are novels that impose themselves on you. Others you have to pull out of a bottomless well. A novel is words. I'd like to show the very slow spasms of a shoot as it emerges from a branch, the violence with which a plant expels its seed, the savage immobility of Paolo Ucello's horses, the extreme expressivity of the androgynous smiles of Leonardo da Vinci's Virgins, the provocative gaze, the most provocative gaze in the world, of one of Cranach's ladies, without eyebrows or eyelashes, wearing a beret, with ostrich feathers, with her breasts outside of her bodice. I haven't gotten that far. It's difficult to write well. By writing well, I mean saying essential things with the maximum simplicity. It's not always possible. To highlight each word; even the most anodyne can shine brilliantly if you put them in the right place. When a sentence comes out with a different twist, I feel a little victorious. Writing depends on choosing the right means of expression, the style. Some writers find it right away, others take a long time, some never find it.]

In the first sentence, Rodoreda likens writing to alchemy. The metaphor is particularly apt, suggesting a combination of magic and dedication, and it's one she comes back to on various occasions. In the conclusion of this same prologue, she describes her efforts to flee from all that is noxious to her soul while cultivating an admiration for all that is uplifting:

> pel quiet poder de les flors que em procuren moments inefables, per la lenta paciència de les pedres precioses, màxima puresa de la terra, pels grans abismes d'aquest cel tan proper i tan llunyà alhora, on brillen i tremolen totes les constel.lacions. (Pròleg, 44)
>
> [for the quiet power of flowers that bring me ineffable moments, for the slow patience of precious stones, the greatest purity of the earth, for the great abysses of this sky, at once so near and so far, where all the constellations shine and tremble.]

Perhaps Rodoreda's interest in the esoteric will allow us to stretch this lyrical description a bit further to suggest that writing represents her search for the philosopher's stone. Or, as she describes the work of other writers she greatly admires: "Homes de gran categoria . . . que van picar pedra a la pedrera de l'idioma i van descobrir-hi vetes d'or" [Men of the highest category . . . who chiseled at the quarry of the language and there uncovered veins of gold]; perhaps she, too, with great dedication, has succeeded in turning stone into gold.[7]

In naming the setting sun as an inspiration, Rodoreda corrects herself: she wants to suggest it, not to describe it. Since she lets this correction stand, we must assume it's for effect, or emphasis, and indeed later in the prologue she discusses how the feelings of a character must be created from within. Colometa, in *La plaça del Diamant,* has to show she's tired of the doves. The author can't just say it, not even Colometa can say it just so. What the author has to do is show, find a manner of expression for Colometa's desperation. Thus, Rodoreda quotes from her own novel: "I va ser aquell dia que vaig dir-me que s'havia acabat . . . tot a passeig!" (Pròleg, 19) [And that was the day I told myself it was over . . . out, everything out!] Colometa's interior monologue then lists a long, rhythmic string of body parts of the doves and household items associated with the doves, punctuating word clusters with the repeated expression "¡tot a passeig!" Rodoreda goes on to explain that the point is to make the language seem simple, and there's nothing simple about that: in her own words, "res de tan alambinat . . . res . . . de més rebuscat" (Pròleg, 20) [nothing so distilled, nothing so elaborated] as *La plaça del Diamant.* The fact that some critics have found Colometa to be simple is a measure of Rodoreda's mastery of this technique.

Some of the other sources of inspiration that Rodoreda names also deserve comment. There are at least two examples of the faces of unknown people reflected in *Mirall trencat:* Teresa Goday inherits the eyes, of indefinite color and with a lot of life accumulated behind them, of a lady looking at Lake Leman in Switzerland; an elderly woman walking her dog suggests the faithful figure of Armanda. Rodoreda lists several artists and paintings as inspirational too, and her love of films is well known. Her own art work, left behind consciously because it interfered with her writing, underscores the strong visual component of her work, and the compelling image which gives title to *Mirall trencat* could be compared to a Cubist painting.

Music is mentioned only in passing here, but it is also an important aspect of Rodoreda's work. Just as Gabriel García Márquez finds ways to incorporate both classical and folk rhythms into his prose, many of Rodoreda's stories are imbued with music of various kinds. The title "Nocturn" suggests a certain kind of composition; as the man jumps out of bed, the sound that follows is "un arpegi de molles" [an arpeggio of springs]; later on the grotesqueness of the plot is underscored by the singing of the drunk German soldier: "Ich hatt'einen Kameraden, / einen bessern find'st du nit . . . / Eine Kugel kam geflogen, / gilt es mir, oder gilt es dir? . . ." [I had a friend, / a better one can't be found . . . / A cannon ball comes, / will it kill you or me? . . .][8] Other stories incorporate music either thematically, structurally, or rhythmically as well, from the classical cadences of "Record de Caux" [Memory of Caux], "Abans de morir" [Before dying], "El gelat rosa" [Pink ice cream], and "Paràlisi" [Paralysis] to the polkas and mazurkas of "El bany" [The bath] to a trumpet being used as an instrument of torture and finally of murder in "Una fulla de gerani blanc" [A white geranium petal]. In light of this brief listing, Anna Murià's words cannot surprise us: "Cantava sovint, la Mercè, cançons catalanes, castellanes, franceses . . ." [Mercè sang often—Catalan songs, Castilian songs, French songs . . .][9]

Murià, who has unlocked a number of mysteries surrounding Rodoreda's complex character, also helps to clarify the life-literature link in her wartime friend. For if Rodoreda took Chekhov's advice very much to heart—she mentions any number of times how important it is to say things in new ways—she also acted in ways that deliberately flew in the face of conventional behavior. Her biographers demonstrate that her life choices were anything but bourgeois, she wore pants at a time when women just didn't do that, at least in her milieu, and Murià describes as a "pallassada" [clowning] the following example of her sense of humor: "allò que jo li havia vist fer a Roissy de caçar una mosca, tirar-la dins del got de vi i empassar-se-la amb un glop, que era, en el fons, una mofa dels prejudicis i les convencions" (Murià, 10) [what I had seen her do in Roissy, catching a fly, tossing it into her wineglass, and downing it, which was fundamentally a challenge to prejudices and conventions]. Real-life behavior, pursued because of love, comfort, or humor, becomes a very serious element in what Rodoreda calls "good writing" and she supplies us with a number of examples. Perhaps some of the most striking instances are to be found in her use of colorful folk language, in set phrases with a twist, and in iconoclastic images: "passi-ho bé tingui" is an untranslatable and ungrammatical combination of two greetings, "passi-ho bé" [have a good time] and "bon dia tingui" [have a good day]; "abraçats com dues pedres" [in an embrace just like two rocks] is even stranger than "happy as a clam" (or a lark), and of course not conventional at all.[10] And while Carme Arnau's point that her great originality might be linked to her lack of formal education and therefore lack of guiding canons is well taken, it is also clear from Rodoreda's own words and her many corrections that her freshness was due to her very great efforts to "escriure d'una manera diferent" [write in a different way.][11]

In light of Rodoreda's constant striving for newness of expression, it is useful to take into account what she said about some of the writers she admired: she names Virginia Woolf and Katherine Mansfield on more than one occasion; she loved the lyricism she found in Charles Dickens; she was fascinated by James Joyce; and she names a number of her Catalan contemporaries as well. One of the writers she mentions who also finds his way into her novels is Marcel Proust, and not surprisingly the topic is the passage of time. As she explains to Montserrat Roig: "Una novel.la no es pot escriure en una tarda. Es un procés llarg . . . I cal saber donar la sensació del temps, una de les meravelles d'en Proust." (Roig, 170) [A novel isn't writen in an afternoon. It's a long process . . . And you have to know how to give the sensation of time, one of Proust's marvels.] As early as *Aloma* she had begun a chapter (2) with a quotation from Proust; in *Mirall trencat* the abysmal differences between Eladi and Sofia are distilled in the fact that Eladi reads Proust and Sofia doesn't; Eladi continues to read Proust as the old papers and photographs are being burned and memories are replacing reality. And even though the passage of time is basically chronological in *La plaça del Diamant,* its flow is interrupted by flashbacks and flash-forwards, in the manner of those great Latin American storytellers, Gabriel García Márquez and Isabel Allende. At the end of the first chapter, for example, Natàlia projects into the future as she says "I en Quimet, al cap d'anys, encara ho explicava com si fos una cosa que acabés de passar." (*Obres completes* 1, 356) [And years later, Quimet was still telling (the story of the slip) as if it were something that had just happened.] Perhaps the most interesting, and also the most poetic, example occurs in chapter 8 with the minute description of Quimet, based, as Rodoreda herself tells us, on the medieval Catalan rendition of Ovid by Bernat Metge. The details Colometa enumerates were observed over time, not all at once, and at the conclusion of the passage, the narrator jumps to the future to announce the episode of the lost key, related in the following chapter. In the even more minute description of the house Natàlia cleans, she virtually apologizes for the detailed description, adding that she couldn't have noticed so much on the first visit: "D'aquestes coses me'n vaig adonar després. (*OC* 1: 414–15) [It wasn't until later that I became aware of these things.] Towards the end of the novel, in chapter 46, there is an explicit reference to the passage of time:

> I vaig sentir d'una manera forta el pas del temps. No el temps dels núvols i del sol i de la pluja i del pas de les estrelles adornament de la nit, . . . no el que posa les fulles a les branques o el que les arrenca, no el que arrissa i desarrissa i colora les flors, sinó el temps dintre de mi, el temps que no es veu i ens pasta. (*OC* 1: 509–10)

> [And I felt the passage of time very strongly. Not the time of the clouds and the sun and the rain and the passage of the stars adorning the night, . . . not the time that puts leaves on branches or takes them away, not the time that curls and uncurls and colors the flowers, but the time inside me, the time you don't see and it kneads us.]

But perhaps even more important than this lyrical description is the author's technique in making the reader feel the time moving in the novel, the passage of Natàlia's life: in the first thirty chapters of *La plaça del Diamant,* the passage of time is nearly imperceptible, while in the last nineteen it passes almost aggressively. Time is structured very neatly in *Jardí vora el mar* [Garden by the sea], with its contrast between summer, when everyone is there and the house is "alive," and winter, when the old gardener/narrator is on his own. But whether the past is remembered, as Proust would have it, or forgotten, as in the quotation from T. S. Eliot for the last part of *Mirall trencat* ("But time past is a time forgotten. We expect the rise of a new constellation" [*OC* 3: 215]), there is no doubt about Rodoreda's mastery of the technique of "giving the sensation of time."

There has been a tremendous amount of new research and criticism on Rodoreda in the last ten years, with posthumous works of the author still being published. My intention in gathering these essays is to hear new voices re-interpreting the classical works from different perspectives, and to address works that have been studied little or not at all.

If Anna Murià tells us that Rodoreda liked to sing, it is Rodoreda herself who says that she also recited poetry: "Em passava hores per casa, amunt i avall, recitant versos en veu alta." (Ollers/Arnau, 5) [I would spend hours at home, (pacing) up and down, reciting verses out loud.] She mentions in a number of her letters to Murià that she is writing poetry, or, as she puts it, "Sí, faig versos. M'ha agafat la malaltia que se'n diu Pansamansa-Minsapinça, i els consonants vénen sols com un vol d'orenetes, però són unes orenetes que em fan bastant la punyeta." (Murià/Rodoreda, 107) [Yes, I'm writing verses. I've gotten the sickness they call "Pansamansa-Minsapinça," and the consonants come by themselves like a flock of swallows, but they're swallows that give me a hard time.] Nancy Bundy's translations and study of the poems published in *Els marges* in 1984 are the first critical recognition of this aspect of Rodoreda's work since she won prizes in the *Jocs Florals* and the title of *"Mestre en gai saber,"* the first woman to receive the latter honor. Bundy finds that loss is the leitmotif of this poetry, with its variant themes of exile, expulsion, desertion, abandonment, and death. Some of the poems take inspiration from biblical or classical themes; many are informed by nature, especially flowers and plants. Other poetry by Rodoreda has been published recently, and it's possible that still more will be found.

Rodoreda discusses her stories at some length in her letters to Anna Murià, saying on the one hand that she could only write stories, given the difficulties of living in wartime France, but on the other hand that she has found that the short story is a "gran gènere" (Murià/Rodoreda, 90) [a great genre], and she has plans for stories "que faran tremolar Déu" (Murià/Rodoreda, 85) [that will make God tremble]. In her conversation with Roig, she compares stories with novels: "M'agradaria haver escrit una novel.la que tingués el to dels meus millors contes, com 'Una fulla de gerani blanca.' De *La plaça del Diamant,* me n'agraden alguns i sobretot el final, que és tan bo com 'El senyor i la lluna' o 'El riu i la barca.'" (Roig, 173) [I'd like to have written a novel that has the tone of my best stories, like 'A white geranium petal.' I like some of *La plaça del Diamant,* especially the end, which is as good as 'The man and the moon' or 'The river and the boat.'] In her prologue to that novel, however, Rodoreda cites another source for *La plaça del Diamant*—her early story "Tarda al cinema" [Afternoon at the movies], in which the protagonist uses a diary with sparse indirect dialogue, showing the great gulf between her thoughts and the exterior world.

In our collection, Nancy Vosburg, Maryellen Bieder, and Mónica Ayala choose short fiction for their focus. Vosburg finds a common thread of mirroring in five of the early stories published in *Vint-i-dos contes* [Twenty-two stories]: "El mirall" [The mirror], "Tarda al cinema," "Abans de morir," "La sang"

[Blood], and "En el tren" [On the train]. Bieder discusses the invisibility of the female protagonists in two stories from *Semblava de seda* [It seemed like silk]: "Pluja" [Rain], and "Paràlisi." While the pieces in *Viatges i flors* [Journeys and flowers] are prose poems or vignettes rather than stories, they do have a narrative thread, and Ayala finds in them a philosophical system, full of lyricism. Rodoreda clearly enjoyed composing these little fictions, and she tells us the first one practically wrote itself, and the others quickly followed (Oller/Arnau, 5).

Just as most of Rodoreda's production was novelistic, so most of the studies in this collection concentrate on the novels. Three of the essays work with *La plaça del Diamant,* and even though there is already an outstanding body of work on this masterpiece, Michele Anderson, Adela Robles, and Vicente Andreu offer us new perspectives. Anderson connects the structure of the novel with processes in Natàlia's mind as she develops her soul and tells her story, breaking from imposed silences and spaces at the same time. Robles contrasts interior with exterior spaces and finds curious hybrids, the semi-protected outdoor spaces and the invaded indoor spaces. She relates Natàlia's rebellions to the regaining of self through space. Andreu's study is linguistic rather than strictly literary, as he examines the two versions in English of this novel: an early British one, *The Pigeon Girl,* and the American *The Time of the Doves.* Rodoreda remarked that the British translation didn't have much success; perhaps this version was unable to find its appropriate public.[12]

Other Rodoreda novels are the focus of several essays. Lisa Vollendorf looks at the "matriarchal" figures in *Mirall trencat* and sees that Teresa's failed "empire" is a result of her adapting herself to the parameters of the patriarchy instead of establishing her own "regime." Sofia's failure is linked symbolically to her distancing from the fantastic elements that appear toward the end of the novel. Josefina González' paper is ambitious in scope, discussing three novels, and painterly in point of view, taking into account the visual aspect of Rodoreda's work. She explores the absences and silences in *Quanta, quanta guerra . . .* [So much war], and two posthumous novels, *La mort i la primavera* [Death and spring], and *Isabel i Maria* [Isabel and Maria], considering the role of Armand Obiols in the editing of Rodoreda's work. Carles Cortés also studies the ritualistic *La mort i la primavera,* using the work of anthropologist Mircea Eliade as an aid in developing possible interpretations, from

Greek and Egyptian mythology to modern psychological theory.

Two essays in addition to González' are devoted to *Isabel i Maria*. Alejandro Varderi, using the work of Proust as a counterpoint, returns to that garden of childhood and explores the shift to the forbidden that leads inexorably to the expulsion from Eden. Jaume Martí-Olivella concentrates on the mother-daughter matrix and motherhood itself, here portrayed as a patriarchal imposition while emerging as an ultimate binding force.

Finally, perhaps the section that readers will turn to most frequently in this book is the meticulous annotated and indexed bibliography compiled by María Isidra Mencos. In the article preceding the actual listing of works by Rodoreda and criticism about her, Mencos explains the state of the entire body of work on Mercè Rodoreda, describing by theme the kind of studies that have been done, and indexing articles according to which works by Rodoreda have been addressed. A more complete version of this tremendously useful work has recently been awarded a prize by the Fundació Mercè Rodoreda in Barcelona, and is sure to be a great help to those who want to know at a glance the current state of Rodoredan studies.

In conclusion, I would like to point out that in spite of the proliferation of criticism on Rodoreda in recent years, there still remain many avenues of exploration for the curious or intrigued critic, particularly in her dramatic work and poetry and certain aspects of her narrative, and perhaps most especially in finding links among them. It is my hope that the articles herein will inspire further study and a deeper appreciation of this fascinating, complex, and prolific writer.

I would like to thank Laia Miret and Carles Cortés for their help in locating certain items on Rodoreda; West Virginia University for letting me have a sabbatical year to work on the project; Mercedes Ugarte for a splendid place to work while gazing at the Mediterranean; Patsy Boyer and Nancy Bundy for a careful reading of some of the essays; and especially Michael Ugarte, for so many things.

NOTES

1. Dolors Oller and Carme Arnau, "L'entrevista que mai no va sortir," *La vanguardia* (Barcelona), 2 July 1991, 4–5. This interview also appeared in *Serra d'Or* 253 (1986): 19–21. Translations are mine.

2. Montserrat Roig, "L'alè poètic de Mercè Rodoreda," *Retrats paral.lels* (Montserrat: l'Abadia, 1976), 2: 168.

3. García Márquez' praise for Rodoreda has been widely quoted. See Carme Arnau's biography *Mercè Rodoreda* (Barcelona: Edicions 62, 1992), 141–42; and Randolph D. Pope's "Mercè Rodoreda's Subtle Greatness," in Joan L. Brown, ed., *Women Writers of Contemporary Spain: Exiles in the Homeland,* (Newark: University of Delaware Press, 1991): 133–34.

4. Mercè Rodoreda, "Pròleg" [prologue] to *Mirall trencat* (Barcelona: Club, 1974): 17.

5. Carme Arnau, "L'escriptura parlada," in *Introducció a la narrativa de Mercè Rodoreda: El mite de la infantesa* (Barcelona: Edicions 62, 1979), 118–21.

6. Montserrat Casals i Couturier, *Mercè Rodoreda: Contra la vida, la literatura* (Barcelona: Edicions 62, 1991). See especially "Tercera part: París-Ginebra 1953–1978," 177–321.

7. Rodoreda, "Pròleg" [prologue] to *Quanta, quanta guerra . . .* (Barcelona: Club, 1980), 24.

8. Rodoreda, "Nocturn," in "Vint-i-dos contes," *Obres completes* (Barcelona: Edicions 62, 1976), 1: 303.

9. Anna Murià, "Mercè Rodoreda viva," in Rodoreda, *Cartes a l'Anna Murià 1939–1956* (Barcelona: l'Eixample, 1991): 36.

10. Montserrat Casals i Couturier, "Conceptes, imatges, dites i frases de collita Rodorediana" in Rodoreda, *El torrent de les flors* (Valencia: Eliseu Climent, 1993), 360. The prologue to this collection of Rodoreda's dramatic work (7–40) by Casals, who also edited the plays, is the most complete and comprehensive of the few studies of Rodoreda's theater.

11. From a letter to her editor, Joan Sales, dated 10 July 1961, quoted by Casals, "Pròleg" to *Torrent,* 89.

12. Sempronio [pseud.], "Cuatro cuartillas: mis mujeres," *Tele/expres* (Barcelona) 10 October 1970, 6.

"L'aventura difícil d'ésser humans": The Problem of Loss in Rodoreda's Poetry

NANCY L. BUNDY

MERCÈ RODOREDA'S NOVELS AND SHORT STORIES HAVE BEEN THE subject of much recent scholarship, but less attention has been given to her poetry, a small but substantial corpus published in the 1940s and 1950s[1] and most likely written after 1939,[2] when she began a forty-year exile from her native Catalonia at the end of the Spanish Civil War. Several critics have mentioned her poetry in passing, but there has not been a close examination of it,[3] despite the fact that she was called a *mestre en gai saber* [master in the poetic art], that her peers recognized her as a poet, and that she won such awards for her poetry as the Jocs Florals and the Premi Maragall.[4]

Rodoreda's poetry shares with her fiction the exilic themes of expulsion, desertion or abandonment, death and dying, time and memory, and existential unrest, all of which have to do with loss, the leitmotif of her poetic work. As Octavio Paz remarks in *The Labyrinth of Solitude,* loss begins when we are expelled from the womb:

> We sense the change as separation and loss, as abandonment, as a fall into a strange or hostile atmosphere. Later this primitive sense of loss becomes a feeling of solitude, and still later it becomes awareness: we are condemned to live alone, but also to transcend our solitude, to re-establish the bonds that united us with life in a paradisiac past.[5]

Birth and subsequent forms of exile are indeed traumatic, but Paz suggests that they can lead to progress through introspection and reconnection. Rodoreda's poetry of loss, expressive of both literal and figurative exile, reflects Paz's exhortation to recollect and move on. Her poems are nostalgic, plaintive, and often lugubrious, yet they contain a dynamism in both content and expression that shows what Rodoreda means by the "aventura difícil d'ésser humans" (63) [difficult adventure of being human,]: while life presents complications, there is value in the challenge that urges us on.

The writer's biography sheds considerable light on her attention to loss. Although she eventually achieved literary recognition and personal contentment, Rodoreda was constantly aware of what Michael Ugarte describes in his study on exile, *Shifting Ground,* as a "here . . . [that] persistently recalls the space of a there, and vice versa,"[6] for she spent most of her life in either psychological or geographical limbo. She led a pleasant but sequestered childhood in her Barcelona house and garden, where she developed a fascination for nature as well as a love for storytelling, both evident later in her writing. Rodoreda's bliss was not unalloyed, though, for she was kept out of school early, and she felt remote first from other children and later from the literati she encountered. At age twenty, she married an older uncle, but she had little contact with him or with the son of that union. Exiled in France and then in Switzerland, she lived with writer Armand Obiols until his death. The long-term liaison was complicated by the fact that he remained in contact with his wife and daughter and that Rodoreda received occasional criticism in her role as the "other woman." When she returned to Catalonia for good after nearly four decades, she continued to feel displaced in an old but unfamiliar environment. Despite all these transitions and deprivations, Rodoreda managed to find challenge and redemption from loss in her writing: *"Potser escric per afirmar-me. Per sentir que sóc."* [Perhaps I write to affirm myself. To feel that I exist.][7] Her poetic "difficult adventure" then seems to have a decidedly autobiographical turn.

All but one of Rodoreda's twenty-five poems are sonnets, a form that traditionally centers on the torments of love and loss, and frames in her poetry what she describes as the *"mots que solquen aquesta soledat"* (57) [words that might penetrate this solitude]. The poetry is divided into four sections, "Sonets" [Sonnets], "Món d'Ulisses" [Ulysses' World], "Albes i Nits" [Dawns and Nights], and "Tres Sonets i una Cançó" [Three Sonnets and a Song]. The "difficult adventure" traced throughout transpires against a backdrop of sea, earth, sky, flora and fauna, natural settings enhanced by Rodoreda's painterly skill with colors, sensations, and symbols. More than a third of the work is based on Homer's *Odyssey,* the story of Ulysses' voyage after the fall of Troy, and one major sonnet, "Adam a Eva"

[Adam to Eve], rests on the biblical account of the couple's flight from paradise. These sonnets on familiar themes, along with the anguished *in utero* poem that follows, and others, are proof of the exile created and/or intensified by loss.

One form of loss is expulsion, an involuntary act of physical or spiritual exile that is as old as Adam and Eve's rejection from the Garden of Eden and as new as one's own banishment from the womb. In the twelfth poem of "Sonnets," Rodoreda depicts the original, universal exile from the mother's warm, secure body, the "flonja cavorca sense claror de dia" (61) [the soft cavern without the light of day]. The fetus makes a dramatic plea before the "primer plor, protegit de dolors" (61) [first tear, protected from pain]:

> deu-me l'alè de viure en les cimes gebrades
> d'aquesta gran tristesa, oblidant els esculls
> de la meva partida vers una nit sens fi . . . (61)
>
> [give me the spirit to live on the frosty peaks
> of this great sadness, forgetting the reefs
> of my departure toward an endless night . . .]

toward what she calls in another sonnet the "vall d'ombres" (57) [valley of shadows]. These lines show Rodoreda's characteristic dynamism in their implied movement out of the womb into the light, then back into darkness, as well as in the ascendant and descendant motif of peaks and reefs as a reflection of the same movement. The reef image itself is one example of Rodoreda's symbolic use of the sea; the rough shoals represent the obstacles along the way from birth to death. The chiaroscuro effect of the entire sonnet, seen in the blackness of the womb, the harsh light of day and its "llampec dels colors" (61) [flash of colors], and the "nit sens fi" (61) [endless night], stresses the nebulous state of the exile caught between here and there, between remembering and adjusting. With this backdrop, the reluctant voyager makes a final appeal against future loss:

> Si em feu, Senyor, només per a morir,
> compadiu-vos d'un cor feixuc d'amor i d'odi,
> buideu-me de l'angoixa en els dies distants,
> i, si això no pot ésser, deixeu que plegat rodi,
> temps y més temps perdut in tebis llimbs flotants . . . (61)

[If you have me born, Lord, just to die,
have compassion for a heart heavy with love and hate,
empty me of anguish in distant days,
and, if that cannot be, let me roll, curled up,
forever and ever lost in warm, floating limbos . . .]

The ninth poem of "Sonnets" takes the prenatal innocence of the previous sonnet to a stage of the life journey enhanced and complicated by adult love. It treats Adam and Eve's banishment from Eden and recalls Rodoreda's relationship with Obiols as well as her longing for her childhood garden, the primary symbol in her work for a paradise lost. Adam implores his partner to flee with him: "Segueix-me, dona meva, pell de rosa estremida, / oh tu que resplendeixes com el primer mati" (59) [Follow me, my lady, with skin of trembling rose, / oh you who shine like the first morning], as the poet again appeals to the senses. The rose, symbolizing love and perfection, connotes Adam's desire for Eve and for the paradise the two have forfeited, and the morning light indicates her beauty and the glory of their old domain. He looks beyond expulsion, trusting that their love will survive the transition: "si el paradís ens llença, l'aspra terra és oferta / al vagareig del nostres entremesclats afanys" (59) [if paradise casts us out, the harsh earth offers itself / for the wandering of our intermingled desires], but the knowledge of the tree of good and evil has made him mindful of loss as well as love:

Ara, incerta i feble, la mort et fa més meva,
la mort que acoloreix com un astre secret
la soma correntia dels nostres dies, Eva! (59)

[Now, uncertain and feeble, death makes you more mine,
death that colors like a secret star
the brief passing of our days, Eve!]

Loss through the death of a loved one is treated with great poignancy in this sonnet. Adam and Eve's dispossession of their earthly paradise is an enormous event in and of itself, so "death" here signifies a spiritual rather than a physical demise. Nonetheless, their exclusion from the Garden puts them in a new and vulnerable state, and their metaphorical brush with death reminds Adam of the brevity of life, the "soma correntia dels nostres dies." Rodoreda expresses in these ninth and twelfth sonnets that love, maternal, romantic, or otherwise, may ease the pain of loss, but the loneliness of exile endures from birth to death.

Being expelled from one's niche, whether it is the womb, the Garden of Eden, or a place or person, is a distressing experience. Being deserted or abandoned is another wrenching kind of loss, as the first and second poems of "Sonnets" reveal. Although based on the *Odyssey,* these sonnets center not on the wanderer himself, but rather on the emotional havoc he has wreaked on two women. Ulysses is a literal exile, wending his long, slow way home to Ithaca; Calypso and Nausica are figurative exiles, suffering from his absence. "Plany de Calipso" [Calypso's Lament] derives from the story of the nymph who loved Ulysses and detained him on her island for ten years. In this sonnet, she imagines the homeland of her departed lover: "Jo veig la teva terra nua i roent, deserta, / vora la mar en fúria sota un penya-segat" (55) [I see your bare and buring earth, deserted, / by the raging sea beneath a steep cliff]. These harsh images of desert and sea continue the here/there dynamic of the earlier poems while reflecting Calypso's desolation and anger at being left behind. She voices her sorrow at being just one more part of transient nature:

> Jo sóc allò que es deixa, allò que fuig i passa:
> l'oreig entre les fulles, l'estel que ha desistit,
> el doll que riu y plora i aquella tendra massa
> dels xuclamels que aturen un instant mès la nit. (55)
>
> [I am what is left, what flees and passes:
> the breeze among the leaves, the star that has dimmed,
> the torrent that laughs and cries and that tender mass
> of honeysuckle that holds off the night a moment more.]

The wind, star, water, and flower symbolize Calypso's ephemeral pleasures with Ulysses, but her jeremiad is complaint as well as plaint. The verses beginning with "your bare and burning earth" and "I am what is left" are certainly mournful, but they also expose her wrath at being deserted, manifested in the violent image of the "raging sea beneath a steep cliff." Her seductive powers, "la meva carn, corba i mel exaltada" (55) [my flesh, curve and exalted honey], do not detain Ulysses from the sea, and she seeks some sort of reaction, passive or aggressive, to the rejection: "Ara voldria ésser lleó que juga i mata / o l'olivera immòbil en son furor retort" (55) [Now I would like to be a lion that plays and kills / or the olive tree immobile in its twisted wrath]. Instead, the loss of Ulysses rankles within her like an "escorpí escarlata" (55) [scarlet scorpion], a passionate symbol for both sex and death.

The second poem of "Sonnets" treats the same type of loss as the first, although the present sonnet is more melancholic than acerbic. Nausica meets Ulysses only briefly in her father's court, but she misses what was never hers when he sets out to sea again. In a moving scene reminiscent of Homer's Ulysses grieving along the shore for his native land,[8] Rodoreda portrays the sad young woman by the nocturnal sea, guided by the reflected light of moon and water, "en aquest mar desert com un desert d'argent" (56) [in this deserted sea like a silver desert]. Both the sea and the desert are lonely and vast, and their combined use here heightens the sense of Nausica's yearning and provides another dramatic chiaroscuro portrait. More innocent about the vagaries of love and desire than Calypso, and more helpless than embittered in her figurative exile, Nausica is a "[d]olç animal ferit pres en xarxa d'estrelles" [sweet wounded animal caught in a net of stars], trapped in her youthful illusions. Despite her guilelessness, however, she experiences her loss profoundly, as an "abisme d'enyor com un ocell cansat / dut per l'ona de sal que esborra els últims passos" (56) [abyss of longing like a weary bird / led by the salty wave that erases its last tracks]; she herself cannot pursue Ulysses, but her desire follows him out to sea, casting her into an exile of the soul.

Although Calypso and Nausica display tremendous anguish at abandonment or desertion, their emotions cannot equal those of Penelope, Ulysses' archetypically patient, faithful wife. "Penelope," the first sonnet of "Ulysses' World," combines the acrimony and the longing of the Calypso and Nausica poems and describes the eponymous character's preoccupation with time and distance since Ulysses' going:

> Em compta el temps la marinada amarga,
> la mar amb son abominable crit!
> La mel dintre la gerra s'ha espessit
> i els brots que vas deixar fan ombra llarga. (62)
>
> [The bitter sea breeze counts the time for me,
> the sea with its abominable cry!
> The honey in the jar has thickened
> and the buds that you left cast a long shadow.]

As in the earlier sonnets, the sea here symbolizes separation and solitude. Nature also provides the subtle eroticism of "mels" and "brots," which hint at both passion and the presence of their son Telemachus. Throughout the long wait, Penelope does and undoes a shroud in progress: "faig i desfaig l'absurda teranyina, / aranya al.lucinada del no-res" (62) [I ravel and unravel the absurd web, / illusory spider of nonbeing]. As she works to fill her emptiness, she becomes absorbed in thoughts of the past and present:

> Un deix d'amor arran de llavi puja
> i mor com una llàgrima de pluja
> al viu del darrer pètal que ha malmès. (62)
>
> [An aftertaste of love rises to my lips
> and dies like a drop of rain
> on the edge of the last ruined petal.]

The tender images of "rain" and "petal" for "tear" and "mouth" are only bittersweet, for, as in "Calypso's Lament," there is rancor mixed with regret. Penelope's meaningless activity reminds her that Ulysses' departure has hurt both husband and wife.

As Rodoreda's biography would suggest, expulsion and desertion or abandonment dominate in her poetry, but death, time and memory, and existential unrest, also play major roles. Death is a concern of the literal exile who suffers a metaphorical death and of the figurative exile who must also face an end to things. The fourth poem of "Sonnets" centers on the literal loss of a cherished companion to death and on the figurative loss of words to describe the tragedy. The first lines describe the utter loneliness and helplessness of the survivor: "I ara tu, només tu, l'àrdua nit i la terra, / i els mots, els mots que solquen aquesta soledat" (57) [And now you, only you, the arduous night and the land, / and the words, the words that might penetrate this solitude]. Rodoreda then portrays with natural images the chilling gloom of grief: "El mar és fet de plors, el món dels morts respira / en cada negra fulla i en cada fred estel" (57) [The sea is made of tears, the world of the dead breathes / in each black leaf and in each cold star]. The mourner deplores the loss of the future as well as the past: ". . . sense demà . . . / haurem d'oblidar el sol, tot el que és or i esclat" (57) [. . . without tomorrow . . . / we will have to forget the sun, all that is gold and bright]. The sonnet ends with words especially poignant coming from a writer:

> Portaré el que fou teu en la teva vall d'ombres
> i viurem sempre més quallats pel passat
> dintre el bosc delirant dels signes i dels nombres. (57)
>
> [I will take what was yours into your valley of shadows
> and we will live evermore corrupted by the past
> within the maddening forest of signs and of names.]

The first line echoes the traditionally consoling words of Psalm 23, but the following two convey only confusion, dejection, and frustration. Comforting recollections of a former life are clouded by names of things which are elusive to someone neither here nor there, lost to two worlds, as is the literal or figurative exile.

"Noia morta" [Dead Girl], the third poem of the fourth section, "Three Sonnets and a Song," has an unnamed persona, perhaps to stress the universality of the experience of loss through death. The sonnet is set in the underworld, a frequent locale in Rodoreda's verse, particularly for *Odyssey*-based poems such as this one.

With the common metaphor of water as life, the girl compares her earlier existence to a placidly flowing stream, a "cinta d'aigua que travessa / l'obaga verda sospirant tot just" (69) [ribbon of water that crosses / the shady green scarcely sighing]. She misses the dynamic life in which she searched for something beyond earth and yet clung to it "sempre passant i sempre romanent / com si fos ala i fos arrel alhora" (69) [always going and always staying / as if it were wing and root at the same time]. In a stark image of the final exile, Rodoreda shows that death surprises even the young:

> . . . l'hivern, el magre rapissaire
> d'allò que es mou, amb argelagues d'aire,
> tort de fumeres agres cap al cel . . . (69)
>
> [. . . the winter, the thin predator
> of that which is moving with gorses of air,
> twisted with bitter clouds of smoke toward the sky . . .]

Winter is a harbinger of death, a raptor in a sinister landscape of thick air and acrid fumes that recalls the darkness and chaos of the underworld. Frozen in space and time, the girl declares that "la mort va deturar-me amb una unglada, / ai l'adormida soledat del gel!" (68) [death stopped me with a claw, / oh the sleepy solitude of ice!], and she becomes irretrievably lost.

A preoccupation with time and memory is another concomitant of loss, as the first sonnet of "Dawns and Nights" illustrates. In a poem of longing for what now exists only in memory, a lonely survivor imagines her dead lover in a setting as eerily silent and empty as her own:

> En quin ombrívol paradís m'esperes
> d'aigües planyents i d'arbres sense vent,
> engelebrit del teu desistiment . . . ? (65)
>
> [In what somber paradise do you await me
> with wailing waters and windless trees,
> made cold by your desisting . . . ?]

Her feelings of sorrow are compounded by the realization of what the other has lost, as well. Again, as in the "And now you" sonnet, there is a comment on the insufficiency of language to express loss: "Enmig de tantes coses passatgeres, / tu sol passaves inefablement!" (65) [Among so many fleeting things, / you alone passed ineffably!"]. The hindsight that loss affords also reveals the difficulties of communication between lovers who are at once unitary and separate: "Sols vaig comprendre el teu llenguatge ardent / quan ja amb les dures albes no vingueres" (65) [I understood your ardent language / only when you came with the cruel dawns no more]. Besides her wistfulness, the survivor feels the passion that does not end abruptly at a partner's disappearance. Driven by the night, she feels the uprooting of the "eura vermella de la [seva] sang" (65) [red ivy of (her) blood]. The green from the garden signifies renewal, the red from the body, passion; together, the colors symbolize the hopeful life that may spring from yet another "difficult adventure."

Loss may lead to existential unrest, to a questioning of our own raison d'être. Without apparent or justifiable reason, we are ejected from the womb, expelled from an earthly paradise, separated from a loved one, deprived of a sense of time or place, and we feel insignificant. "Elpenor," the third sonnet of "Ulysses' World," treats this idea of the "lleu sospir que sóc" (60) [light sigh that I am], the futility of human effort. The poem begins with the young sailor's bacchanalian hymn: "De l'odre fins a la resseca gorja / feres, oh vi, tants de camins vermells!" (63) [From the wineskin to the parched throat / you made, oh wine, so many red paths!]. In his inebriation, he makes a mortal leap from a rooftop and finds that death offers no similar chance for celebration: "Ara, si em moc, no sento mon trepig, / car ombra sóc dins la sauleda borda" (63) [Now, if I move, I do not hear my footfall, / for I am a shadow within the empty willow grove], with the tree as a symbol of death. Elpenor questions his being with "Viure? Per què?" (63) [Live? Why?], but his own answer is ambiguous, since "Fregar . . . ribatges impossibles" (63) [To graze . . . impossible shores] describes life's frustrations as well as its call to adventure. The last three lines may give the lie to the second interpretation:

> Desig, renom, virtut, triple quimera!
> Germans de rem, jo enfilo la drecera:
> vindreu amargs, cansats, i d'un a un. (63)
>
> [Desire, renown, virtue, triple chimera!
> Brothers of the oar, I take the shortcut:
> You will come bitter, tired, and one by one.]

As Elpenor cautions from beyond the grave, one's "difficult adventure" in life has an inescapable end that no amount of illusion can allay or dismiss.

Rodoreda imbues her poetry with a sense of loss by offering expulsion, desertion or abandonment, death, time and memory, and existential unrest as unsettling matters for consideration. Through her artistic skill and vast exilic experience, however, she reminds us of the usefulness of memory and courage in surviving our own losses, in feeling "that we are," to paraphrase her own assertion.[9] Reading her poetry is an arduous emotional project, but that very difficulty offers us a chance for lofty adventure.

Notes

This essay is dedicated to the memory of Montserrat Vilarrubla (1945–1995).

I am grateful for Anna Sánchez Rué's kind assistance in the translation of some poems.

1. Mercè Rodoreda, "Obra poètica," *Els Marges* 30 (1984): 55–71. Unless noted otherwise, all page references are to this source.

2. Nancy Vosburg, "Mercè Rodoreda," in Linda Gould Levine, Ellen Engelson Marson, and Gloria Feiman Waldman, ed., *Spanish Women Writers: A Bio-Bibliographical Source Book* (Westport, Conn.: Greenwood Press, 1993), 416.

3. See, for example, Kathleen McNerney and Nancy Vosburg, eds., *Garden Across the Border: Mercè Rodoreda's Fiction* (Selinsgrove, Pa.: Susquehanna University Press, 1993), 12; "The Most Significant Writer in Catalan," in Janet Pérez, *Contemporary Women Writers of Spain* (Boston: G. K. Hall, 1988), 74.

4. Rodoreda, "Obra poètica," 71.

5. Octavio Paz, *The Labyrinth of Solitude. Life and Thought in Mexico,* trans. Helen R. Lane (New York: Grove Press, 1961), 195.

6. Michael Ugarte, *Shifting Ground: Spanish Civil War Exile Literature* (Durham, N.C., and London: Duke University Press, 1989), 22.

7. Mercè Rodoreda, "Pròleg" to *Mirall trencat,* in *Obres completes* (Barcelona: Edicions 62, 1984), 3:32, quoted in Randolph Pope, "Mercé Rodoreda's Subtle Greatness," in *Women Writers of Spain: Exiles in the Homeland,* ed. Joan L. Brown, (Newark: University of Delaware Press, 1991), 131.

8. Homer, *The Odyssey* (Garden City, N.Y.: Doubleday Anchor Books, 1963), 85. "[H]e sat on the rocky shore / and broke his own heart groaning, with eyes wet / scanning the bare horizon of the sea," ll.32–34.

9. See "Ulisses en l'illa de Circe" and the second paragraph of this essay.

Poems by Rodoreda, translated by Nancy L. Bundy

Sonets

1

(Plany de Calipso)

Jo veig la teva terra nua i roent, deserta,
vora la mar en fúria sota un penya-segat,
el teu palau de pedra com una boca oberta
i l'erm on brunz la vespa i on famejà el ramat.

Jo sóc allò que es deixa, allò que fuig i passa:
l'oreig entre les fulles, l'estel que ha desistit,
el doll que riu i plora i aquella tendra massa
dels xuclamels que aturen un instant més la nit.

T'he volgut meu per sempre, cansat de mar i onada,
segur en la meva carn, corba i mel exaltada,
estranger que t'entornes cap a la teva mort.

Ara voldria ésser lleó que juga i mata
o l'olivera inmòbil en son furor retort,
però al pit m'agonitza un escorpí escarlata.

Sonnets

1

(Calypso's Lament)

I see your bare and burning earth, deserted,
by the raging sea below a steep cliff,
your stone palace like an open mouth
and the wasteland where the wasp buzzes and the flock
starves.

I am what is left, what flees and passes:
the breeze among the leaves, the star that has dimmed,
the torrent that laughs and cries and that tender mass
of honeysuckle that holds off the night a moment more.

I have wanted you mine forever, tired of sea and wave,
secure in my flesh, curve and exalted honey,
stranger returning to your own death.

Now I would like to be a lion that plays and kills
or the olive tree immobile in its twisted wrath,
but in my heart there riles a scarlet scorpion.

2

L'espatlla nua et lluu d'un raig de lluna encesa,
un àngel compadit resta prop teu fulgent,
en aquest mar desert com un desert d'argent
només un bleix de vent vetlla per tu, princesa.

El teu nom, com un plany, es perd de mica en mica,
seràs ben sola a dir-lo, cara al mar, dins la nit,
un sospir de ressaca te'l durà repetit,
irresistible i pur com tota tu, Nausica.

Dolç animal ferit pres en xarxa d'estrelles,
verda sang del teu cel, inútils meravelles
per als teus ulls que cerquen l'ombra que els ha deixat,

l'alta aurora cruel et posarà en els braços
un abisme d'enyor com un ocell cansat
dut per l'ona de sal que esborra els últims passos.

2

Your bare shoulder lights up with a flash of fiery moon,
a sympathetic angel stands shining by you,
in this deserted sea like a silver desert
only a gust of wind watches over you, princess.

Your name, like a lament, is lost little by little,
you must say it all alone, facing the sea, at night,
a shuddering sigh roughly repeats it to you,
irresistible and pure as all of you, Nausica.

Sweet wounded animal caught in a net of stars,
green blood of your sky, useless marvels
for your eyes which look for the shadow that has left them,

the high cruel dawn will lay in your arms
an abyss of longing like a weary bird
led by the salty wave that erases its last tracks.

3

Submarina claror, nit breu, esquinç de seda,
genoll fugaç i somnis, neu dura de les dents,
el sol neix desesmat i et taca la mà freda,
l'alba espadada encela els òpals defallents.

Set àngels i set roses i set estrelles blanques
vetllaran, trist amor, el teu son enllaçat,
per retrobar més purs els càndids ulls que tanques
sagnant de tu suscito el dolç fantasma amat.

I quan vindràs als fons de la cova encisada
on l'aigua acerba crema l'arrel més obstinada,
el serpent adormit en el llot del meu cor,

madeixa que embullà l'ungla ardent de la ira,
pel laberint llacós de la innombrable espira
ablamarà els magentes i els verds pigallats d'or.

3

Submarine clarity, brief night, rustling of silk,
fleeting knee and dreams, hard snow of your teeth,
the sun rises dejectedly and touches your cold hand,
the breaking dawn shrouds the dimming opals.

Seven angels and seven roses and seven white stars
will keep watch, sad love, over your muddled sleep,
to meet again the innocent eyes you close, more pure,
bleeding from you I revive your sweet beloved ghost.

And when you come to the bottom of the enchanted cave
where the bitter water burns the most stubborn root,
the serpent asleep in the mire of my heart,

skein tangled by the ardent claw of anger,
through the muddy labyrinth of the unnamable spark
it will inflame the magentas and the greens touched with
gold.

4

I ara tu, només tu, l'àrdua nit i la terra,
i els mots, els mots que solquen aquesta soledat;
sota un torrent de llunes el darrer cel enterra
les flors aponcellades, l'àngel inviolat.

El mar és fet de plors, el món dels morts respira
en cada negra fulla i en cada fred estel,
en els teus ulls d'espectre tremola una guspira
de joventut enterca presa en un llac de fel.

Oh pare que em dugueres per un camí tan tendre,
ara, sense demà, enllà del freu de cendra,
haurem d'oblidar el sol, tot el que és or i esclat.

Portaré el que fou teu en la teva vall d'ombres
i viurem sempre més quallats pel passat
dintre el bosc delirant dels signes i dels nombres.

4

And now you, only you, the arduous night and the land,
and the words, the words that might penetrate this solitude;
beneath a torrent of moons the last sky buries
the unopened flowers, the inviolate angel.

The sea is made of tears, the world of the dead breathes
in each black leaf and in each cold star,
in your spectral eyes there trembles a spark
of stubborn youth trapped in a lake of gall.

Oh father who led me down such a tender path,
now, without tomorrow, beyond the ashen channel,
we will have to forget the sun, all that is gold and bright.

I will take what was yours into your valley of shadows
and we will live evermore corrupted by the past
within the maddening forest of signs and of names.

5

El vent neix amb el dia sobre el camp de batalla,
Judit! escolta el bleix d'aquest soldat morent
que les darreres ombres s'emporten lentament;
del cel, secret i fred, un vol de corbs davalla.

La nit deixa entre nacres un últim diamant,
un tendre riu vermell tot l'horitzó decora
i súbit, missatger d'una pútrida aurora,
renilla, mig de l'ombra, el fer onagre errant.

Tu avances com un astre i et gires fascinada,
punyent pantera groga, d'oblit assedegada,
els peus color d'oliva coberts de llot i sang.

Tots els càntics d'un poble no et trauran de les nines
l'acer ni els ulls atònits del teu cadàver blanc,
petita flama brusca que et consums i t'inclines.

5

The wind is born with the day upon the battlefield,
Judith! listen to the gasping of this dying soldier
whom the last shadows carry away slowly;
from the sky, secret and cold, a flight of crows comes down.

The night leaves among nacres a last diamond,
a soft red river adorns the whole horizon
and suddenly, messenger of a dreadful dawn,
there brays amid the shadow the wild, wandering onager.

You advance like a star and spin around fascinated,
penetrating yellow panther, thirsting for oblivion,
your olive-colored feet covered with mud and blood.

All the songs of a nation will not bring from your pupils
the steel or the astonished eyes of your white corpse,
small rough flame that burns away and bends.

6

Per un camí que fuig i et mena presonera,
amb lentituds de somni, floten esparsos vels,
als salzes amargueja un glop de primavera
i ploren, vora l'aigua, els rossinyols fidels.

Tornaràs amb la nit, blanca nadala trista,
entre els verds moribunds i la boira naixent,
la gespa es cobrirà de pètals d'ametista,
als joncs i a l'argelaga hi haurà un gemec de vent.

I amb els cabells cenyits de trèvols i d'ortigues
coronaràs de flames subtilment enemigues
la juvenil follia dels amants innocents,

perduda i retrobada per la lenta camèlia
que abalteix els estels i exalta els mar lluents,
oh passatgera, en seda esquiva, dolça Ofèlia.

6

Down a road that flees and takes you prisoner,
with the slowness of dreams, float loose veils,
a draft of spring embitters the willows
and, near the water, the faithful nightingales weep.

You will return with the night, sad white narcissus,
among the dying greens and the nascent mist,
the grass will be covered with amethyst petals,
among the rushes and the furze there will be a moaning of
the wind.

And with your hair wreathed in clover and thistles
you will crown with subtly inimical flames
the young folly of innocent lovers,

lost and found again by the slow camellia
that lulls the stars to sleep and lifts up the shining seas,
oh fleeting, in elusive silk, sweet Ophelia.

7

Rosa

Exhausta rosa pura, ardència setinada
d'innúmers pètals dats al matí candorós,
duus un perfum de nits feixugues d'estelada
entre llunes passives i vacillants verdors.

Fràgil al sol, de perles, de diamants cansada,
un vol d'ocell escampa la teva lluïsor;
oh, la breu innombrable en la tenebra nada,
tanta claror rotunda et corba de dolçor.

Sang de la tarda llences en giravolt de fulles,
adéu als cels nacrats, en expirar despulles
el teu esclat de porpra, el teu tresor de foc.

Fremeix un darrer pètal tenaç en son reialme,
només et resta el cor i l'implacable joc
de llunes i llavors dins l'hivern blanc de calma.

7

Rose

Pure exhausted rose, satiny ardor
of countless petals given to the fresh morning,
you wear a perfume of nights heavy with stars
among passive moons and wavering greens.

Fragile in the sun, weary of pearls, of diamonds,
a bird in flight scatters your brightness;
oh, inexpressible brevity swims in the gloom,
so much round clarity cradles you in sweetness.

You cast the blood of the afternoon in a whirlwind of leaves,
farewell to the nacred skies, as your burst of purple,
your treasure of fire, fade away bare.

A last insistent petal quivers in its kingdom,
and there remains only heart and the implacable play
of moons and seeds within the white, calm winter.

8

Amor novell

Arbres, fullatges tristos sota la nit immensa
i tu, lluna gebrada sobre els fruits i les flors,

vetlleu aquests carmins d'un amor que comença,
infant malalt de somnis, infant malalt de plors.

¿Per quin desert de vents menaràs els teus passos
quan les càndides roses absents s'esfullaran?
Pels nostres ulls velats passaran ocells lassos:
el llac del notre amor llurs ombres cobriran.

Màgics palaus de boira, extrems eixams d'estrelles
no deixaran morir aquestes flames velles,
i l'antic paradís brunzent d'abelles d'or

es dreçarà amb les dàlies i els mars d'espigues gerdes,
amb els purs diamants, secrets al fons del cor,
dels nostres besos joves sota les frondes verdes.

8

New Love

Trees, sad foliage under the immense night
and you, frozen moon above the fruits and flowers,
watch over these paths of a love that begins,
a child ailing with dreams, a child ailing with tears.

Through what windy desert will you take your steps
when the fresh absent roses shed their leaves?
Past our veiled eyes weary birds will cross:
their shadows will cover the lake of our love.

Magic palaces of mist, extravagant swarms of stars
will not let these old flames die,
and the ancient paradise buzzing with golden bees

will arise with the dahlias and the seas of fresh spikes,
with the pure diamonds, secreted at the bottom of the heart,
of our young kisses under the green fronds.

9

Adam a Eva

Segueix-me, dona meva, pell de rosa estremida,
oh tu que resplendeixes com el primer matí
i els lliris dintre l'aigua mires embadalida,
lleu de tot el que encara resta de teu en mi.

Oblida l'àngel, l'arbre, l'alta vela deserta
dels matins molls de llum, de les nits sense danys;
si el paradís ens llença, l'aspra terra és oferta
al vagareig dels nostres entremesclats afanys.

L'ala lluent del foc m'ha lliurat ta nuesa,
oh tu, la inesperada, ¿de quina absència empesa
cap a mi pel serpent, rel del nostre destret?

Ara, incerta i feble, la mort et fa més meva,
la mort que acoloreix com un astre secret
la soma correntia dels nostres dies, Eva!

9

Adam to Eve

Follow me, my lady, with skin of trembling rose,
oh you who shine like the first morning
and look entranced at the lilies in the water,
light of all that still remains of you in me.

Forget the angel, the tree, the tall deserted sail
of the mornings soft with light, of the nights without harm;
if paradise casts us out, the harsh earth offers itself
for the wandering of our intermingled desires.

The shining wing of fire has freed for me your nakedness,
oh you, the unexpected one, from what absence are you
  thrust upon me
by the serpent, root of our dilemma?

Now, uncertain and feeble, death makes you more mine,
death that colors like a secret star
the brief passing of our days, Eve!

10

Ocell

Sobre una branca baixa, silenciós, reposes;
amb les ales esteses has planejat suau,
abans que el teu reialme es desfés de les roses
i en els teus ulls morissin espurnes de cel blau.

T'embriaga el silenci, t'inquieten les ombres,
gires el bec esquiu vers l'orient desert;
mai no sabràs per què amb el teu vol aombres
una llença de terra i una mica de verd.

Ara t'esglaia el vol d'una fulla despresa,
el crit desesperat d'un llunyà ocell de presa
i la nit infinita que plana damunt teu.

Et fascina una estrella dintre l'aigua somorta
i les llances dels joncs, sota la claror lleu
d'aquesta flor d'argent que la tenebra porta.

10

Bird

Upon a low branch, silently, you rest;
with your wings extended you glide softly,
before your kingdom loses its roses
and the sparks of blue sky die in your eyes.

The silence inebriates you, the shadows disturb you,
you turn your timid beak toward the deserted east;
you will never know why you darken with your flight
a strip of earth and a bit of green.

Now the flight of an unfettered leaf frightens you,
the desperate cry of a distant bird of prey
and the infinite night that spreads out above you.

A star in the dying water fascinates you
and the spears of the rushes, under the gentle light
of this silver flower that the darkness brings.

11

Embadalit estol d'ombres acollidores,
la nit final comença dintre un gran llac d'estels,
reialme pur, espai tot bategant d'aurores,
tres claus d'or crucifiquen la volta dels teus cels.

La terra d'on sóc filla és lluny i sembla morta:
una flor ran del marge, una petja al sorral
i, sobre el blau de l'aigua, un bleix d'oreig que porta,
floc de perles desfetes, la boira matinal.

Vora la mar i un arbre el meu cor las reposa,
una rosa de verms com neu ardent es posa
damunt la trista platja deserta del meu cos.

Tot és oblit de tot. Res no cal que defensi
el lleu sospir que sóc en el glaçat repòs
d'aquesta paorosa congesta de silenci.

11

Enchanted band of welcoming shadows,
the final night begins in a great lake of stars,
pure realm, space all pulsating with dawns,
three golden keys crucify the arch of your skies.

The earth of which I am a daughter is distant and dead-
seeming:
a flower along the edge, a footstep in the sand
and, over the blue of the water, a puff of breeze that bears,
a string of pearls undone, the morning mist.

By the sea and a tree my heart lays them to rest,
a rose of worms like shining snow settles
upon the sad deserted beach of my body.

All is oblivion. There is nothing to keep back
the light sigh that I am in the glacial repose
of this swollen frightful silence.

12

Senyor, abans de néixer fer-vos un prec voldria;
abans del primer plor, protegit de dolors,
en la flonja cavorca sense claror de dia;
abans de veure el món i el llampec dels colors.

Ara que ja tinc ossos, les mans al pit plegades
i sota les parpelles tot el vidre dels ulls,
deu-me l'alè de viure en les cimes gebrades
d'aquesta gran tristesa, oblidant els esculls

de la meva partida vers una nit sens fi . . .
Si em feu néixer, Senyor, només per a morir,
compadiu-vos d'un cor feixuc d'amor i d'odi,

buideu-me de l'angoixa en els dies distants,
i, si això no pot ésser, deixeu que plegat rodi,
temps i més temps perdut en tebis llimbs flotants . . .

12

Lord, before I am born I would like to make a plea to you;
before the first tear, protected from pain,
in the soft cavern without the light of day;
before I see the world and the flash of colors.

Now that I have bones, my hands folded to my chest
and under my eyelids all the glass of my eyes,
give me the spirit to live on the frosty peaks
of this great sadness, forgetting the reefs

of my departure toward an endless night . . .
If you have me born, Lord, just to die,
have compassion for a heart heavy with love and hate,

empty me of anguish in distant days,
and, if that cannot be, let me roll, curled up,
forever and ever lost in warm floating limbos.

13

Boques de rosa i vori on dues serps lascives
continuen eternes el dolç combat d'amor,
castament devoreu les vostres flors, salives
més pàl.lides que els astres. Aquest diví licor,

fresc com la mel antiga, beveu, tristos amants,
adorables cadàvers que un sol desig confina.
Déu us pastà de fang i refeu amb les mans
de vostres flancs reials la corba que s'afina.

Retuts per la fatiga dormiu junts en la pau;
la rosada que irisa un cel amarg i blau
desfà les seves perles en la claror daurada.

Pròdigs de somnis verges no us desvetlleu mai més,
la dea de l'oblit, damunt vostre vinclada,
gelosament us sotja i us pren el darrer bes.

13

Rose and ivory mouths where two lascivious serpents
continue eternally the sweet combat of love,
you chastely devour your flowers, saliva
paler than the stars. Drink this divine liquor,

fresh as ancient honey, sad lovers,
adorable cadavers that a single desire confines.
God molded you from clay and fashioned with his hands
from your royal flanks the curve that is refined.

Worn by fatigue you sleep together in peace;
the dew that lights up a bitter blue sky
scatters its pearls in the golden brightness.

Prodigal with virgin dreams you never again awaken,
the goddess of oblivion, bending over you,
jealously lies in wait for you and takes from you the last
kiss.

MÓN D'ULISSES

1

(Penèlope)

Em compta el temps la marinada amarga,
la mar amb son abominable crit!
La mel dintre la gerra s'ha espessit
i els brots que vas deixar fan ombra llarga.

Oh xaragall lluent! La seda blanca
serà la lluna de la meva nit;
l'arbre cairat, capçal del nostre llit,
estén encar un pensament de branca.

Esquerpa, sola tota fel i espina,
faig i desfaig l'absurda teranyina,
aranya al.lucinada del no-res.

Un deix d'amor arran de llavi puja
i mor com una llàgrima de pluja
al viu del darrer pètal que ha malmès.

ULYSSES' WORLD

1

(Penelope)

The bitter sea breeze counts the time for me,
the sea with its abominable cry!
The honey in the jar has thickened
and the buds that you left cast a long shadow.

Oh, shining stream! The white silk
will be the moon of my night;
the awned tree, mast of our bed,
spreads still a thought of the branch.

Harsh, just bile and thorn alone,
I ravel and unravel the absurd web,
illusory spider of non-being.

An aftertaste of love rises to my lips
and dies like a drop of rain
on the edge of the last ruined petal.

2

(Ulisses en l'Illa de Circe)

En la barreja d'un folcat d'oprobi
ara ja sou sota rasposa pell
amb boques afuades en musell,
grinyoladissos al voltant de l'obi.

Haurà bastat, oh companyons, la quera
incessant de la fam, tota cabdell
pel laberint feréstec del budell,
la malvestat d'una deessa artera!

Que us valguin totes les viltats rebudes
quan sereu verticals sobre els peus rudes,
braços capçats per les forcades mans!

En cims d'honor o en conca de servatge,
recomenceu amb pacient coratge
l'aventura difícil d'ésser humans.

2

(Ulysses on Circe's Isle)

In the midst of a disgraceful band
now you are under a rough skin
with mouths sharpened into muzzles,
howling around the feeding trough.

Oh companions, it is enough, the incessant
gnawing of hunger, a whole ball of thread
through the savage labyrinth of the intestine,
the evildoing of a cunning goddess!

May all the vile deeds received help you
when you are standing on your rough feet,
arms shaken by strong hands!

At the height of honor or in the hollow of servitude,
may you begin again with patient courage
the difficult adventure of being human.

3

(Elpènor)

De l'odre fins a la resseca gorja
feres, oh vi, tants de camins vermells!
Veia dansar les llunes a parells
en un cel enfurit com una forja.

Quin salt, el meu, de ràfec a llamborda,
sense relleix, sense graó entremig!
Ara, si em moc, no sento mon trepig,
car ombra só dins la sauleda borda.

Viure? Per què? Oh corba dels periples!
Fregar, tot just, ribatges impossibles,
voltar un mar amb alirets damunt.

Desig, renom, virtut, triple quimera!
Germans de rem, jo enfilo la drecera:
vindreu amargs, cansats, i d'un a un.

3

(Elpenor)

From the wineskin to the parched throat
you made, oh wine, so many red paths!
I saw the moons dance in pairs
in a sky raging like a forge.

What a leap I made, from the eaves to the paving stone,
without a stair, without a step between!
Now, if I move, I do not hear my footfall,
for I am a shadow within the empty willow grove.

Live? Why? Oh curve of the periplus!
To graze, barely, impossible shores,
to round a sea with cries above.

Desire, renown, virtue, triple chimera!
Brothers of the oar, I take the shortcut:
you will come bitter, tired, and one by one.

4

(Mort d'un pretendent)

Oh mos companys esbarrellats de cara,
ja sóc del vostre immòbil escamot!
Amb un súbit xisclet de falziot
una sageta en el meu coll s'enllara.

T'he envescat amb la sang més amagada,
pern de la porta fosca de la mort!
Sigui més curt el plany en ma dissort
que quan vaig botre a vida colorada.

Reial corser, quin déu et desembrida?
Com flama brusca en mata agemolida,
ixes del vil parrac espès de polls.

Adéu! La Parca em gela la ferida.
Que la fidel et renti, esbalaïda,
la sang que t'ha esquitxat els dos genolls.

4

(Death of a Suitor)

Oh my companions with shattered faces,
I am now of your immobile group!
With the sudden cry of a swift,
an arrow lodges in my neck.

I have smeared you with the most secret blood,
bolt of the dark gate of death!
May my lament be briefer in my misfortune
Than when I gamboled in the good life.

Royal courses, what god unleashes you?
Like a rough flame in a hidden grove
you rise from the vile rag thick with lice.

Farewell! Fate chills my wound.
Let the faithful one wash from you, astonished,
the blood that has spattered your two knees.

ALBES I NITS

1

¿En quin ombrívol paradís m'esperes
d'aigües planyents i d'arbres sense vent,
engelebrit del teu desistiment,
espectre de les meves primaveres?

Enmig de tantes coses passatgeres,
tu sol passaves inefablement!
Sols vaig comprendre el teu llenguatge ardent
quan ja amb les dures albes no vingueres.

Ara estic sola en la presó de l'aire.
Amb una mà indecisa de captaire,
oh nit, ja fregues mon indúctil fang,

fins que, convulsa, arrencaràs tot d'una,
entre tu i jo feréstega vedruna,
l'eura vermella de la meva sang.

DAWNS AND NIGHTS

1

In what somber paradise do you await me
with wailing waters and windless trees,
made cold by your desisting,
specter of my springs?

Among so many fleeting things,
you along passed ineffably!
I understood your ardent language
only when you came with the cruel dawns no more.

Now I am alone in the prison of the air.
With an indecisive beggar's hand,
oh night, already you graze my stubborn clay,

until, convulsed, you will uproot all at once,
between you and me, wild border,
the red ivy of my blood.

2

Sang sense esclat, afany secret de l'arbre,
fronda que el vent de la tardor consum,
sobre el meu pit, oh somni pres en marbre,
un déu reneix embriagat de llum.

Címbals bateu, el meu orgull em deixa!
Quina pluja d'amor nodreix l'arrel?
Vençuda i tot, vull ésser jo mateixa,
abella furiosa de sa mel.

Tant se val, tant se val que l'amagada
mà de l'aurora hagi escanyat en cada
bardissa un pobre rossinyol cansat,

incendiada nit, oh fugissera,
que em deixes panteixant per la sendera
de joia, en el meu rost emmetzinat.

2

Blood without bursting, secret fervor of the tree,
frond that the wind of autumn consumes,
upon my heart, oh dream captured in marble,
a god is reborn drunken with light.

You beat cymbals, my pride abandons me!
What rain of love nourishes the root?
Vanquished and all, I myself want to be
a bee fervent about its honey.

It doesn't matter, it doesn't matter that the hidden
hand of the dawn has choked in each
bramble a poor tired nightingale,

of fleeting, fiery night,
that leaves me panting along the pathway
of joy, on poisoned slope.

3

Negra ciutat de la malenconia
que estrenys encastellada en un tombant
els teus pollancs de fulla delirant
i el gemec adollat que te'ls destria!

Inesperada al cim dels teus pendissos
entre plomalls de boira que es desfan,
l'alba sempre aturada al teu voltant
sense crit, sense foc ni ocells feliços!

¿Quina oblidada música, quin plany
a penes dit, llença el secret tirany
fins al súbits carreus d'ombra aglevada?

Ciutat d'enlloc on tota cosa va!
afany obscur del buit que vol salvar
l'últim somni d'una aigua dispersada.

3

Black city of melancholy
towering over a creek you embrace
your poplars of delirious leaf
and the pained moaning that separates you from them!

Unexpectedly at the peak of your slopes
among the plumes of mist that fade away,
the dawn ever holding still around you
without a cry, without fire or happy birds!

What forgotten music, what lament
scarcely said, casts the secret hook
to the sudden ashlers of congealed shadow?

City nowhere where everything goes!
dark desire for the emptiness that tries to save
the last sleep of a scattered water.

4

Oh ressaca estel.lar del violeta,
esborronada minva de la nit
que ratlla amb la ferida del seu crit
el vol crucificat de l'oreneta!

El verd s'esmuny pels brins, el blau s'alzina,
murs de la llum i torres de l'esglai
amb iris que es despleguen en desmai
com si el cel fos el buc d'una petxina.

Entremesclat panteix, doble agonia,
l'espasa irrefutable que ens destria
ens ha tallat d'un branc de somni, sols,

presos en tosca plenitud sobtada,
oh lenta soledat, arremorada
pel tomb de l'or tranquil dels gira-sols!

4

Oh starry undercurrent of the violet,
horrifying loss of the night
that the crucified flight of the swallow
grates with the wound of its cry!

The green slips through the brine, the blue arises,
walls of light and towers of fear
with iris that open out into a swoon
as if the sky were the belly of a shell.

Intermingled gasping, double agony,
the irrefutable sword that separates us
has carved us from a branch of dreams, alone,

caught in rustic surprised plenitude,
oh slow solitude, agitated
by the tranquil gold turning of the sunflowers!

TRES SONETS I UNA CANÇO

(Evocació dels morts)
Anticlea

No pas de l'home que em va estrènyer el flanc
tot emportat en remolí de febre,
ans meu, que et vaig maurar dins la tenebra
ambs les ressaques de la meva sang,

car, closa encara, m'enrosaren lentes
marors d'encís que no sabé ningú:
del costat de la fosca ja eres tu
que cercaves la llum a les palpentes.

Seré pagada de mai més no haver-te,
d'haver estat un congost de carn oberta,
crit al llindar de l'aire i la claror,

si en puges d'ombra, pacient falena,
sóc el calfred que et ressegueix l'esquena
quan rera el ventre de l'escut tens por.

THREE SONNETS AND A SONG

(Evocation of the Dead)
Anticlea

Not of the man who pressed my hips
all carried away in a whirlwind of fever,
but rather mine, who grazed you in the darkness
with the undertow of my blood,

because, still closed, slow waves of magic
that no one knew brushed by me:
you are now on the side of the dark
who looked gropingly for the light.

I will be thankful for having you no more,
for having been a narrow pass of open flesh,
a cry upon the threshold of air and brightness,

if in raising shadows, patient phaelena,
I am the shiver that runs up and down your back
when behind the belly of the shield you are afraid.

(Evocació dels morts)
Agamèmnon

No els va fer por la meva barba saura.
El primer cop l'espatlla em mig obrí
com una mossegada de mastí.
Em vaig girar i al segon cop vaig caure.

Ella després va acoltellar-me mentre
tot de costat veia el pedrís lluent:
el sol arbora—vaig pensar—ponent,
i a glops la sang m'anava eixint del ventre.

Jo m'afanyava per morir, debades:
tantes de maltraçudes coltellades
reblat m'havien a la llum atroç.

Encar vivent, a frec d'aurora brava,
mon panteig amb el d'ella es barrejava,
igual que abans damunt el llit de flors.

(Evocation of the Dead)
Agamemnon

My golden beard did not frighten them.
The first blow half-opened my back
like a bite from a mastiff.
I turned around and at the second blow I fell.

Then she stabbed me while
on my side I saw the shining threshold:
the setting sun—I thought—lights up the west
and in spurts the blood came running out of my gut.

I strove to die, in vain:
so many clumsy slashes
have riveted me in the terrible light.

Still living, very near the wild dawn,
my panting with that of hers was mingled,
just as before upon the bed of flowers.

(Evocació dels morts)
Noia morta

Com una cinta d'aigua que travessa
l'obaga verda sospirant tot just
i és tota adéus en el seu roc adust
i en el pendís enganyadora pressa

sempre passant i sempre romanent
com si fos ala i fos arrel alhora
fidel al branc que es gronxa al seu devora
i a l'ocell que el deixà ploma-batent

i ve l'hivern, el magre rapissaire
d'allò que es mou, amb argelagues d'aire,
tort de fumeres agres cap al cel,

a llunyanies meves decantada
la mort va deturar-me amb una unglada,
ai l'adormida soledat del gel!

(Evocation of the Dead)
Dead Girl

Like a ribbon of water that crosses
the shady green scarcely sighing
and is all good-byes on harsh rock
and on the slope deceiving captive

always going and always staying
as if it were wing and root at the same time
faithful to the branch that swings around her
and to the bird that abandons it with beating feather

and winter comes, the thin predator
of that which is moving with gorses of air,
twisted with bitter clouds of smoke toward the sky,

to my distances inclined
death stopped me with a claw,
oh the sleepy solitude of ice!

(Cançó de les molineres)

1

Als molins on el temps mol
només hi ha farina negra:
—ara el blat, com indecís,
ens verdeja ran de terra.

L'ombra en pren tota la flor
i la maura amb aigua freda;
—ai que el blat es va gronxant,
abrinat, en mar espessa.

Ni una engruna de llevat
i en un forn que és ple de cendra!
—cada espiga rossa estreny
un grapat de grana tèbia.

Als molins on el temps mol
tot serà farina negra.

2

Als molins on mol la nit
tot serà farina blanca;
—un blat fosc ens treu arrel
al vessant ombriu de l'aire.

A llevant l'esventaran
crits de gall i batecs d'ala;
—com s'espiga amb grans d'argent
ran la mola entenebrada!

I tindrem un pa tot ros
al prestatge net de l'alba;
—el minvant rellisca, prim,
per la feixa que es decanta.

Els molins on mol la nit
cremaran amb flama blanca.

3

Als molins on tant maldem
només hi ha grana vermella;
—al pedrís, els dos genolls,
se'ns encasten amb sang presa.

Maurarem a trenc d'estels
pels potents que senyoregen;
—amb el fel que els escopim
més que amb aigua de cisterna.

Dents lluents dels asseguts
boques dures que ens desdenyen!
—aquest pa, quan entri a dins,
sigui un mos de brasa encesa.

Sota l'arbre blau del cel
que us ajegui mort vermella.

(Song of the Millers)

1

In the mills where time grinds
there is only black flour:
—now the wheat, as though indecisive,
makes us green along the earth.

The shadow takes from it the entire flower
and kneads it with cold water;
—oh the wheat is swaying,
thinning out, in a thick sea.

Not one crumb of leaven
and in an oven that is full of ash!
—each blond spike clutches
a handful of warm grain.

In the mills time grinds
everything will be black flour.

2

In the mills where night grinds
everything will be white flour;
—a dark wheat takes root in us,
on the shadowy slope of the air.

In the east will rise
cries of cock and beatings of wing;
—as it sprouts with grains of silver
along the darkened millstone!

And we will have a bread all fair,
on the clean shelf of dawn,
—the ebb tide slides thinly
through the strip of draining land.

The mills where night grinds
will burn with a white flame.

3

In the mills where we struggle so much
there is only red grain;
—at the threshold, the two knees,
stick to us with captive blood.

We will graze at the breaking of the stars
through the powerful ones who dominate;
—with the bile that they spit out
more than with well water.

Shining teeth of the seated
hard mouths that disdain us!
—this bread, when it enters within,
let it be a bite of burning embers.

Under the blue tree of the sky
may red death lay you low.

Reflections: Spaces of Self-Knowledge in Rodoreda's Fiction

NANCY VOSBURG

In me she has drowned a young girl, and in me an old woman/ Rises toward her day after day, like a terrible fish.
—(From "Mirror," by Sylvia Plath)

ONE OF THE STRIKING CHARACTERISTICS OF MERCÈ RODOREDA'S FICtional prose, repeatedly underscored by critics of her most widely-acclaimed novels *La plaça del Diamant* (1962; *The Time of the Doves*, (1980) and *El carrer de les Camèlies* (1966; *Camellia Street*, 1993), is the awkward and deceptively naive conversational style of the narrative voice. The reader, situated as an eavesdropper to a conversation directed at an unknown interlocutor, is drawn into the confusing reflections of a narrator who retells the circumstances of her past, trying to make sense of the meaningless, incoherent, or indecipherable events and emotions she evokes. As the narration progresses, the reader often seems to experience simultaneously with the narrator revelations made possible only through the dialogical process of narrating. The act of narrating, with its concomitant ordering and attempt at coherency, functions as a metaphorical mirror for the speaking subject; as she constructs the events of her past for another, she also becomes an otherness to herself, a projected image which is reflected back to her through her externally directed speech.[1]

Mirrors, and acts of mirroring, play an important role in Rodoreda's fiction. Critics such as Busquets and Varderi have offered psychological interpretations of specific mirror scenes in Rodoreda's novels, and the duality of the mirror has been evoked by Carme Arnau in her *Miralls màgics* as a metaphor for Rodoreda's narrative evolution. Rodoreda herself explained the significance of the titular mirror in her prologue to *Mirall trencat:*

> Què és un mirall? L'aigua és un mirall. Narcís ho sabia. Ho sap la lluna i ho sap el salze. Tot el mar és un mirall. Ho sap el cel. Els ulls són el mirall de l'ànima. I del món. Hi ha el mirall de la veritat dels egipcis que reflectia totes les passions; tant les altes com les baixes. Hi ha miralls màgics. Miralls diabòlics. Miralls que deformen. Hi ha mirallets per caçer aloses. Hi ha el mirall de cada dia que ens fa estrangers a nosaltres mateixos. Darrera el mirall hi ha el somni. Tots voldríem atènyer el somni, que és la nostra més profunda realitat sense trencar el mirall. (3:21)[2]
>
> [What is a mirror? The water is a mirror. Narcissus knew it. The moon and the willow tree know it. The whole sea is a mirror. The sky knows it. The eyes are the mirror of the soul. And of the world. There is the Egyptian mirror of truth that reflected all passions; the most elevated and the lowliest. There are magical mirrors. Diabolical mirrors. Mirrors that deform. There are little mirrors to hunt skylarks. There is the mirror of each day that makes us strangers to ourselves. Behind the mirror is the dream. We would all like to achieve the dream, which is our most profound reality, without breaking the mirror.]

The centrality of the mirror and other reflecting devices, such as water, windows, and display cases, has been underscored in feminist discussions, which probe questions of female identity, recurring themes of alienation and victimization, and the fictional characters' search for self-knowledge in Rodoreda's fiction. These studies suggest a common ground with Jenijoy La Belle's observation that "[t]hrough the mirror, we can gain insight into the reciprocal interchanges between interiority and exteriority as these create what a woman is to herself and to her culture."[3] In Anne Hollander's analysis of mirrors in paintings throughout the ages, she observes that mirrors "seem likely witnesses to the critical moments in moral and sexual life,"[4] a theme running throughout La Belle's *Herself Beheld* and applicable to Rodoreda's fiction as well.

My purpose in this essay is to explore the relationship between the catoptric and the semiotic, i.e., between the symbolic functions of a diversity of mirroring devices which appear in Rodoreda's 1958 collection, *Vint-i-dos contes,* and her development of the oral narrative style which will be the predominant characteristic of her subsequent works. Representative stories from *Vint-i-dos contes* reveal a linkage between the narrators' confrontations with explicit catoptric devices and with what could be considered implicit mirroring devices, or the dialogic self-reflections of diaries and letters. The similarity between diaries/letters and mirrors has been noted by others such as La Belle, who postulates that

> [b]oth looking into mirrors and reading/writing are attempts to create the self without another person literally present. In the reflection or in the book, there is another presence. Once you objectify yourself into a mirror or onto a page, then that image has a separate reality. (155)

I will further argue that dreams, in which one sees oneself in a modified or distorted reality, function as reflecting surfaces as well, offering the speaking subject an additional "mirror" in which to perceive herself. In the mirror reflection, on the page, and in the dream reflection, the presence of an "other" creates a space of dialogic interaction akin to the living conversation directed at an interlocutor. As precursors to *La plaça del Diamant,* the stories in the 1958 collection reveal Rodoreda's emerging mystery of the essential narrative techniques of her award-winning novels. As Carme Arnau has noted:

> Però si *Vint-i-dos contes* és una peça important dins la producció de la Rodoreda, ho és gràcies al fet que, en els tempteigs de la seva escriptura, l'autora efectua un assaig que carregarà de conseqüències per a la seva producció posterior. Es tracta de la descoberta d'un tipus d'escriptura, que seguint Barthes podem denominar parlada, i que serà el comú denominador de la prosa rodorediana a partir de *La plaça del Diamant.* (*Obres completes* I:14)

> [But if *Vint-i-dos contes* is an important piece within Rodoreda's [literary] production, it is due to the fact that, in the trials and errors of her writing, the author carries out an experiment that is loaded with consequences for her later production. It is the discovery of a type of writing, which according to Barthes we can call spoken, and that will become the common denominator of Rodoredian prose beginning with *La plaça del Diamant.*]

The *Vint-i-dos contes* collection, winner of the 1957 Víctor Català Literary Prize, marked what might be considered the "resurrection" of the exiled writer. Having published five novels prior to the Civil War, Rodoreda's novelistic pursuits were virtually truncated by the harsh conditions of her itinerant exile, first near Paris, then in Limoges, later in Bordeaux, and finally in Geneva. Rodoreda's letters to her friend Anna Murià reveal that during her war years in Barcelona and her early exile in France, she was writing poems and short stories, some of which appeared in Catalan journals in France and Mexico.[5] In general, the stories in *Vint-i-dos contes* relate the characters' increasing sense of isolation and failed dreams as they struggle to understand or articulate a newly perceived void. Jealousy, domestic entrapment, exile, lost youth, poverty, abandonment, cruelty, death, adultery, and deceit figure prominently as contributing factors that intensify the theme of solitude, alienation, and the struggle for self-knowledge. Only six of the stories are narrated in first person; one story alternates between first and third person; the rest are rendered in third person but from the interiorized point of view of a single, in most cases female, character.

Of special interest in discussing the symbolic functions of the mirror is, of course, the story entitled "El mirall" [The mirror]. In addition, I will be focusing on Rodoreda's use of the diary and/or letters as self-reflective devices in "Tarda al cinema" [An afternoon at the movies] and "Abans de morir" [Before dying]; the dream sequence in "Abans de morir" and "La sang" [Blood]; and Rodoreda's experiments with an unidentified interlocutor in "En el tren" [On the train] and "La sang." As I stated in my opening paragraph, the mute and unidentified interlocutor serves a catoptric function similar to that of the mirror in that the speaking subject defines herself and comes to greater self-knowledge through her encounter with an "other," whose mere presence (implied but never visible) allows her to shape an external image of her complex interior world. Carmen Martín Gaite, in her ruminations on the intrinsic necessity of an interlocutor for both oral and written narratives, has observed that

> employed well or not, this [literary] recourse, every time it appears, is a reflection of an intrinsic necessity of a narrative . . . I interpret it almost as a transposition to the plane of writing of the "are you still listening?" or "I hope this isn't putting you to sleep" that, also spontaneously, frequently stake out our oral narrations when they start to falter; eloquent examples of this desire to find the shape of a listener—real or invented—a desire which constitutes, I repeat, the original motive and the perennial incentive of any narration.[6]

First let's examine the role of mirroring scenes in the 1958 collection, most explicitly developed in "El mirall," the fifth story in *Vint-i-dos contes.* Like the majority of Rodoreda's short stories, the surface plot of "El mirall" is deceivingly simple: an aged, diabetic woman leaves the doctor's office, stops to buy cookies in open defiance to the doctor's recommendations, returns to the home she shares with her son and his family, and takes refuge in her room, where she proceeds to consume her purchase. Yet interspersed with the third person narration of these simple events are the protagonist's reflections on her past, rendered in first person, which add layers of complexity to the story while providing the reader with clues to the old woman's rebellious, and life-threatening, defiance of her doctor's orders.

Reflecting surfaces are central to the shifts from third-to first-person narration, and create a temporal shift between present and past. The first mirroring device is introduced shortly after the protagonist leaves the doctor's office: she pauses to gaze into the display window of the jewelry store. Initially, it is the sight of the jewelry that, like Proust's madeleine, evokes memories of the past and begins to provide the reader with clues to the personality and vital circumstances of the character: she has had to sell off the jewelry, piece by piece, that her now-deceased husband had given her. Yet her attention is immediately captured by the reflection of her hand in the display-case window: "El vidre de l'aparador reflectí la mà: una mà llarga, solcada de venes fosques, amb els dits deformats a les juntures, lenta com una bèstia malalta." (1:200) [The display window reflected her hand: a long hand, furrowed with dark veins, with the finger joints deformed, slow like a sick animal.] The presence in the reflecting window, seemingly inhuman and yet privileged with the truth of her physical and psychic state, disrupts the equation between self and image normally associated with the mirror. The voices of two girls who have stopped to gaze into the display case provide another vital clue to the circumstances of the main character: not totally familiar with French, she still dreams of returning one day to Barcelona. The reader is struck by the accumulation of signs of alienation encoded vertiginously in the opening paragraphs—an elderly, diabetic widow who has suffered a declining socioeconomic status, exiled and linguistically marginalized in a foreign country. The accrual of these significant sign-posts and the question the old woman poses to herself—"Què faig plantada aquí?" (1:200) [What am I doing stuck here?]—point to a fundamental crisis of identity. The confrontation with the mirroring surface, characterized by disunity between self and reflected image, allows the author to dramatize and literalize a metaphor of alienation from self and society.

After stopping at a pastry shop to buy half a kilo of cookies, the small, slightly curved figure arrives at the home she shares with her son, daughter-in-law, and grandson. Irritated by her daughter-in-law's probing questions, she deliberately lies about having visited the doctor, and seeks refuge in her room. "La cambra era el seu món, ple de secrets, de retrats de persones que ni el seu fill ni la jove no coneixien. Quan hi entrà, el mirall de l'armari reflectia el jardí verd, misteriós, a penes visible darrera les ballestes de la persiana tirada, com un paisatge de somni." (1:201–2) [The bedroom was her world, full of secrets, of photographs of people that neither her son nor the young woman knew. Upon entering, the wardrobe mirror reflected the green garden, mysterious, barely visible through the slats of the closed Persian blinds, like a dream landscape.] Rodoreda's articulation of the significance of the mirror in the prologue to *Mirall trencat,* cited previously, befits the mirror's reflection in this scene. Alejandro Varderi, in his exploration of the dream landscape of the garden in Rodoreda's prose, has found inside/outside scenes such as this to be a recurring motive: "Positioning oneself inside the house implies leaving outside the garden . . . in order to embark on a labor of introspection about the objects within the house" (263), one of which is frequently a mirror. The old woman removes her shoes, contemplating her bony, tight-skinned feet, and begins to eat the forbidden cookies: "Que vagin a passeig els metges i els seus règims . . ." (1:202) [To hell with doctors and their diets . . .] The revolt, presaged by the disunity between self and reflected image in the display case, is now clearly under way.[7]

As the unnamed protagonist runs her tongue over her teeth to free the sticky pastry cream, she picks up a hand mirror, a wedding gift associated with the past. She contemplates the wrinkled and slightly congested face, the soft blue bags under her eyes. The image in the mirror no longer substantiates her identity, an identity that, in spite of being imposed on her by another, she has interiorized: "'Té els ulls verds i els cabells negres . . . Per a fer-te fer una bogeria . . .' Ho havia dit un dels seus pretendents a Roger, quan Roger encara no la coneixia"

(1:202) ["She has green eyes and dark hair . . . enough to drive you mad." One of her suitors had said this to Roger, even before he knew her.]

As she continues to gaze in the mirror and munch on a cookie, the narration again shifts to first person, creating once more a disjunction between present and past. She sees herself at a dance, enjoined in a waltz with her future husband while she watches Roger dance with another—his lover, she had found out just days before—and remembers her one afternoon with Roger, the drops of blood on the sheet, his last embrace.

Another narrative shift brings us back to the present, as the old woman contemplates her ears in the mirror. One of them bears a scratch, where her infant son—Roger's son—had torn off her earring while breast-feeding, and continued to suck on her blood-splattered breast. She remembers the white lilies at her wedding, her fear, her desire to escape. The narration shifts again to first person, and we are plunged back into the past made present. A confusing stream-of-consciousness monologue follows in which the reader infers a panoply of events and emotions: the character's continuing desire for Roger, the son born of their single union, her cold disdain for the other man, whom she subsequently married. But the exterior presence in the mirror brings her abruptly back to the present: "Ara sóc vella i estic malalta i la meva joventut . . ." (1:205) [But now I'm old and I'm sick and my youth . . .] Again she searches in the mirror for the reflection of her previous identity: "Aquest mirall ho sap tot. Els meus ulls verds i els meus cabells negres encara són a dins, amagats, però a dins . . ." (1:205) [This mirror knows everything. My green eyes and dark hair are still inside it, hidden, but they're there . . .] It is the same mirror that they held up to her husband's mouth to see if he was still breathing after he attempted to hang himself. The disjunction between past and present reaches a culminating point as the narrator experiences a definitive split between herself, what she has become, and the image hidden within the mirror: "Quan va morir, al cap d'uns quants anys, no vaig plorar gens. I deu ser l'única persona que m'ha estimat . . . A mi no, a l'altra, a la que havia viscut aquí dintre . . ." (1:206) [When he (her husband) died, a few years later, I didn't shed a single tear. And he must have been the only person who ever loved me . . . Not me, the other, the one that he saw there inside . . .] She tosses aside the mirror and, as her son approaches her room, brushes off the cookie crumbs.

The mirroring surfaces in "El mirall" serve an obvious narrative function of facilitating the shift from present to past, reinforced by the accompanying shift from an exterior third person narration to the interior first person narrative. But in the interplay between exteriority and interiority, the protagonist becomes increasingly aware of the disjunction between self and image, and consequently between past and present. Her self-contemplation in the mirror, with its objective reflectivity, leads her to a revelation, a confrontation with a truth that has just come into focus: "No res. Ningú. He viscut sola. Estic sola. Sola amb tot aquest feix de records morts, que podrien ser meus o no ser-ho, inútils, sòrdids." (1:206) [Nothing. No one. I've lived alone. I am alone. Alone with this whole bundle of dead memories, that could be mine or not, useless, sordid.] The reader understands simultaneously with the protagonist that she has wasted her entire adult life pining away for a lost love, incapable of accepting her husband's affection and now repulsed by the sight of her son, who resembles too closely his father. Does her rejection of the mirror at the end of the story—not breaking it, but rather tossing it onto the bed—signal a willful distancing from that "other" woman whose past now seems so futile? Or is her decision not to break the mirror a sign that she will remain under the power of the looking glass? The significance of mirror scenes for other Rodoredian heroines, such as Natàlia-Colometa, Cecília Ce, and Teresa Goday,[8] suggests the positive power of the mirror, in that those heroines do succeed, after experiencing a similar doubling of the reflected "I," in recuperating their "lost bearings" (Varderi, 271), in claiming a new and empowering sense of identity through the self-knowledge they have acquired.

At the end of "El mirall," the protagonist gathers up the cookie crumbs—the last vestiges of her rebellion—that have fallen on her lap, opens the blinds, and tosses them into the garden. Initially, the reader is left awash in the accumulation of details which construct a complex portrait of physical, cultural, emotional, and psychological alienation from self and society, details that seem to portend a tragic, although unspoken, ending to the narrative. Yet in the catoptric confrontation, which produces the to-and-fro between past and present, interiority and exteriority, the protagonist seems to arrive at a self-knowledge that has the potential to save her from her self-destructive behavior. Her final actions—casting aside the mirror and tossing the cookie crumbs into the garden—suggest a more positive denouement, again unspoken. Her rebellion, initially understood as one against the present, becomes reconfigured as a revolt against her stultifying past, perhaps finally transcended.

"Tarda al cinema," the seventh story in *Vint-i-dos contes,* presents another variety of self-reflectivity. This very short narrative is structured as a diary entry, in which a young woman, Caterina, reflects on her relationship with her boyfriend, Ramon. The catoptric function of the diary entry is first made apparent in a parenthetical aside that reveals a shift from interiority to exterior contemplation. It is the beginning of a shift from monologism to dialogism: "(Ara m'adono que he escrit tot aquest tros seguit, i la mestressa sempre em deia que de tant en tant fes punt i a part. Però com que això només ho escric per mi és igual.)" (1:214) [I've just realized that I've written all this nonstop, and my teacher always told me that now and then, I needed to start a new paragraph. But since I'm only writing this for myself, it doesn't matter.] La Belle postulates that

> [t]exts and mirrors can perform similar psychological functions for women, particularly during periods in their lives when objectification and consciousness of self become necessary. (160–61)

Caterina's subsequent ramblings confirm that she is indeed at a critical junction in her life. She thinks she loves Ramon and hopes to marry him, despite her parents' disapproval and the fact that Ramon seems more interested in his black marketing activities than in her. The celluloid screen in the movie theater reflects back to her yet another image that adds to her confusion, as she realizes that she and Ramon do not love each other with the same kind of passion and commitment as the idealized couple in the movie.

Caterina once again steps back and gazes into the mirror of her writing. The encounter is marked by a disjunction between interior and exterior, between self and reflected image: "Ara he llegit tot això que acabo d'escriure i veig que no és ben bé el que volia dir." (1:215) [I've just read everything that I've finished writing and I realize that it is not exactly what I meant.] Her self-conscious struggle to articulate her thoughts and feelings dramatizes even more profoundly her confusion and struggle to understand her thoughts and emotions. Yet in the dialogic interstice between narrator and text, the reader glimpses a greater self-understanding than the narrator professes. More than anything, "Tarda al cinema" posits the act of writing, of narrating, as a means of making sense of the world.

In some ways, Caterina is a prototype of the artless and naive narrators of *La plaça* and *El carrer,* whose transformation from events lived to events told allows them to come to terms with these same events. Caterina, however, while seeming to grasp intuitively the need for a more objective interlocutor—"qualsevol que llegís aquest diari diria que penso que en Ramon no m'estima i jo crec que sí que m'estima" (1:215) [anyone who read this diary would think that Ramon doesn't love me and I do believe that he does]—does not succeed in clarifying fully her thoughts and feelings. While her diary has the potential to create a separate reality that can be evaluated more objectively, she seems, at least for the moment, incapable of realizing it. Perhaps it's because Caterina is still under the sway of an externally imposed identity: "[j]o ja ho sé que sóc una tanoca" (1:215) [I know full well that I'm a nitwit.] Nevertheless, her narration, as refracted to the reader, suggests that she is more clear-sighted than she thinks. The ellipsis at the end of the narrative clearly indicates that her story has not ended; the process of self-understanding has only begun.

If Caterina's diary reflects back to her an image of dull-witted confusion, the diary entries in "Abans de morir" are significant sign-posts for another narrator who is trying to make sense of her past. The last story in the collection, "Abans de morir" makes explicit the correlation between the catoptric and the semiotic, and the potential power of the reflective surface in achieving self-knowledge: "Abans de morir, voldria fixar els dos darrers anys de la meva vida, explicar, per explicar-m'ho a mi mateixa, tot el que m'han obligat a no poder viure." (1:329) [Before I die, I would like to put my last two years of life on record, to explain, in order to explain to myself, everything that has kept me from living.] What follows is the story of Marta Coll, who, unlike Caterina, Natàlia-Colometa, or Cecília Ce, is a self-consciously unconventional woman with an artistic bent. Marta proceeds to relate the significant events of the past two years and her feelings about them in what reveals itself, over half way into the narration, to be a letter. The person whom she is addressing is Roger, the best friend of her husband Màrius and perhaps, the reader infers, even Marta's lover. The catoptric devices are multiplied even further by the inclusion of a dream sequence and, as in

"Tarda al cinema," the narrator's contemplation of another couple (not celluloid, but rather the housekeeper's niece and her husband) who, in their intimacy, reflect back to Marta her unsatisfied desire in her own marital relationship.

Marta recalls in her letter her initial encounter with her future husband, and the somewhat odd development of their budding romance. A turning point in their relationship seems to occur when Màrius sends her two white pigeons, which she promptly converts into a dinner entree. The pigeons reappear to her in a dream shortly after their marriage: she is travelling, and everywhere she goes she encounters two white pigeons with bloody feathers around their necks. While dreams are essentially interior monologues that surge from the unconscious, perhaps reflecting unresolved fears and anxieties, the conscious confrontation with the dream, the attempt to make sense of it through narration, transforms it into an exterior "presence" that reflects back to Marta an enigmatic yet ominous foreboding. This is followed by the discovery of a bundle of letters in her husband's briefcase that makes her initially suspicious and increasingly obsessed with the possibility that he loves another. Marta's inclusion of the dream in her epistolary narrative emphasizes its haunting psychological presence; in retrospect, she finds in it a foreshadowing of the death she is now planning to bring about.

Marta incorporates into her epistle five diary entries she had written in the past, each set apart by the subtitle "Del meu diari" [From my diary]. They do not differ substantially from the rest of the narration, and seem to serve essentially as a sign-post for Marta's reconstruction of events in her letter, folding themselves into the epistolary narration. Yet, upon closer inspection, the reader discerns certain contradictions between what the narrator had written to herself in the past, and what she is now writing to Roger. For example, in the first entry, she writes: "M'he acabat de conèixer. No crec en res. Però penso que el mínim que es pot demanar a les persones intel.ligents és que sàpiguen ésser felices, que sàpiguen viure i que sàpiguen acceptar." (1 : 332) [I have finally come to know myself. I don't believe in anything. But I think that the least one can ask of intelligent people is that they know how to be happy, that they know how to live and to accept.] Certainly Marta couldn't have been leveling with herself, since she is now preparing to commit suicide, unable to accept that Màrius might still love another woman.

The diary's lack of veracity is underscored again when the narrator, reflecting on the third interjected diary entry, confesses to her narratee that what she wrote there was not true: "No era veritat. No vaig cremar-les." (1:338) [That wasn't true. I didn't burn them (the letters).] Like Caterina's diary, in "Tarda al cinema," Marta's does not appear to serve as a valid mirror of reality. While narrative reflection, in the form of a diary, allows both Marta and Caterina to project themselves as an otherness that can be observed, Rodoreda seems to suggest that the power of this solipsistic contemplation, like that in a mirror, is prone to subjective deformation. Often a mirror gazer cannot escape putting self-acceptable expressions and poses into the frame, as Hollander has suggested (392). In this sense, the reflective surface may only corroborate an idealized, not an authentic, sense of identity. Nevertheless, the interplay between the diary entries, directed at herself, and the letter, directed to another, adds another layer of psychological depth to Marta's character, a depth necessary to understand her suicidal intentions. In a final catoptric twist, Marta's last hope is that Màruis's closely-guarded letters will forever reflect back *to him* his responsibility for her suicide.

"En el tren" and "La sang," the penultimate and first stories, respectively, are experiments with the anonymous interlocutor who will be present in Rodoreda's novels of the 1960s. They are written as one-sided dialogues delivered by awkward, naive narrators who, like Natàlia-Colometa and Cecília Ce, reconstruct their pasts. In both cases, the reconstructed past is fraught with emotional undertones of which the narrators seemingly are unaware until, in the case of "La sang," the moment of the telling. In contrast to "La sang," the pathos of "En el tren" is achieved primarily through the ironic disjunction between the innocent, seemingly happy-go-lucky narrator and the tragic events that she narrates. As the train pulls into Barcelona, she concludes: "Quan penso en els que no tenen tanta sort com jo, mare meva!, i en les tragèdies que els passen que quasi fa escruixir . . ." (1:327) [When I think about those who have not had the luck I have, goodness!, and the tragedies they suffer that almost make me shiver . . .] Initially, her discourse, like Caterina's diary, fails to fulfill its potential as a catoptric device to this narrator, even as it refracts to the reader the tender tragedy of the character's apparent emotional distancing from her own sorrowful experiences. Yet the "shiver" she experiences as the train pulls into Barcelona suggests that, through the voicing of her own story, the abyss between event and emotional reaction may be in the process of being bridged.

In "La sang," however, the narrator's discourse does perform a metaphorically mirroring function as it reflects back to her an exteriorized image of herself that allows her to articulate more clearly her suffering. The narrator begins by telling her unknown interlocutor, addressed formally ("Veu?"), about the dahlias her husband used to plant in her now-empty flowerbed. Her explanation acquires a stream-of-consciousness character as one image or reference evokes another, taking narrator, interlocutor, and reader back to the early, happy days of her marriage. The mirroring power of the interlocutor is established early on, as the narrator self-consciously acknowledges the exterior image she must be projecting to the other: "Vostè em mira i potser es pensa que sempre ha estat així, oi? Si sabés com era bonica . . ." (1 : 170) [You look at me and perhaps are thinking that I was always like this, aren't you? If you only knew how pretty I was . . .]

If in "El mirall" the narrator has identified more closely with the previous "self" hidden within the reflected image, the narrator of "La sang" is clearly situated on the other side of the bifurcated image: "No és que fos allò que en diuen una noia vistosa, no, però tenia els ulls molt lluents i dolços: com de vellut . . . dispensi, però en puc parlar perquè ja és com si parlés d'una filla que hagués tingut i se m'hagués mort, sap?" (I:170) [It's not that I was what you would call a beautiful girl, no, but I had very brilliant, soft eyes, like velvet . . . pardon me, but I can say this because it's as if I were talking about a daughter that I once had who had died, you know?] Perhaps it is the interlocutor, an authentic "other," rather than the solipsistic reflective devices employed in the other stories studied, that underlies this important shift in how the speaking subject perceives her identity. With its emphasis on the narrator's full identification with the external image, which represents her present self, rather than the interiorized self of the past, "La sang" marks a direction in Rodoreda's writing that she will adhere to in her subsequent novels.

Nevertheless, in creating the portrait of her younger "self" for her interlocutor, the narrator of "La sang" seems to experience a moment of revelation, a newly perceived connecting link between the past and the present: "I em penso que tot el mal va venir perquè vaig ser dona de molt joveneta, sap?, i tot va començar quan vaig deixar de ser dona." (1 : 170) [And I now believe that all the bad things that happened were due to the fact that I became a woman at a very young age, you know?, and everything started when I stopped being a woman.] Her ensuing story relates the gradual disintegration of her marital relationship, a perhaps inevitable process given the way in which this woman defines herself in accordance with her biological potential and physical appearance. The onset of menopause brings with it an escalating series of psychic disorders, the most severe of which are her mounting suspicions that her husband is unfaithful and her increasing sense of guilt about her father's death.

The constant "presence" of the protagonist's father in her narration suggests a reading of "La sang" as a narrative of women's condition within a patriarchal society, particularly in the ways that women define themselves in relation to men. The narrator confesses to her interlocutor that she married against her father's will, and when he died a year later, "vaig pensar que s'havia mort perquè era vell, però a mida que va anar passant temps vaig veure que era el disgust de la meva desobediència el que l'havia matat . . ." (169–70) [I thought he had died of old age, but as time went by I understood that what killed him was the displeasure of my disobedience . . .] She attributes her frequent crying spells to a lingering sense of guilt for having "abandoned" her father, although her narration refracts to the reader a perhaps more pressing emotional trauma: the narrator's feelings of her own abandonment in relation to her husband.

Waiting anxiously for her husband to return from work, the protagonist realizes that she is repeating a disquieting paternal gesture: "Mentre l'esperava, de vegades pensava en el meu pare: quan jo era menuda m'enviava a comprar a casa de l'adroguer, m'esperava arrepenjat a la barana del balcó. I no m'agradava. Gairebé no sabia caminar perquè sabia que, allà dalt, hi havia la mirada del meu pare que no perdia ni un gest meu." (171) [While I waited for him, I sometimes thought about my father: when I was little he would send me to buy something at the pharmacy, and he would wait for me leaning on the balcony railing. I never liked it. I could hardly walk because I knew that, there up above, was my father's gaze, a gaze that didn't miss even one of my gestures.] She seems to intuit that the "gaze," and the ensuing power to reassure or criticize, is a male privilege, and although she flees into the house at the first sight of her husband, she continues her spying each evening. Her reward is the confirmation of her suspicions; she finally sees him accompanied by the young woman who lives down the street, who is the cashier at the cafe where he works. While there is nothing suspect about their behavior, the words of her friend, Roser, which the protagonist dismisses as inappropriate to her situation, nevertheless seem to add to her mounting paranoia: "Els homes, com més fas, pitjor. Quan et tenen vella i gastada se'n busquen una de jove . . ." (172) [The more you sacrifice for men, the worse. When a woman is old and used up, men always look for a younger woman . . .]

The commentary that the narrator adds to her narration of past events emphasizes her state of isolation and incommunication, the underlying motives that propel her discourse: "I quan una dona sent aquestes coses voldria una mà que li estrenyés la mà i una veu que molt baix digués: 't'entenc!' Però, com vol que una dona com jo trobi una veu que digui les paraules que es necessiten, si amb prou feines m'entenc jo, comprèn?" (1:174) [And when a woman has these feelings she would like a hand to squeeze hers and a voice that would whisper to her, "I understand you!" Yet how do you expect a woman like me to find a voice that will say the words she needs, if I can barely understand myself, you know?] The fact that she has found a way to finally voice this need, to project externally her interior dilemma, indicates that, thanks to the presence of a valid interlocutor, she has broken through the barrier of incommunication. As she unfolds her story of alienation and self-absence to the mute interlocutor, she is engaging in a process of social engagement and self-creation.

An additional catoptric device is incorporated into the protagonist's self-narration as she relates a disquieting dream. Rodoreda displays an attention-grabbing mastery at capturing the illogical temporal and spatial ruptures that occur in dreams, and the disconnected images that surge to the forefront as one tries to bestow narrative coherence on what is dredged up from the unconscious. The dream is indeed a distorted mirror image, rich in symbolic suggestions, of the narration that has preceeded it: bodies of water, apparently dead fish that then resuscitate, descending staircases and ascending ladders, the narrator dropping a jug of water and realizing she has killed someone, fruit stands in the marketplace, disappearances and reappearances of both her husband and her father, a party celebration with waiters bearing large trays of food in a hotel-like space, and an injured, disguised figure whom she takes into her arms and leads away upon realizing he is her father.

Although unable to interpret the dream, the narrator is left with "un gran molestar" (1:176) [a great discomfort] that has a psychological effect on her subsequent actions. As if to fulfill the dream's "prophecy," she turns increasingly away from her husband and toward her deceased father: "buscava el retrat del meu pare . . . Des d'aquell dia vaig començar a viure amb el meu pare. Parlava amb el retrat" (1:179) [I searched for the photograph of my father . . . From that day on I began to live with my father. I spoke with his photograph.] The photograph becomes a stand-in for her husband; the narrator recreates her identity for the masculine observer, the original and ever-present authority figure.

While "La sang" tells a tragic story of a woman's inability to escape from the male gaze in order to create for herself a new and empowering identity, I think we must be attentive to the *form* that the narrative takes. The very fact that the woman is telling *her* story to another, *voicing* feelings that she was unable to articulate before and *shaping* her own discourse, suggests an attempt at self-creation that is ultimately more important than the events narrated. If, at the end, she confesses that "si veig dàlies en un aparador em ve com una mena de mareig i tinc ganes de vomitar, dispensi," (1:180) [if I see dahlias in a window display I become a little nauseated and I feel like vomiting, if you'll forgive me] she has also spewed forth the psychological demons of her past. Perhaps now she, like Natàlia-Colometa or Cecília Ce, can begin to recover her lost bearings.

Besides its standing as an important precursor to the conversational discourse developed in subsequent writings, "La sang" is an eloquent, masterful critique of a culture in which women have come, or are forced, to define themselves in relation to their biological function, whether or not that function has been realized. Bearing in mind the distinctions made by Geraldine Cleary Nichols between the two types of female characters who inhabit Rodoreda's fictional world, the victims and the *triomfadoras,* the protagonist of "La sang," as well as the protagonists presented in the other stories explored here, seem to me to fall within the latter category. This is because they are all willful women who are attempting to impose the shape of their desire on the world around them (Nichols 171). Their power to seize control of the signifier depends, to a large part, on their power to transcend the doubled "I," the identity imposed from without and the muted sense of self emerging from within. The various catoptric devices do not merely serve a narrative function; they are metaphors of the disjunctive identities that they must reclaim in order to escape from their self-alienation. The catoptric devices, in their ability to create a dialogic interplay between exteriority and interiority, provide a means of self-scrutiny essential to the process of self-creation.

Notes

1. As Mikhail Bakhtin argues, "every word is directed toward an *answer* and cannot escape the profound influence of the answering word that it anticipates. The word in living conversation is directly, blatantly, oriented toward a future answer-word: it provokes an answer, anticipates it and structures itself in the answer's direction. Forming itself in an atmosphere of the already spoken, the word is at the same time determined by that which has not yet been said but which is needed and in fact anticipated by the answering word. Such is the situation in any living dialogue." Mikhail M. Bakhtin. "Discourse in the Novel," in *The Dialogic Imagination: Four Essays by M. M. Bakhtin,* ed. Michael Holquist, trans. Caryl Emerson and Michael Holquist (Austin: University of Texas Press, 1981), 280.

2. Page numbers of this and subsequent citations of Rodoreda's works correspond to the three-volume *Obres Completes,* ed. Carme Arnau (Barcelona: Edicions 62, 1984).

3. Jenijoy La Belle, *Herself Beheld: The Literature of the Looking Glass* (Ithaca and London: Cornell University Press, 1988), 9.

4. Anne Hollander, *Seeing through Clothes* (Berkeley: University of California Press, 1993), 407.

5. Emilie Bergmann has analyzed several of Rodoreda's wartime stories in "Fragments of Letters: Mercè Rodoreda's Wartime Fiction," in *The Garden Across the Border: Mercè Rodoreda's Fiction,* ed. Kathleen McNerney and Nancy Vosburg, (Selinsgrove, Pa.: Susquehanna University Press, 1994), 223–39. These stories, written between March 1937 and July 1938 and published originally in *Meridià, Companya, Catalans!,* and *Moments,* appeared subsequently in the 1981 anthology *Contes de guerra i revolució,* 2 vols., introducció, selecció, i notes de Maria Campillo (Barcelona: Laia, 1981).

6. Carmen Martín Gaite, "La búsqueda de interlocutor," *La búsqueda de interlocutor y otras búsquedas* (Barcelona: Destino, 1982). "Bien o mal empleado, este recurso, cada vez que aparece es reflejo de una intrínseca necesidad del relato, . . . Lo interpreto casi como una transposición al plano de lo escrito de los '¿me oyes todavía?' o 'no te habrás dormido' que, también espontáneamente, jalonan con frecuencia nuestras narraciones orales cuando decaen; elocuentes muestras ambas de ese afán por buscar el bulto del oyente—real o inventado—, afán que constituye, repito, el originario móvil y perenne acicate de toda narración." (28)

7. La Belle has observed that, in a number of literary works, mirror scenes characterized by a disunity between self and reflected image almost always signal either a revolt or a psychological disturbance. (22)

8. Natàlia-Colometa, Cecília Ce, and Teresa Goday are the primary female characters of, respectively, *La plaça del Diamant, El carrer de les Camèlies,* and *Mirall trencat.*

Silent Women: Language in Mercè Rodoreda

MARYELLEN BIEDER

> Què és? Es un peix? No. És una senyora. I, encara prenent el pols a Rafael, es va cargolar de riure. ("Paràlisi")
>
> What is it? Is it a fish? No. It's a woman. And, still taking Rafael's pulse, he burst out laughing.

QUESTIONS OF REPRESENTATION AND SELF-REPRESENTATION, OF A woman as seen by a man and as seen by herself, underlie much of Mercè Rodoreda's fiction.[1] What, she asks in these works, does it mean to be a woman, to be the object of the male gaze and the subject of one's own attempts at representation? In a brilliant *mise en abîme,* her short story "Paràlisi" [Paralysis] figures both this tension between representation and self-representation and the tension between reading and misreading. The female narrator/protagonist of "Paralysis" has painted a picture "a la boja, amb draps mullats i amb el paper xop" [wildly, with moist rags and wet paper]. A man, looking at the picture, guesses it to be a fish. The narrator corrects him: it is a woman. An innocent mistake, perhaps, but the viewer in this case is a doctor, a man trained to observe, to analyze, and to diagnose the human body. At the very moment he comments on the painting, he is taking the pulse of the narrator's male companion. The man of science thus fails to recognize the protagonist's representation of a woman. What escapes him is not only the human subject, but the portrayal of interiority. He can detect the deceit beneath his male patient's symptoms, but when looking at the picture he seeks only a superficial realism. Seeing only the picture's surface, and not the alienation and anguish it figures, the doctor accepts his misdiagnosis with a laugh.

Since "Paralysis" is narrated in the first person, the reader perceives the painting through the gaze and language of the unnamed woman narrator. Contemplating her own work through her woman's eyes, she recreates it in language, painting it with words: "Blava i lila, rosada. El cap un triangle i mitja cara ratllada amb ratlles fines trencades de tant en tant per un cop de drap mullat." (103) [Blue and lilac, pink. The head, a triangle, and half the face striped with thin lines broken here and there by the imprint of a damp rag].[2] This scission of the woman's face—one half broken by stripes—emblemizes the narrator's self-representation within the story. The visible, unshaded half is the face the woman presents to the gaze of others. It is the carefully constructed self that she prepares to elicit and receive the male gaze. In contrast, the veiled and partly effaced half hides the inner self, unseen, unknowable, perhaps even to herself. As an act of violence committed by a woman against herself, the painting makes visible the invisible and communicates what language itself cannot. Outwardly, the protagonist appears to move freely and confidently in the world: she has friends and lovers, she works, she takes walks, and she expresses her creativity in painting and writing. Inwardly, however, she is disconnected, estranged, blurred, invisible. The doctor's response to his misdiagnosis, his laughter at his mistake, marks the distance between subject and object, between creation and reception, between female and male in Rodoreda's story. This in turn mirrors the distance that necessarily arises between author and reader, between writing a text and reading a text, making the story a self-conscious meditation on its own reception.

The tension conveyed by the narrator-painter in "Paralysis" between women as visible social being and the invisible inner woman, between representation and self-representation, surfaces in many of Rodoreda's other narratives. The central component of Rodoreda's fiction, as Carme Arnau has observed, is "una figura femenina que, intensament, viu i contempla el món que la rodeja" (84) [a female figure who with great intensity lives in and contemplates the world around her].[3] In privileged moments her protagonists, almost always women, see themselves simultaneously both from within and from the outside, as if they were watching themselves. The two halves of their experience as women stand revealed to them, as the narrator's painting makes explicit.[4] Such a moment embodies the radical solitude of the women in Rodoreda's fiction. It is the moment of epiphany in which Rodoreda's women recognize the failure of language and the impossibility of communication. In "Paralysis," this failure is triply figured through the language of art, of the body, and of writing, making the story one of Rodoreda's most complex and most self-conscious meditations on language and representation.

Another story, "Pluja" [Rain], also from Rodoreda's 1978 collection, *Semblava de seda* [It Seemed Like Silk], similarly explores the dialectic between the female protagonist's visible public self and invisible private self. Both stories are superbly crafted to capture moments of privileged awareness in which the protagonist sees herself mirrored in an object, text, or scene in the world around her. This essay will examine both stories. The two protagonists—one a single woman, the other living with her partner—are at that age when, as Rodoreda said of herself, "allò que m'interessa més es la llibertat interior i exterior"[5] [What interests me the most is personal and external freedom]. The two stories offer opposing, but nevertheless similar, resolutions to the decisive moment when a woman faces the need to define her life for herself. One woman may seek refuge in solitude and silence, while another may rebel against the limitations that circumscribe her.[6] Differences of technique and style, as well as implicit differences in the ages of the protagonists, suggest that "Rain" may have been written before "Paralysis."[7] Whatever the chronology of composition, given the order of the stories in the collection it is possible to read the narrator/protagonist of "Paralysis" as a response to and rewriting of the protagonist of "Rain." The emblematic confrontation of perception between the narrator and the doctor in "Paralysis" dramatizes the impossibility of communicating a woman's inner self—its erasure and invisibility—that is the silent text of Rodoreda's fiction.

Narrated in the third person, "Rain" transmits only the actions, thoughts and mental processes of its protagonist, Marta. Using predominantly indirect style, the narration follows the flow of her thoughts, which almost never coalesce into spoken language. Put another way, this is a focalized narration, in which objects, people, events, and even words are seen exclusively through Marta's eyes and received by her consciousness. The transcription of this third-person mental flow signals the presence of an undramatized narrator who controls and transmits the narration. Designated "narrated monologue" by the critic Dorrit Cohn,[8] this technique allows for the faithful reproduction of the protagonist's mental language even though this language remains in an unuttered state. Every narrated monologue implies the existence of a narrator whose mediation serves to distance the narration temporally and emotionally from the experiences that give rise to it. This mediation between the character who perceives and the language that transmits perception distinguishes narrated monologue from a first-person monologue, such as occurs in "Paralysis." Rodoreda uses narrated monologue to position the reader to share the perceptual and conceptual processes of a protagonist who does not exercise linguistic control within the story. (In this story, I would posit, narratee and implied reader, like Rodoreda and her protagonist, are implicitly female; they are the recipients, respectively, of the covert narrator's communication and of the implied author's vision, both also coded female.) In spite of seeing exclusively through the protagonist's eyes and understanding through her perceptions, the reader follows Marta from a plane at both a temporal and spatial distance from her. To some extent this distance parallels the tension within Marta herself: at once inside and outside, subject and object, observer and observed, of her own life. By means of this narrated monologue, the implied reader of "Rain" experiences with Marta, although distanced from her, a decisive day in her life: the day Albert will enter her apartment for the first time.

If initially Marta appears to embody the industrious domesticity of her Biblical namesake, a quality that seems to embody the promise of a wife willing to sacrifice herself for her husband's happiness, her resistence to internalizing this model soon manifests itself. Marta reviews the preparations she has made for Albert's arrival as if she were viewing from outside herself: "Anà fins a la porta i mirà quin efecte feia." (67) [She stood in the doorway and looked at the result of her efforts]. She has arranged the house as a backdrop to create the desired effect, having neutralized all signs of her individuality: "l'escriptori amb els llibres ben arrenglerats, amb el tinter net i el secant rosa bombó, sense una taca de tinta" (67) [her desk with its books neatly arranged, its clean inkwell and spotless pink blotter]. The world of Marta's apartment is a world of things, of objects carefully chosen and arranged; taken together, they represent a prudent, if impersonal, well-being. Surveying her world with a critical eye, Marta concludes to herself: "Tot estava en ordre." (67) [Everything was in order]. Having taken herself out of the room, Marta tries to project onto it the gaze for which it has been prepared, Albert's male gaze.

The stage set for Albert's entrance, Marta gets ready to play the role of the welcoming girlfriend, constructing the identity that she wants Albert to read when he views her for the first time in her own world. She goes through her wardrobe, choosing the dress that will send the appropriate message; she rejects an alluring blue dressing gown, in favor of a more respectable brown dress, thus placing her social role ahead of her sexual attraction. She chooses a book for the end table, attempting to identify in literature an objective correlative for the role she embodies. Fearing that Albert will misread her and think her pretentious, she rejects her first choice, *Othello,* a drama that foreshadows the playing out in the story of the dichotomy between reality and illusion, between anticipation and experience. One of the central motifs of Rodoreda's story is the greeting the returning Othello gives to his wife: "'Bella guerrera!' Cap compliment de soldat per a la seva dona no pot ésser més patèticament pur." (68) ["My fair warrior!" What more pathetically pure compliment could a soldier give his lady?] This same greeting from warrior to warrior, with its implication of equality in difference, carries with it as well the play's promise of jealousy and death. Othello's words echo in Marta's mind throughout the afternoon, giving voice to her desires and fears. When she chooses *Du côté de chez Swann* for the end table, Marta breaks the sense of anticipation that Albert's visit has aroused in her up to this point and instead opens the door to her past and to memories. With these two books, the intertextual frame of Rodoreda's story opens up to foreground texts through which Marta can contextualize herself. She can become the warrior-spouse in a play of passion, envy and deception, or she can decide to withdraw into memory and live off the re-creation of past emotions. These intertexts mark the dichotomy between present and past, between desire and memory, between being for herself and being for another.

In Marta, Rodoreda has created a protagonist who exercises control over her economic and material circumstances. An inheritance from her mother (the passing of wealth through the maternal line) and her job as a secretary give Marta a financial independence that makes marriage an option and not a necessity. She has a few close friends, "bons i desinteressats amics" (68) [good, unselfish friends], with whom to share her life. Yet within this material and emotional well-being Marta feels the weight of solitude and desire. Breaking with the conventional plot of the marriageable young woman on the verge of a lifetime commitment, Rodoreda interjects an unexpected complication into the familiar story: the memory of an earlier passionate affair that led to an abortion. With the recollection of that first love, Marta ceases to project Albert's arrival in terms of a new future. His visit becomes instead both a forecaste of and a return to deception, anguish, and death. This association of love with death—anticipated by the reference to *Othello*—has its roots in her past, in the death of her lover, her abortion, and consequently her own fear of death. For Marta, love is a contradictory sign, both pleasure and danger/death. Leaving ajar the door to her past, Marta begins to feel the weight of her role as the object of desire and to assume the consequences of a new amorous, sexual relationship. To allow Albert to enter her world is to open herself up anew to pain. She glimpses the absence of control over her life, the destructive emotions, and the lack of autonomy that life with Albert portends. The dialectic that begins to ferment in Marta is reflected not only in the opposition between past and present, but also in the tension between the space of her home and the world outside, between self-sufficient solitude and sexual love, between silence and communication.

In an abrupt and unexpected transition, Marta abandons her apartment before Albert appears, fleeing from the violation of her private world, her memories, and her body that his presence has come to represent. She suddenly finds herself outside on the street, walking aimlessly, and looking at the world around her, instead of at the self she has constructed. Loosing herself in this anonymous world, she sheds the attempt to make herself into the object of Albert's desire. Whereas earlier she put on perfume in order to please him, now she breathes in the smells of the streets, enjoying the memories these other smells evoke. She has ceased to be the Biblical Martha and she now lives for herself. On the other hand, this contact with the larger world brings back the reality of a routine, monotonous, and unexceptional day. In the words of Maria Campillo, for Rodoreda's protagonists the experience of quotidian reality "es resolia concèntricament, a l'entorn d'ells mateixos i de les seves topades—involuntàries, inevitables—amb el món exterior, experiència, per tant, només referida al propi cas"[9] [ripples in concentric circles around them and their involuntary but inevitable encounters with the external world; it is therefore an experience that refers only to their own situation]. If the world around her exists only as a function of herself, Marta's trajectory is not in essence outward but, despite her having left her apartment, a journey inward.

This dual physical and emotional trajectory takes place against a backdrop of fine, monotonous rain that falls from before the story begins until its end. Maria-Aurèlia Capmany has noted that in Rodoreda's fiction "hi ha alguna cosa constant i segura que s'escola al marge de la vida desorbitada dels homes: les flors que esberlen la terra, el pas fidel de les estacions, el fred i la calor, les pluges i el sol"[10] [there are certain constant things that unfold on the margin of people's unregulated lives: the flowers that break through the earth, the faithful passing of the seasons, cold and warmth, rain and sun]. The rain rescues Marta from waiting and from losing herself in the inanimate objects that comprise her domestic world; it puts her in contact with the timeless external world and submerges her in the flow of life. Taking up the thread of her own life, she searches for reflective surfaces in which to see and define herself. Through Marta's readings of herself as objectified on these surfaces, the reader in turn reads Marta.

These objective correlatives give structure to Marta's journey away from the apartment and into herself. Interspersed along her directionless flight, these emblematic moments allow the reader to share Marta's self-projections. From the street she sees a cat inside a house peering out at the rain: "A l'àmpit d'una finestra lligat amb un cordill al coll hi havia un gat petit: cada vegada que una gota d'aigua li queia al nas, alçava el cap. A dintre se sentien crits de criatures." (71) [From behind a window sat a little cat with a string around its neck. Every time a drop of water fell on its nose, it looked up. Inside she could hear children screaming]. The kitten, with its collar and confinement, lives the constricted life from which Marta has escaped into the rain.

Other correlatives take the form of images and texts: remembered scenes from a movie about Queen Elizabeth, with its reflection of the queen in the mirror; the Desdemona evoked by Othello's words; and Queen Dido calling out to a "fleeing Aeneas" (71–72). If Marta is unable to put herself into language, she is nevertheless able to bring other texts to life by transfusing them with her own anguish. Anchored in her pre-verbal consciousness, Marta responds to the language and emotions of others to contextualize her feelings. Similarly, in her work as a secretary, she routinely transcribes the words of others, words that frequently convey no meaning to her. Without her own language, Marta is locked in her own inner silence.

Marta's trajectory in "Rain" is circular, tracing out the double displacement of escape and return. If her first response is to flee from her housebound identity, her second instinct is to return to the absolute solitude of her own home. During her journey, a number of polarities struggle within her: memories of a former passion and the contemplation of a new relationship, the desire for another and the defense of her own self, the longing for love and the need to be free. Something in her is stronger than her desire for Albert or her fear of being alone; her inviolable sense of self will not allow her to become the person others seek in her. On returning home many hours later, Marta looks for some sign of Albert's emotional passage along her street or in her building: "El carrer no deia res: ni si ell havia arribat feliç ni si n'havia entornat tristíssim. L'ombra del fanal es trencava sobre la paret i un aparell de radio escampava les onades d'un vals." (73) [The street said nothing: neither that he had arrived happy nor that he had left very sad. The shadow of a streetlamp broke into fragments on the wall and a radio sent out waves of waltz music]. Albert has left no trace of his passage through her world. Faced with the danger to herself that he embodies, Marta "aborts" the possibility of a relationship and its destructive consequences. Evading the deceptions and pain of a shared life, she takes refuge in herself, in her solitude and silence.

For the women in Rodoreda's fiction, control over the body is intimately associated with control over language, as Geraldine Cleary Nichols recognizes when she tellingly observes that "a woman's power can evaporate if she stops listening to her own voice and attends to the world's."[11] Powerless without her own voice, Marta has to create her own language to empower herself, a process that in her case builds on borrowed words. Once back in her own apartment, she experiences the power of language and with this power, the subordination of her body. Home again, Marta allows Proust's words to replace her direct contact with the world, submerging her existence in the experience of the text. The book she selected to define herself for Albert's gaze elicits the thought: "les *aubepines* dintre el llibre de Proust devien ser més boniques que mai" (73) [the *aubepines* in Proust's book were surely more beautiful than ever]. Having eschewed communication and taken refuge in silence, Marta creates her own linguistic realm. In this realm, to *think* a world is to grant it physical existence: "Allò que ignoro no ho poc pensar; per a mi no existeix. Xina existeix tot d'una, quan hi penso, quan dic: cirerer florit, Dragó de foc . . ." (73–74) [I cannot think what I do not know; for me it does not exist. China suddenly exists when I think of it, when I say: flowering cherry tree, Fire dragon . . .] Proust has named the hawthorn trees; for Marta they are alive because she thinks of them. This epiphany reveals to her the primacy of language, its power to bring into being, the precedence of the word over the thing named. From this insight into linguistic power, associated with her memory of Proust, comes the power with which to define her own emotions.

Marta finds in a Mallarmé poem a defense of her own expression of solitude: "Oui, c'est pour moi, pour moi/ que je fleuris, déserte!" (74). Creator and recipient, Marta encloses herself in language, encircled and safe. Her sense of self-preservation, her defense against pain—"alguna cosa més forta que ella mateixa" (72) [something stronger than herself]—has come between her and the future Albert represents. "'¿Per què aquesta por d'un nou amor, per què aquest egoisme de persona cansada i vella?'" (72) ["Why that fear of a new love? Why that self-absorption, as if you were a tired old person?"][12] All her preparation for Albert, now signs without a receiver, are subsumed into her double role of sender and recipient. For herself alone, Marta puts on "la camisa de dormir més bonica, la més etèria, la més nuvial" (74) [her prettiest, most diaphanous, most bridal nightgown]. Her wedding night will be a night spent alone; her body will be warmed not by a man's presence but by three drinks. The world into which Marta retreats is the world of things, not of bodies. The brandy fills her with the warmth of the missing man, lulling her to sleep in her dual role as subject and object, a duality created by unspoken words over which she finally has gained control. Pleasure, like everything else, is for her a verbal creation, in a play of silence.

Once she takes refuge in the creative power of language, Marta uses it to transform her verbal and corporal solitude: "Ara tindria besos a les espatlles; en tindria al braços, als llavis: podria guardar-los perquè li fessin companyia a la nit. Podria deixar-los sota el coixí i potser en sortirien mentre dormiria per tornar, precisos, al braços, a les espatlles." (74) [Now she would have the imprint of kisses on her shoulders, her arms, her lips; she could hold on to them so they would keep her company at night. She could slip them beneath her pillow and maybe they would come out while she was sleeping, returning to the same spots on her arms and her shoulders]. Marta avoids the commitment that Albert's visit represents, resolving the double tension of passion/solitude and language/silence with the power of unspoken words dependent only on her own will. If she does not name something, it ceases to exist; if she gives something a name, it comes into being. She will not become the woman Albert desires; he will instead become her creation. By taking control of the word, she creates at least the illusion of taking control of her world. Her trajectory is at once outward, inward, and towards a disembodied lover; if she flees from the man she has invited to her own home, she receives the one she creates in her own imagination.

Marta does not utter a single word in "Rain," except when she orders a cup of coffee, and this single attempted communication fails because the coffee machine is broken. She only manages to transform language into the thing it names on her second attempt, when she requests an herbal tea. The narrative transmits those thoughts that Marta consciously formulates by using direct style, enclosing them in quotation marks, as in her closing reflection: "'M'emborratxaré'" (74) [I'll get drunk]. Like the rest of the narrated monologue, these are unspoken words that she addresses to herself. Language begins for Marta as another system of subordination; she relates to it passively. When her mind scripts possible scenarios for Albert's visit, she always imagines herself as an object dependent on his words and moods. When she searches for a language with which to define herself, the words that come to mind are those already recorded by others. In this sense, "Rain" narrates Marta's textualization or literaturization, her coming into subjecthood through the models she identifies in visual and literary texts. She is distanced from the spoken word in the same way that the story's use of narrated monologue maintains the reader at a distance from Marta. Silence is the space of her self-representation, her escape from being represented by another, even if this is purchased at the price of solitude and made bearable by numbing effect of alcohol.

In her study of Rodoreda's *La plaça del Diamant,* Frances Wyers insightfully identifies the novel's underlying paradox; it is a verbal text which, although constructed with words, communicates the impossibility of communication on the part of a protagonist whose language evaporates in the very moment that it takes shape.[13] The paradoxes multiply in the short story "Rain." In the first place, the transcription of Marta's mental monologue necessarily occurs subsequent to its momentary existence in her consciousness. Even more significantly, Marta ends up transforming her silence into a language, an operation carried out by means of two complementary discoveries: the autonomy of the word from the physical existence of the object it names, and the control exercised by the bearer of a word.

Whereas in "Rain," Rodoreda explores the language of silence, in "Paralysis," multiple languages interweave, all of them implicating silence in some way. On a critical day in her life, the unnamed protagonist narrates the flow of her consciousness as she keeps an appointment with the doctor, relives memories, and imagines a resolution to her crisis. A creative woman, she attempts to communicate herself through painting and writing, as well as through flowers, clothing, and her body. The story's conflict arises from the clash between her desire for subjectivity and her sense of objectification with its paralyzing physical, emotional, and expressive consequences. The similarity between the protagonists of the two stories is striking. Both women face a personal decision that will set the limits of their subjectivity. "Paralysis" deals with a mature woman trapped in what might be the very same circumstances that Marta feared and aborted in "Rain." The relationship that Marta foresaw between herself and Albert seems to characterize the corrosive tension between the older protagonist of "Paralysis" and her companion Rafael:

> Si fos fidel exigiria, seria sever, seriós, es faria vell amb pausa. Si no ho fos, seria condescendent, comprensiu, patiria del cor i es tancaria en un món del qual ella en seria exclosa. (69)
>
> [If he were faithful he would be demanding, he would be severe, serious, he would slowly become old. If he were not, he would be indulgent, understanding, he would have heart trouble and he would close himself up in a world from which she would be excluded.]

Reversing the ending of "Rain," "Paralysis" traces out the failure of communication in a destructive relationship. Because the narrator/protagonist is also a writer, the story in fact articulates the triple failure—sexual, artistic and literary—of her attempts to break out of the silence that encloses her. In spite of the multiple codes she manipulates, the protagonist does not find her desired interlocutor; communication always falls short, as it does when the doctor cannot identify the woman's face in her painting.

When the doctor misreads the signs that convey the experience of being a woman, he misreads the shape of woman in a man's world. His diagnosis of the painted text—a fish—severs the identification between the painter and the painting, between the body and the text. The word "fish" floats in the air between narrator and doctor, a sign without a referent. Instead of transmitting her inner reality, the painting releases two free-floating linguistic signs: woman and fish. Repeating the two words, the narrator reverses their order, disassociating them from their initial referent, the painting: "Què és? Es una senyora? No. Es un peix. No. Es una senyora." (103) [What is it? Is it a woman? No. It's a fish. No. It's a woman]. Devoid of reference, the painting signals only the absence of communication.

The confusion over the painting is a memory overlaid onto the present of the narrator's monologue, which centers on her appointment with the doctor about the immobilizing pain in her foot. In this exchange, communication again fails between the woman and the doctor. He sees her as part of a pair, as his patient's "wife," rather than as a separate individual. According to his diagnosis, she is the cause of her "husband's" illness, but the reader comes to perceive the reverse, that Rafael is a cause of hers. The narrator is equally unsuccessful in her attempt to make herself physically attractive to the doctor; he reads her only as a patient, not as a woman. This time the text that does not communicate her desired message is her own body, which she cannot code as an object of desire to a man.

In contrast to "Rain," the narrative of "Paralysis" is a first-person mental monologue. In the opening sentences of the story, the temporal plane is just slightly posterior to the action: "He mirat en el diccionari 'didalera.'" (99) [I've looked up "didalera" in the dictionary]. Language is thus the subject—as well as the medium—both of Rodoreda's story and of the protagonist's interior monologue. Throughout most of "Paralysis," however, the representation of the protagonist's thoughts and actions coincides with the moment in which they occur, without any apparent mediating narrator. The result is an autonomous interior monologue which, as Cohn has shown, is, "paradoxically, a nonnarrated form of fiction."[14] Thus in "Paralysis" the implied (female) reader comes into direct and immediate contact with the closed circle of the autonomous monologue, in which voice and listener are one. In the protagonist's conscious mind, thoughts, memories and overheard phrases, fragments of conversations, city sights, readings, plans, desires, and dreams all intertwine. The implied presence of a mediating narrative voice occurs only in the frame to the monologue, enclosing it between the story's opening lines and its closing paragraph.

In the middle of the autonomous monologue, in the second of its three sections, the protagonist unexpectedly identifies herself as an author in the act of writing. The revelation shifts our perception of the relationship between character and language, by reinserting the mediating presence of a narrator/writer into the previous mental flow and granting the protagonist/writer the power of the written word. Thus in "Paralysis" the distance between reader and protagonist varies at different points, from the minimal but marked distance of the narrative frame, to the erasure of distance in the (apparently) unmediated monologue, to the invisible but controling hand of the protagonist/writer whose presence can be projected back to the beginning of the story. In the third section, the protagonist/writer again picks up the thread of her consultation with the doctor, thus preserving her double voice as monologuist and author. Rodoreda further intertextualizes the functions of narrating and reading/decoding through a musical motif: the sounds of Beethoven's Kreutzer Sonata accompany the protagonist as she recreates her experiences in words. The Sonata inspired Tolstoy's eponymous novel of jealousy, adultery, and death, in which the male narrator cannot escape the need to retell obsessively the story of his marriage. With this motif, Rodoreda suggests the imperative of interlocution and the difficulty of interpretation, compulsions about dominate human response.

The shifting of linguistic signs that denotes Rodoreda's destabilizing of linguistic reference first occurs in the opening sentence of "Paralysis" with the word "didalera." It is a word that resonates on multiple levels throughout the story, in its dual meanings of foxglove and digitalis, thus signaling overlapping facets of the narrator's fragmented self. The protagonist, as monologuist, narrator, and writer, peoples her linguistic world with the objects and experiences that define her and her verbal codes. An American critic has observed that in a Virginia Woolf novel even ordinary words can take on a "paradigmatic dimension within the text."[15] In Rodoreda's story, words like "foxglove," "fish," "paralysis," and "blue underwear," take on a paradigmatic function in the protagonist's verbal self-representation. For her, these words set different codes into play and embody different representations of herself: her youth (foxglove), her inner self (woman/fish), her sexual self (underwear). Like Marta preparing herself for Albert's visit, the protagonist tries to communicate herself as a readable text. Her lost blue underwear, for example, becomes for her the objective correlative of her powers of sexual attraction. The foxglove is the talisman that opens the door to the lost paradise of her childhood; it is the touchstone that will identify an ideal interlocutor, someone with whom to share her world. The question repeated in some form in each sentence of the story—"Saps que són didaleres?" [Do you know what foxgloves are?]—encapsulates the search for communication that defines the protagonist's monologue. In a subtle way Rodoreda manages to layer onto one word the story's two central but contradictory motifs: flowers (emotions) and medicine (body). The word "didalera" simultaneously carries the protagonist into the past, back to the flowers in her childhood garden[16] and into a present dominated by the pain that is paralyzing her, "l'angoixa com una bèstia grossa se m'instal.la sota del cor i no em deixa respirar" (102) [like a huge beast, anxiety has taken up residence under my heart and doesn't let me breathe]. While evoking an escape from her solitude, "didalera" also suggests the possibility of a cure for the pain and paralysis that accompany it.

Paralysis is the principal trope for the protagonist's feeling of entrapment. It is at once a physical paralysis that impedes her movements, an emotional paralysis that thwarts her self-representation, and a psychic paralysis that blocks her resolve to abandon a destructive relationship. From her memories of Catalonia, emblems surface of the powerlessness she feels. The leashed dog and the grafted rosebush are the objective correlatives of her bodily and emotional paralysis. The dog's subordination to his mistress is such that he is tied "amb una corda invisible en un pal invisible" (102) [with an invisible leash to an invisible stake], as she feels herself tied to Rafael. The mediocre rose that as a child she once grafted onto a first-class rosebush killed the healthy plant: "l'empelt . . . se li va menjar tota la saba per alimentar-se només ell" (105) [the graft absorbed all the sap just to feed itself]. The devouring graft figures her own feelings of annihilation and death as her life with Rafael absorbs her strength and kills her autonomy. Fear of losing control is also figured in the underclothing that seems to slide down her body. To exhibit one's private self, to lose one's protective covering, is to violate social codes and reveal the vulnerability of the intimate self.

The elastic band that threatens to come loose and release hidden undergarments, the trope of the sexual body, constitutes an archetypal experience for Rodoreda's women. Writing of *La Plaça del Diamant,* Wyers reminds us that when the elastic on Natalia's slip gives way at the dance, she lets the garment fall to the floor and runs away, in an ambiguous gesture of flight from the danger embodied by Quimet's pursuit of her.[17] Neus Carbonell further observes that Natalia's pain of abandonment—she is a daughter without a mother—"is felt through the elastic waistband of her petticoat."[18] Similarly, in "Paralysis," deep emotional anxiety and the resulting physical pain manifest themselves as a preoccupation with the staying power of an elastic band. The fear of immobility, of not being able to escape, intensifies the protagonist's sense of entrapment and lays bare her insecurity at the door of the very doctor whom she desires to attract.

Unlike Marta, who needs the words of others to give voice to her reality (Proust's *aubépines,* for example), the protagonist of "Paralysis" can control language and make words her own. Her attempts at interlocution fail, however, and she rejects further dialogue with Rafael. Instead, she increasingly loses herself in dialogue with other texts, ceding her creative word and responding to the language of other authors. A passage from Plutarch's *Demonology,* in which a nymph affirms the astounding longevity of Nereids over all other beings, seems to constitute a moment of recognition for the narrator. The enigmatic lines affirm life and counter her building disillusionment and sense of incapacity. Together with the now-recovered blue underwear, the words propel her to construct her own future in language. Both visually and auditorily, the long quote from Plutarch interrupts the flow of her monologue and breaks the text. The remainder of "Paralysis" reinscribes its narrative frame and reestablishes the temporal distance between narrator and narration.

Projecting a new day and new plans, as did the story's opening, the ending brings the day full circle. The protagonist imagines the sequence of actions that will enable her to leave the apartment and abandon her relationship with Rafael, but these actions remain at the level of language. As the framing narrative's greater distance makes clear, the protagonist is trapped not only in her body, but in time and in the sterility of her words. She fails to construct a verbal path out of her dead-end situation; her language has no referential potential, no power to become movement. The words that record her contemplated actions are narrated after the fact, making her flight only an unrealized mental projection, forever postponed by language.

In the final paragraph, the narrator moves from mimetic summary—"He dormit malament" (111) [I slept badly]—to performative anticipation—"El primer de tot és curar-me el peu malalt" (112) [The first thing is to cure my bad foot]. With the disappearance of the first-person pronoun, however, the autonomous monologue merges into a totally impersonal and atemporal closing declaration: "La farmacia és a la vora de casa" (112) [The pharmacy is just around the corner]. The story increasingly disengages itself from the protagonist in its final sentences, in spite of the fact that she is narrating her own excision. Having lost the link between word and motion, as well as control of her body, she is left immobile, silenced, and invisible at the story's close. The verb tenses of this final paragraph repeat the conjugation of her past, present, and future "I," all of which paralyze her. Her body defeats her linguistic projection of escape, as paralysis insinuates itself between her desire to leave home and the act itself, deferring its realization. The trip to the pharmacy, the taking of medicine, the recovery from pain: the moment of departure recedes in the face of the many obstacles to be overcome first. By the time the reader reaches the last word of the story, the narrator's escape is farther removed than when she first enunciated it. After all, the desired escape from place cannot release her from her own body or from the psychic pain that entraps her.

Like the doctor in his passing assessment of the painting, Rafael and Albert have misread the woman in their lives; they look at her but they do not see her. Fish or woman, words are empty signs. Whereas in "Rain" Marta escapes the potential oppression of marriage by withdrawing inward to embrace herself as both subject and object of her own desire, in "Paralysis" the protagonist comes to the brink of breaking out of her immobility and escaping outward, into subjectivity. Her language, however, remains subordinated to her body, which blocks her escape at the very moment that her words plot the path to initiate it. The divided self that her painting represents continues unhealed. Although she enjoys the power of self-expression that Marta lacks, she cannot use language performatively to enact what it names. In this way, she is as trapped in silence as Marta. In *A Room of One's Own,* Virginia Woolf imagined her woman novelist overcoming women's customary "concealment and suppression" and catching "those unrecorded gestures, those unsaid or half-said words, which form themselves, no more palpably than the shadows of moths on the ceiling, when women are alone, unlit by the capricious and coloured light of the other sex."[19] This is what Mercè Rodoreda brilliantly does in "Rain" and "Paralysis"; she makes visible the invisible female body and gives language to silent women.[20]

Notes

1. An earlier version of this study appeared in Spanish in Jane White Albrecht, Janet Ann DeCesaris, Patricia V. Lunn and Josep Miquel Sobrer, eds., *Homenatge a Josep Roca-Pons: Estudis de llengua i literatura* (Montserrat: l'Abadia, 1991), 91–110.

2. All page references for quotations from Rodoreda's stories are to *Semblava de seda* (Barcelona: Edicions 62, 1978). The translations are mine.

3. Carme Arnau, "Mercè Rodoreda o la força de l'escriptura" in Isabel Segura, et al., ed., *Literatura de dones: Una visió del mòn,* (Barcelona: laSal, 1988), 84.

4. Geraldine Cleary Nichols analyzes another of the story's metaphors of excision in "'Mitja poma, mitja taronja': génesis y destino literarios de la catalana contemporánea," *Anthropos* 60–61 (1986): 120.

5. Lluís Busquets i Grabulosa, "Mercé Rodoreda, passió eterna i fràgil" in *Plomes Catalanes Contemporànies* (Barcelona: Mall, 1980), 59.

6. In her study of female characters as writers in Rodoreda's fiction, Nichols also divides them into two, albeit different, groupings: victims and willful women; "Writers, Wantons, Witches: Woman and the Expression of Desire in Rodoreda," *Catalan Review* 2, no. 2 (December 1987): 171–80.

7. Although these two stories appeared in print for the first time in the 1978 collection *Semblava de seda,* they seem to have been written at different times. Nichols includes "Paralysis" among stories that reflect the experience of exile following the end of the Spanish Civil War and dates it to the early 1960s; "Exile, Gender, and Mercè Rodoreda," *MLN* 101 (1986): 408.

8. Dorrit Cohn discusses narrated monologue in *Transparent Minds: Narrative Modes for Presenting Consciousness in Fiction* (Princeton: Princeton University Press, 1978), 99–140.

9. Maria Campillo, "Mercè Rodoreda: la realitat i els miralls," *Els Marges*, 21 (1981): 129.

10. Maria-Aurèlia Capmany, "Mercè Rodoreda o les coses de la vida," *Serra d'Or* 10, no. 104 (May 1968): 49.

11. Nichols, "Writers, Wantons, Witches," 179.

12. In "Rain" and more intensively in "Paralysis," the protagonist's journey toward silence and solitude runs parallel to her growing perception of aging. Mercè Clarasó has studied Rodoreda's use of the anaphoric article to introduce a new noun, rather than to refer back to a previous use of the noun. Through this technique Rodoreda implicates her reader in the memory of something that the reader is in fact encountering for the first time; "The Angle of Vision in the Novels of Mercè Rodoreda," *Bulletin of Hispanic Studies* 57 (1980): 149.

13. Frances Wyers, "A Woman's Voices: Mercè Rodoreda's *La Plaça del Diamant*," *Kentucky Romance Quarterly* 30 (1983): 304.

14. Cohn, 1978. For a discussion of autonomous monologue, see 217–65.

15. Nancy Armstrong, "A Language of One's Own: Communication Modeling Systems in *Mrs. Dalloway*," *Language and Style* 16 (1983): 357.

16. For a discussion of the significance of the garden in the construction of female identity in Rodoreda's fiction, see my "The Woman in the Garden: The Problem of Identity in the Novels of Mercè Rodoreda," in *Actes del Segon Col.loqui d'Estudis Catalans a Nord-Amèrica*, ed. Manuel Duran, et al. (Montserrat: l'Abadia, 1982), 353–64.

17. Wyers, 303.

18. Neus Carbonell, "Beyond the Anxiety of Patriarchy: Language, Identity, and Otherness in Mercè Rodoreda's Fiction" (diss., Indiana University, Bloomington, 1992), 10. See also her *"La Plaça del Diamant" de Mercè Rodoreda* (Barcelona: Empùries, 1994), 19.

19. Virginia Woolf, *A Room of One's Own* (New York: Harcourt Brace Jovanovich, 1957 [originally published 1929]), 88.

20. In the light of Randolph D. Pope's discussion of the relationship between Rodoreda, her companion, Armand Obiols, and writing, it is tempting to read "Paralysis," and especially the oppressive figure of Rafael, as a response to Obiols's presence: "*Aloma*'s Two Faces and the Character of Her True Nature" in *The Garden Across the Border: Mercè Rodoreda's Fiction*, ed. Kathleen McNerney and Nancy Vosburg (Selinsgrove, Pa.: Susquehanna University Press, 1993), 135–47.

Spaces and Aromas in *Viatges i flors*

MÓNICA AYALA

A DISCUSSION OF THE CONFIGURATION OF SPACE AND THE DYNAMIC of the garden in Mercè Rodoreda's *Viatges i flors* requires a reading of the text based on two tangents: the sense of the fantastic and its manifestations in the narrations in the first section, "Viatges," and the proposal of an ethic contained in the symbolism that determines the characteristics of the flowers in the second part, "Flors."

With this double focus, following the division within the text, I will first study the links between space and the fantastic, between the "once upon a time" towns or provinces and the beings that inhabit them and whose customs give them form; then I will propose a moral of the aromas or an aromatic of the virtues, the evils, and the vicissitudes of the human soul, as an interpretive guide to the stories/descriptions which form the garden of the second part of the text.

FANTASTIC WANDERINGS

The point of departure for my interpretations of Rodoreda's work does not depend on a previous definition of the fantastic in order to prove its appearance in the stories; it does not assume the presence of the supernatural or the marvelous as elements to arrive at the fantastic in *Viatges i flors*. Instead, it is informed by a textual axis woven through the narrations that continuously confronts the real with the imaginary. This confrontation and its constant questioning create a ludic context in which the fantastic appears in several ways. Two elements in particular inform the shaping of the fantastic in these stories: wanderings and revealings.

In spite of the differences that separate and individualize each of the stories in "Viatges"—the specific architecture of each town, the activities of the inhabitants and their gender—

a common thread unites them all: the link that the wanderer who travels through them establishes among their spaces. The presence of a wandering narrator constitutes the fundamental axis that binds the stories together through his gaze and his language, defining a textual dynamic based on the trilogy of travel, observation, and narration.

The narrative device of wandering is not greatly elaborated: from the first tale the reader discovers a narrator whose existential and textual foundation is, in fact, travel. Nevertheless, there is no explanation of this condition and in only one of the stories is he named as such, indicating the perception that others have of him, when one of the characters says to him, "Fes via, vianant. Més amunt trobaràs una passera."[1] [Go on, wanderer. You'll find a stepping-stone up yonder.]

These stories assume the risk implicit in all tautological or self-referential structures: they are constructed on elements without external referents to justify their presence in the text, since the narration itself determines their worth. In the case of these stories, a dynamic is established between the wandering and the narrating that defines the material offered to the reader. It is fundamental to describe and narrate what happens in each town, but this is only possible because of the continuous movement of the narrator. Nevertheless, the related material maintains greater value and interest than the wandering itself.

The first story manifests this dynamic through its very title: the reader is taken to the "Poble dels guerrers" (Town of the warriors), without reference to the wandering condition of the narrator, and is told of the characteristics of the place. The narrator simply finds himself in the town full of soldiers with lances, horses, flags, drums, trumpets, and beautiful, solitary women; he observes this reality and describes and wonders about it, manifesting the sensations it arouses in him. In some of the later stories, references to the wandering condition of the narrator are directly associated with the action, and many verbs evoke movement. However, words such as "arrive," "accompany," "run," "fall," "cross through forests," and " sleep in a valley" suggest continuous movement without elaborating on its cause or reason.

In some of the stories, the inhabitants do recognize the narrator as a traveler, for example, in the towns "de vidre" [of glass], "dels homes ganduls" [of lazy men], and "dels cargols i del llot" [of snails and mud]. In these cases, the townspeople clearly see the narrator as a wayfarer. His motive for wandering is never questioned; it is simply a fact, a condition that defines him and is natural for him. The narrator does address the question of his mobile nature in one of the stories: when a voice that could belong to a listener, an inhabitant, or to the narrator himself asks: "Per què, si va enamorar-se'n, no s'hi va establir?" he replies, "Perquè la meva feina no és aturar-me sino anar sempre endavant; continuar la infinita busca i captura de cors obscurs i de costums ignorats." (41) [Why didn't you settle down, if you fell in love? Because my job is not to stop, it's to keep on going, to continue the unending search and capture of dark hearts and unknown customs.] In another story, the justification is more direct. In the town of the "penjats" [hanged], he assures the listener that the boredom and monotony of his own town are what push him to keep moving: "Li vaig explicar que a casa meva m'hi avorria perquè la gent anava pels carrers, volta que volta, cridant sense parar 'Llibertat! Llibertat!' i que me n'havia anat a córrer món, és a dir que, de moment, era un home sense poble." (48) [I told him that where I was from I got bored because people kept going up and down the streets, around and around, always yelling "Freedom! Freedom!" and that I'd left to see the world, and that at the moment, I was a man without a place.] It would seem, then, that the narrator is saying that he came from a submissive, monotonous, and homogenous place and left to look for differences, for the other. What he finds is different, but equally homogenous and monotonous.

The narrator's task requires that he travel so that he can reveal realities hidden to the everyday gaze, but what is the connection between the wandering and the fantastic, or, what meaning does the fantastic contain within this wandering? For even though the stories do not begin with the traditional opening "Once upon a time," nor do they prepare the reader to enter into a fantastic universe, the stories in *Viatges i flors* do belong to that world, since they are constructed in imaginary spaces and they contain a sense of time similar to fantastic stories.

All the stories in "Viatges" show a sense of space that transcends the concrete and real and becomes signification. The towns in these stories are more than geometric spaces, represented places, proposed by the narrator to the reader as spaces full of meaning in which the architecture and geometric design take on significance with their interrelation with the inhabitants and their customs. They are thought, lived, and named by the imagination, and as Bachelard points out, "space that has been seized upon by the imagination cannot remain indifferent space subject to the measures and estimates of the surveyor. It has been lived in, not in its positivity, but with all the partiality of the imagination."[2]

Throughout the narrator's trajectory of different towns, there is a spatial poetics that defines them as fantastic places, even though in the words of the narrator, the stories propose a limited sense of the fantastic: that of the unusual, the little known. The stories of dark sensibilities and strange customs are offered to the reader through the gaze of an errant narrator who describes and names them to familiarize the reader with them. In this way, the wandering character and poetic creation of spaces are directly associated with the form of presentation of the fantastic in "Viatges."

Certain temporal coordinates also form a part of this configuration of the fantastic. The narrator is characterized by his movement, which implies both a spatial and temporal displacement, but the emphasis is on the spatial. That is, the narrations propose a notion of time only with respect to space, so that instead of a lineal or continual perception of time, there is a condensation of time as it is lived, an almost imperceptible constituent of the text. It is a subtle element that travels through space implicitly, lurking in the corners of the houses, secondary to the narrative imagination. This treatment of time is characteristic of fantastic stories that avoid measuring the concrete duration of events and instead offer abstract time, the private experience that each individual makes of it, counting not the passing of hours but the condensation of a space that constitutes a different meaning.

Revelation

The traveler in these stories is dedicated to discovering unsuspected realities, and an aspect of his task has an ethical character. In this sense the tales are not unlike the traditional stories of fantasy that often contain elements encouraging certain kinds of behavior, even though they are not strictly speaking didactic, since they are usually self-contained and without extratextual referents.[3]

One of the most outstanding characteristics of *Viatges i flors* is the narrator's descriptions of the towns he visits. The customs of the inhabitants define the towns, rather than their topography or temporal references to the trips. Each town is characterized by a kind of work that differentiates it from the others and defines it as a closed, complete, and self-sufficient universe, determined by rules that balance and shape it. The inhabitants can define themselves as beings with identical behavior; each one accepts the task assigned and adapts to the norms of the community. The differences among them, basically of gender and age, create a sense of equilibrium and make up the closed character of these communities. In each of the towns, the impossibility of change is apparent, as if each reiterated the idea that everything that happened there corresponded to a pre-established order whose objective was self-preservation.

This does not mean that the stories have a moralizing intention, nor that they reproduce the pattern of traditional fantastic stories. But it is possible to see a revelation of behaviors that contrast with that of the narrator and the readers, for whom these are "ignorant customs" and people with "dark hearts" who therefore constitute "the other." These people and their ways transgress and contrast with the patterns of behavior the narrator and readers are accustomed to. The narrator's task is ethical in that it reveals to the world other possibilities with a complexity that comes from contrast, from the encounter with otherness, making evident differences and variations in feeling and acting and questioning the parameters of normality and the limits that define good and evil, what is accepted or permitted and what is not.

Since the task is not to propose a model of behavior, it is not strictly moralizing. Rather it is a deconstructive task that uncovers the senselessness of pre-established order and social differences because it shows the conservative nature of the "other" communities, even though they are transgressors of the familiar patterns. Moral teaching becomes impossible even though customs constitute the theme. The inclusion of elements from didactic models similar to those in the classic tales of fantasy shows mulitiplicity and differences in identity rather than perpetuating the earlier didactic lessons.

The narrator's task of revelations is related to the fantastic in two ways: it introduces customs that contain a certain didactic model, as in fairy tales, fables, and legends, and it shows the sense of strangeness or unusual of the fantastic. These two links with the fantastic demonstrate the double dynamic that characterizes these stories: on the one hand, a traditional element is recovered, and on the other, the didactic possibility is deconstructed by the critical position vis-à-vis human customs.

The narrator travels through the towns to discover and demonstrate their idiosycrasies and differences, and his work would be impartial if he limited himself to describing them. However, in many stories he inserts his own commentaries or those of other characters who express their opinions about what is described; he finds one town to be the prettiest, he describes the faces of happiness or sadness of the inhabitants, he wonders why certain things happen. His judgements cannot change anything, since the communities are completely closed, tautological societies. They not only reject the permanent presence of outsiders, but they also refuse any possiblility of change; no option for transformation exists. The traveler's only relationship with them is one of observaton and description of the collective behaviors that entrap and immobilize the townspeople, and never of full assimilation.

These tales do not contain the mythical element of the voyage in which the traveler goes through a series of tests in order to be recognized by the community. The content of the stories and the towns described are fantastic universes in which the effects of absolute homogeneity can be seen: the absence of differences, the total acceptance of the established regime, produces completely passive beings lacking in any kind of imagination. The only possibility of a liberating force is suggested in the visit to the the town of "bruixeria" [witchcraft], the prettiest town in the world, in which the inhabitants' dreams of liberation keep them from quotidian monotony.

Through the devices of wandering and revealing, Mercè Rodoreda thematicizes the fantastic in these stories. The first allows the displacement from one fantastic place to another within a specific time and space, reproducing certain aspects of traditional tales. The second describes fantastic towns and customs, not to propose them as prototypes of behavior but to demonstrate the danger of a life of obedience which nullifies the imagination and hinders the liberating exercise of creativity.

AN ETHICO-MORAL GARDEN

The second part of *Viatges i flors* is made up of thirty-eight brief descriptions of various flowers, categorized according to orientating and moral values, as is indicated in the title "Flors de debò" [Real flowers]. This second part has no voyaging narrator, and the descriptions have an individual character that makes them independent units. Nevertheless, they place the reader in the situation of a trip through a fantastic garden in which each flower described takes on human characteristics.

The traditional floral language, according to which each is attributed with significance depending on color and aroma, and placed in a sensual context as a fundamental framework, is here subverted by Rodoreda. This subversion is achieved by assigning each flower a specific value and an independent, autonomous role; first, by naming them, and then, by designating some of them as "real," implying that the others are false.

The name game that Rodoreda creates for her flowers subverts the traditional rhetoric surrounding them. There are no flowers in this garden that correspond to common names: no roses, jasmines, tulips, or sunflowers. This is a garden of imaginary flowers whose titles do not follow a single criterion for naming. Not only is the traditional nomenclature of floriculture rejected, but new denominations are invented. Some flowers have adjectival designators, such as "ferida" [wounded], or "dolenta" [bad], and three carry names of colors: "vermella" [red], "blava" [blue], and "negra" [black].

Other flowers are indicated by nouns: "felicitat" [happiness], "vergonya" [shame], "disfressa" [disguise], and "fantasma" [ghost]. Still others receive a name from their material makeup: "foc" [fire] and "mel" [honey]. A few do not fit into the above categories, such as the "flor sense nom" [nameless flower].

The largest group is the adjectival one, with most of the flowers displaying anthropomorphic characteristics and representing human emotions and actions. No logical principle organizes the selection of these adjectives or justifies the grouping proposed here. Instead, as in the previous section of "Viatges," the author seems to play, within a fantastic context, games determined only by laws of dreaming and the unconscious. From that perspective, she offers a portrait of the human condition in which each of the characteristics represented by the flowers is specific and at the same time captures a part of the social and textual dynamic.

The flowers named by nouns tend to appear toward the end, and they form a more coherent pattern. All are linked to pain and absence, and three of them (ghost, shadow, and disguise) allude to some sort of simulacrum or to the reality/appearance dichotomy.

This dichotomy is a fundamental axis of the textual dynamic throughout the work, but in the "Flors" section it becomes the actual presentation of the fantastic in the stories, for the fantastic here calls into question the exactness of the true/false limits through a narrative process that selects real and common objects—flowers—offering them as real only within their redefinition. They are no longer entities full of color and perfume; their significance comes from their representation of human emotions.

The other kinds of designations are in the minority for the small number of flowers named. Those that refer to the matter they are composed of would presumably not exist outside the confines of that matter, singular though it is—fire, honey, and perhaps life itself. "Flor cavaller" [Gentleman flower] stands alone as a masculine presence among the others, and its gender is emphasized by its activities: it is a general in constant defense of the feminine flowers. This male flower, "morat amb un pistil de color de safrà . . . vestit de color de bisbe i amb el pistil trompeta" (83–84) [purple with a saffron-colored pistil . . . dressed in bishop's color and with a pistil like a trumpet] lives in constant battle with his eternal rival, the wind, who wants to smell the flowers and spread their perfume around.

One of the most interesting flowers is precisely the nameless one; a very affectionate flower, it is nonetheless exposed to the tragedy of chaos and linguistic confusion. Its leaves and petals contain language, each representing a letter, but they are irremediably disarranged and changed into riddles because of the wind. The flower is incapable of naming itself and cannot be designated under any rubric because it cannot organize its own language. Including a nameless flower within this text underscores the naming game Rodoreda is playing, because it introduces flexibility into the dynamic she has created: in "Flors," the assigning of names is not unilateral. The language of the flowers names and unnames, it organizes and disorganizes, it constructs and deconstructs gardens of emotions, of feelings, and of words.

Flowers that are Really Real

The name game is inscribed in yet another way which gives title to part of the text, "Flors de debò." Such a designation would seem to establish a criterion by which some other flowers—unnamed—would have to be false. This dichotomy is not simple either, because we see no parameter assigning the value of "real" to certain flowers and excluding others, presumably those common flowers that the reader would know, to designate them as "false." Such a recourse would not work within the rest of the textual dynamic.

What, then, is the significance of the label "de debò"? The concept of truth is associated with the problem of knowledge; it is a logical category with certain consequences at the moral and therefore at the behavioral level. It is a traditionally exclusive designation, which would opt for "the good," "the beautiful," "the credible," leaving aside their opposites, and this is characteristic of the fantastic. What do these "real" flowers do? From the beginning, the reader finds them different, uncommon, and this constitutes the initial form of presentation of the "truth." These real flowers are anthropomorphic and they lack aroma. They are real because they are different, because they have human characteristics, and because they have no perfume, in ironic opposition to the reality of the floral universe.

This irony might tempt the reader to interpret the game in simple terms. But Rodoreda is not exchanging true for false; the text surpasses the limits of a game that would merely change the positions of the elements, thereby putting into question the bases of the categories. The false does not become true, rather the true becomes relative within a context of signification that produces certain conditions of validation for itself.

Nothing in this garden is definitively true; conventions and agreements are established on the basis of language to allow the construction of a reality. Within this reality, truth is a category directly linked to the fantastic which here takes the form of an imaginary space in which the human condition is revealed as defined by language. The human becomes a symbolic universe in which the exclusive dichotomies are merely methodological categories for the exercise of knowledge. Within this system, the limits between sadness and happiness, true and false, health and illness cannot be clear. The garden of "flors de debò" contains sensations, notions, and realities of humankind, and its space of symbolization, to propose a reading through the body of flowers. The distance provided by the prism of the garden, the stems and petals of flowers, allows a new reading of the human condition.

Aromatic Ethics

Rodoreda's garden here does not correspond to a pre-established order, nor is it a paradisiacal place within an esthetic or moral order, nor is it the lost, idealized garden of childhood or innocence. Rather it is a garden with a great variety of emotions, attitudes, and sensations in which human reality is revealed as complex, multiple, contradictory, and ambivalent. The text is not an anguished desire to uncover the mystery of reality, nor does it correspond to a wish to idealize reality, which would surely be rejected as partial and imcomplete. The second part contains a clear and direct ethical proposal only suggested in the first part, for it alludes more directly to characteristics peculiar to human beings.

A distance must be made between morality and ethics; the ethics discussed here is a proposal which does not define patterns of behavior to follow, with bases in absolute criteria of good and evil, acceptable and unacceptable. It is a proposal that allows a reading of humanity, understanding it as a territory defined by will and desire, by active and reactive forces in constant interaction.

The fantastic world of the garden puts this proposal into play through the language of individual flowers recognizable within the wide spectrum of their symbolism in relation to other flowers. This interior garden offers a tender, satirical, cruel, and sweet image of the human condition, accepting it, criticising it, letting it be seen in all its fundamental ambivalence and complexity. "Viatges," in the travels through fantastic towns, also describes diverse aspects of the human condition and reflects its contradictions and multiplicity, always reiterating the risk of submission and homogeneity. The two parts of the text can be read as proposals of interpretation of humanity from an ethical-esthetic perspective which strive to discover a poetic of desire and will inhabiting the fantastic gardens and towns in which human beings live.

Notes

This essay was translated from Spanish by Kathleen McNerney.

1. Mercè Rodoreda, *Viatges i flors* (Barcelona: Institut d'Estudis Catalans, 1990): 37. All citations are from this source unless noted otherwise and were translated from Catalan by Kathleen McNerney.

2. Gaston Bachelard, *The Poetics of Space* (New York: Orion Press, 1964), introduction, xxxii.

3. See Ana Rueda, "Mercè Rodoreda: From Traditional Tales to Modern Fantasy" in *The Garden across the Border: Mercè Rodoreda's Fiction, ed.* Kathleen McNerney and Nancy Vosburg. (Selinsgrove, Pa. Susquehanna University Press, 1994): 201–22.

Time Within Space in Mercè Rodoreda's *La plaça del Diamant*

MICHELE ANDERSON

IN MERCÈ RODOREDA'S *LA PLAÇA DEL DIAMANT* THE NARRATOR/PROtagonist, Natàlia, recounts her lost youth—a time in her life that was marked indelibly by the severe deprivations of the Spanish Civil War. Unlike the author, Natàlia is not politically engaged in the conflict. In fact, she associates her husband Quimet's involvement in the Republican cause with her own "big headaches." Covering the period of time from just before the Second Republic of Spain to the 1950s, Natàlia's first-person memory narrative describes the central events of her life: adolescent courtship, marriage and motherhood, war and widowhood, re-marriage and survival. While the time structure of the novel is linear, the passage of time is not well-indicated by historical dates or specific, real events. For Natàlia this tragic time is enclosed in the confined spaces that become her obsession.

As Enric Bou points out, Rodoreda's use of space in this novel "is particularly striking because it introduces analogy with estrangement."[1] In his study of the relationship between the physical and the psychic space of the novel, Bou examines the streets and the houses in *La plaça del Diamant* as "a physical extension of what the main character cannot utter; Barcelona becomes an allegory of the unspeakable."[2] I wish to carry Bou's interesting study a step further by examining Natàlia's descriptions of enclosed spaces—her father's lonely house, the *plaça* of her first meeting with Quimet, her dove-infested apartment, the labyrinthine mansion of her employers, the womb-like shelter of Antoni's house—in order to demonstrate that these enclosures, imposed on Natàlia by events that threaten her happiness or survival, force the apparently passive protagonist to make choices. Despite the limited options available to a working-class woman of a traditional society in a country torn by civil war, Natàlia not only undergoes what Bou terms an "internal evolution,"[3] she has moments of choice or "revolution" that save her from being a mere victim. As in the poetically descriptive central section of Virginia Woolf's *To the Lighthouse,* time is conceived, memory is preserved, in the spaces in which human beings have lived in intimacy. As Gaston Bachelard states in his phenomenological study of spatial imagery, *La Poétique de l'espace,* it is space, not time, that animates memory: "For the knowledge of intimacy, determination of place in the spaces of our intimacy is more urgent than the determination of dates."[4]

Frances Wyers sees the spaces of Natàlia's life as enclosures that suggest the imprisonment of her existence:

> It is a woman's story about a life turned in and imprisoned within itself. It looks out through doors, windows, cages and in at cracks in the woodwork where dust and the crumbs of wood borers accumulate and lie still and inert. The novel is not the story of a person who moves in a world with or against others, with or against forms of thought or feeling shared or disputed on the level of action. It is a reversed tapestry where the muted colors trace a pattern different from the outside design of historical events and acts.[5]

Wyers also cites the connection between past time and the enclosures of Natàlia's life: "Past time is encased in memory whose course she [Natàlia] attempts to retrace, circling back to a house and a past to which she cannot return, to a plaza whose enclosure suggests the shape of her life."[6] Examining the language of the narrative, Wyers sees Natàlia's spoken "lament" as the "only exterior projection" of the novel.[7] Nevertheless, I intend to demonstrate that the cruel confinements of Natàlia's existence press upon her to such a degree that, even within her apparently passive silence, Natàlia reacts against her prison.

The spaces of Natàlia's life are so confining that life does seem to happen to her. In the very first paragraph of the novel, she characterizes herself as a passive person: "Però em va fer seguir vulgues no vulgues, perquè jo era així, que patia si algú em demanava una cosa i havia de dir que no." [But she made me come even though I didn't want to, because that's how I was. It was hard for me to say no if someone asked me to do something.][8] Natàlia is explaining why she went to the dance in the plaça del Diamant although she did not really want to go. The tense of the verb *era* indicates, however, that Natàlia is looking back at how she was in her youth. Of course, she does not tell the reader that she was to become any less passive with maturity. In fact, during the first half of the novel, Natàlia seems unable to overcome her passivity enough to resist the enclosures of her life. Had she been totally passive, however, Natàlia might not have survived the hardships and the tragic events that "happened" to her. While her moments of "revolution" are incomplete, or even illusory, they are moments of "choice" that keep her afloat in a sea of events that are often incomprehensible to her.[9]

The novel begins with Natàlia's first important choice—Quimet, who sweeps her off her feet at a dance in the plaça del Diamant, the first of the spaces that stand out in Natàlia's memory. Quimet's authoritative personality both fascinates and dominates Natàlia. She looks back on their first meeting with a mixture of nostalgia and regret:

> I jo amb aquells ulls al davant que no em deixaven com si tot el món s'hagués convertit en aquells ulls i no hi hagués cap manera d'escapar-ne. I la nit anava endavant amb el carro de les estrelles i la festa anava endavant i la toia i la noia de la toia, tota blava, giravoltant . . . La meva mare al cementiri de Sant Gervasi i jo a la plaça del Diamant . . . (22)

> [And me with those eyes in front of me that wouldn't go away, as if the whole world had become those eyes and there was no way to escape them. And the night moving forward with its chariot of stars and the festival going on and the fruitbasket and the girl with the fruitbasket, all in blue, whirling around . . . My mother in Saint Gervasi Cemetery and me in the Plaça del Diamant. . . .] (18)[10]

From the beginning, Quimet's "monkey eyes" imprison Natàlia. Her entrapment is suggested by the captivating, circular motion of the waltz, a movement conveyed by "giravoltant" and by the rhythm of the paratactic sentence structure with its repetitions—"i . . . i . . . i . . . i" and "anava endavant . . . anava endavant"—and even with its rhyme—"i la toia i la noia de la toia."[11] While the rhythm recaptures the festive atmosphere of the plaza, the circular spatial phenomenon of the waltz offers Natàlia only an illusion of freedom.[12] Her colloquial language, characterized by parataxis and ellipsis, suggests that she is a person who does not really try to analyze her life or the causes of her actions. Rodoreda often juxtaposes her narrator's thoughts rather than using subordination to show causality and relationships. Gene Forrest notes also that this use of the conjunction *i* indicates passivity and lack of fixed direction.[13]

Instead of explaining that her mother was not present to give her advice at this crucial time of adolescence, Natàlia merely juxtaposes the Saint Gervasi Cemetery, where her mother is buried, with the plaça del Diamant. Rodoreda sets off this sentence of juxtaposition by ellipses, which allow the reader to conclude that advice from Natàlia's mother might have made a difference. Had her mother been alive, Natàlia might not have broken her engagement to the "safe" Pere in order to marry the unstable, impatient, self-centered—but more exciting—Quimet.

The memory of the plaça del Diamant is associated with another illusion of freedom, Natàlia's loss of her tight petticoat as she runs away from Quimet and barely escapes being struck by a streetcar. What appears to be a release from confinement is only an embarrassment for Natàlia and an incident that Quimet will turn into a repeated joke years later.

Just as the plaça del Diamant represents the paradox of freedom and confinement that Natàlia's choice of Quimet destines for her youth, the couple's apartment begins as a place of security but eventually becomes a prison. At first the apartment is an escape from the insecurity Natàlia feels as a quasi-orphan living with her father, who has remarried. Her father's house is frightening to her:

> I quan al cap d'uns quants anys el meu pare va tornar a casar-se, a casa meva no hi havia res on jo em pogués agafar. Vivia com deu viure un gat: amunt i avall amb la cua baixa, amb la cua dreta, ara és l'hora de la gana, ara és l'hora de la son; amb la diferència que un gat no ha de treballar per viure. A casa vivíem sense paraules i les coses que jo duia per dintre em feien por perquè no sabia si eren meves . . . (34)

> [And when my father remarried a few years later there was nothing left for me to hold onto. I felt the way a cat must feel, running around with his tail between his legs or sticking out. Now it's time to eat, now it's time to sleep. With the difference that a cat doesn't have to work for a living. We lived without words in my house and the things I felt inside scared me because I didn't know where they came from. . . .] (28)

By "les coses que jo duia per dintre" Natàlia may be referring to an inner space of loneliness which, according to the traditional idea of woman's role, should be filled by love and marriage. Carol Gilligan cites Erik Erikson's view (1968) that the female adolescent "holds her identity in abeyance as she prepares to attract the man . . . by whose status she will be defined, the man who will rescue her from emptiness and loneliness by filling 'the inner space.'"[14]

Quimet temporarily rescues Natàlia from the loneliness of her family home. He literally defines her by giving her a name of his choosing, "Colometa," little dove, a name to which Natàlia becomes accustomed. According to Joan Triadú, this naming by the man who is to become Natàlia's husband is the beginning of a kind of "systematic alienation."[15] In other words, as Frances Wyers affirms, Natàlia "loses quite literally her self and her life in the arms of Quimet."[16]

The traditional view of woman's role—a trading of self for love and security—is implied in the advice that Natàlia receives from her neighbor, Senyora Enriqueta: "'Necessites un marit i un sostre.'" (37) [You need a husband and a roof over your head. (29)] The roof that Natàlia does acquire, with its breeze and its view of the rooftops of Barcelona, at first holds some promise of freedom. It is the saving feature of an apartment that, otherwise, is roach-ridden and in need of new wallpaper. Of course Quimet disappears after assigning the task of remodeling to Natàlia and his friends Cintet and Mateu. Natàlia silently tolerates Quimet's evasion of work. While Natàlia rebels, at least initially, at Quimet's jealous obsession with her boss, she eventually accepts Quimet as an authority figure in her life, as if he were an adult and she a child.

A small detail in the description of their apartment suggests the inequality in their relationship. Like a child, Natàlia likes to run her hand along some scales carved into the wall between their landing and the second floor: "L'un dels plats penjava una mica més avall que l'altre. I vaig passar el dit pel voltant d'un dels plats." (39) [One side of the scales hung down a little lower than the other. I ran my finger along one of them. (31)] Gene Forrest attributes the sensation of time passing in this novel to Rodoreda's use of objects as "signposts to which Natàlia turns when she wants to assure herself of the permanence and security of existence."[17] Her instinctive habit of touching these scales is a manifestation of this intimate relationship that Natàlia has with objects she observes around her—proof, according to Forrest, that she is not totally passive.[18] I agree with Forrest's perceptive observation, but I would add that the imbalance of the scales represents what marriage and life in this apartment are to become for Natàlia—security but imbalance in her relationship with the dominating Quimet.

This imbalance seems to take the form of a master-slave relationship in the sex life of the young couple. Natàlia relates two ambiguous incidents illustrating her physical entrapment by Quimet inside their apartment: first, the wedding night that lasts a week because Quimet bars the door and, second, his habit of pushing Natàlia under the bed with his feet, jumping on top of the bed, and slapping her on the head when she tries to get out. Natàlia's comment on the latter incident reveals that it was a regular occurrence: "Aquesta broma, després, me la va fer moltes vegades." (56) [From then on he played that joke a lot. (44)] Natàlia's language reveals that Quimet is the subject and that she is the object of his "joke." For her, sex with Quimet seems to mean little more than fear and difficult pregnancies.

The apartment becomes more of a prison for Natàlia when Quimet decides to raise doves. At first Natàlia passively acquiesces when her laundry shed on the roof is converted into a place for the dovecote. She even does the painting. The doves give her a false sense of security, described at the end of Chapter 13: "i aquella vegada, quan els antics van fer ous, tot va anar bé." (87) [and then the old ones started laying eggs and everything went well. (69)]

This atmosphere of security continues into the beginning of the next chapter. Chapters 13 and 14 illustrate the unity within individual chapters and the skillful transition between chapters in *La plaça del Diamant.* Each chapter is a small episode in the life of Natàlia. Rodoreda often ends the chapter with a kind of revelation for the narrator or with a sentence or paragraph that leads into the next chapter, or memorable episode, of Natàlia's life. A description of the open space of the market place, with an emphasis on smells, opens Chapter 14. Natàlia evokes nostagically the familiar smells of fish and the brightness of the sunshine on the sidewalk of the market square. The scene embodies a time of happiness and prosperity, a condition that changes with the beginning of the Republic. Natàlia refers to this time of change in a brief description of the world outside her "woman's space"—a world that extends only as far as the flowers, the street where Quimet is marching and the fresh air:

> Encara em recordo d'aquell aire fresc, un aire, cada vegada que me'n recordo, que no l'he pogut sentir mai més. Mai més. Barrejat amb olor de fulla tendra i amb olor de poncella, un aire que va fugir i tots els que després van venir mai més no van ser com l'aire aquell d'aquell dia que va fer un tall en la meva vida, perquè va ser amb abril i flors tancades que els meus maldecaps petits es van començar a tornar maldecaps grossos. (90–91)

> [I still remember that cool air, an air that—every time I think of it—I've never smelled again. Never. Mixed with the smell of new leaves and the smell of flower buds; an air that couldn't last, and the air that came afterwards was never like the air on that day—a day that made a notch in my life, because it was with that April and those flowerbuds that my little headaches started turning into big headaches.] (70–71)

The narrator reiterates her negation, "mai més"; she seems obsessed with "aire"; she insists on the demonstrative juxtaposing space and time, "l'aire aquell d'aquell dia." By the end of the chapter the doves are allowed to fly on the roof. More of her woman's space is taken from Natàlia: "I des d'aquell dia no vaig poder estendre la roba al terrat perquè els coloms me l'empastifaven. L'havia d'estendre a la galeria. I gràcies." (92) [From then on I couldn't hang clothes on the roof because the doves would get them dirty. I had to hang them on the balcony. And be grateful for that. (73)] This limitation of space—from the roof to the balcony—tightens the enclosure of Natàlia's life. The recurrence of the demonstrative, "aquell dia," suggests that the doves with their filth have deprived Natàlia of her breathing space and made a turning point in her life—a change associated in her mind with Quimet's marching for the Republic.

The coming of the Republic brings another big headache for Natàlia. Quimet's business does not go well since people cannot afford to have furniture made. Natàlia's ignorance of Quimet's activities suggests that he is involved in politics, about which she knows nothing. Concerned with feeding her two children, Natàlia finds that her world has become more and more separate from her husband's. She makes a decision to look for part-time work, although it means leaving her two children alone, locked in the dining room.

The house of Natàlia's employers is a forbidding, labyrinthine space characterized by bad plumbing, mildew, dust, and termites. Natàlia refers to it as "la casa soterrani" (112) [that basement house (88)]. The employers are as dark and sinister as the house. (It is not surprising that, later in the novel, the patriarchal son-in-law becomes a Fascist.) Natàlia describes, with almost obsessive detail, both the house and its furnishings. Her description is from the perspective of one who has spent hours cleaning the place; however, she attributes her long description to feelings of puzzlement and isolation: "I si parlo tant de la casa, és perquè encara la veig com un trencaclosques, amb les veus d'ells que, quan em cridaven, no sabia mai d'on venien." (109) [And if I've spent so much time talking about the house it's because it's still a puzzle to me with those people's voices that when they called me I never knew where they were coming from. (87)] The narrator expresses here in spatial terms the class barriers that separate her from her employers, who treat her condescendingly.

Always anxious to return home to her children, Natàlia derives little autonomy from her houscleaning job. Ironically, while she is cleaning her employers' house, the children allow the doves to take over the apartment. Quimet, like a child himself, finds it amusing that the children play happily among the doves. He calls the dovecote "el cor, d'on surt la sang que fa la volta al cos i torna al cor i que els coloms sortien del colomar que era el cor, donaven la volta pel pis que era el cos i tornaven al colomar que era el cor" (122) [the heart where the blood comes from that goes through the body and returns to the heart and how the doves left the dovecote which was the heart and went through the apartment which was the body and returned to the dovecote which was the heart. (97)] In this circular motion, the doves in her home represent for Natàlia just the opposite of the life-force that they signify to Quimet. For Natàlia the doves are like an infection that spreads through her home and threatens to poison her. Quimet even makes a trap door connecting the dovecote to a small, dark room, thus extending the space occupied by the doves. Natàlia becomes a slave to everyone since she must clean up after the doves, her husband, her children, and her employers. Unable to get rid of the stench of doves that permeates her hair, her skin and her clothes, Natàlia has absolutely no space of her own. The claustrophobia and dehumanization of this total imprisonment finally cause Natàlia to rebel, to destroy the doves' eggs.

It is noteworthy that this rebellion takes place in Chapter 25, at approximately the middle of the novel. Natàlia's rage, however, has been building. In Chapter 24 she is angry with Quimet, not only because of the doves but also because of his plans to join a military patrol. In the same chapter Natàlia has a conversation with Mateu, whose blue eyes attract her. Although he calls her his sister, they seem to share an invisible bond of suffering and mutual compassion. Natàlia goes up on the roof, amid the usurper doves, to watch the sunset. That night she has thoughts of Mateu's eyes, which are the color of the sea:

> El color que tenia el mar quan feia sol i amb en Quimet corríem amb la moto, i, sense adonar-m'en, pensava en coses que em semblava que entenia i que no acabava d'entendre . . . o aprenia coses que tot just començava a saber . . . (136)
>
> [The color of the sea when the sun was shining on it and Quimet and I went out on the motorcycle and without realizing I thought about things I understood but that I hadn't understood completely . . . or things I was learning and just beginning to find out about.] (109–10)

The open spaces of the roof and the sea juxtaposed with thoughts of Mateu, who treats her with so much more respect than Quimet does, suggest that, for the first time, Natàlia is aware of growth, and perhaps even of sexual feelings, in herself. This carefully written transition prepares the reader for Natàlia's silent revolution in Chapter 25.

After being obliged to pay for a glass that she has accidentally broken, Natàlia reaches a breaking point, and must assert herself. Natàlia becomes, temporarily, what Sandra Gilbert and Susan Gubar call the "witch-monster-madwoman"—a woman who rejects "the submissive silences of domesticity."[19] Men have traditionally seen such a woman as a terrible monster, because her assertiveness is considered unfeminine. From a female point of view, she is "simply a woman who seeks the power of self-articulation."[20] In her secret and silent killing of the doves, Natàlia seeks to regain her space, and, in the process, the part of her self that she has surrendered in her marriage to Quimet. This self-assertion causes guilt pangs. She has difficulty sleeping and wakes up feeling as if someone is tugging everything out of her through an umbilical cord.

Ironically, the deprivations of war assist Natàlia in her "gran revolució amb els coloms" (141) [great revolution with the doves. (113)] A shortage of birdseed causes the doves to start leaving. The war, however, also means the loss of her job, starvation, and the absence of Quimet. Natàlia must make a very difficult choice. She sends her son to a camp outside the city since she cannot obtain enough food for all three of them. Meanwhile Natàlia receives word that Quimet and his friend Cintet have both been killed. She goes up on the roof to breathe. It is windy. The clothesline is swaying and the door of the shed keeps slamming. When Natàlia goes to shut it, she finds a dead dove inside the shed:

> Tenia les plomes del coll mullades per la suor de la mort, els ullets enlleganyats. Ossos i ploma. Li vaig tocar les potes, tot just passar-li el dit pel damunt, plegades endintre, amb els ditets fent ganxo avall. Ja estava fred. I el vaig deixar allí, que havia estat a casa seva. (171)

> [His neck feathers were still wet from his death sweat, his eyes were cloudy. Feathers and bones. I poked his feet, barely touching them with my finger. They were folded toward him, with the claws hanging down like hooks. He was already cold. And I left him there in what had been his home.] (138)

Despite the departure of the doves, this space on the roof, which once gave Natália an illusion of freedom or escape, now seems haunted by the death that fills the atmosphere.

Natàlia does not say that she cried at the death of Quimet nor at the return of her son, starving and diseased, from the camp, nor at the loneliness of her sudden widowhood in the face of starvation. What she does say is that she had to harden herself, to become like a cork with a heart of stone, "perquè si en comptes de ser de suro amb el cor de neu, hagués estat, com abans, de carn que quan et pessigues et fa mal, no hauria pogut passar per un pont tan alt i tan estret i tan llarg" (173–74) [because if instead of being a cork with a heart of stone I'd been like before, made of flesh that hurts when you pinch it, I'd never have gotten across such a high, narrow, long bridge. (138)] The spatial metaphor of the high, narrow, long bridge embodies this most difficult time of Natàlia's life. She describes her chaotic inner space in terms of familiar household furnishings, all turned topsy-turvy:

> A la nit, si em despertava, tenia tots els dintres com una casa quan vénen els homes de la conductora i ho treuen tot de lloc. Així estava jo per dintre: amb armaris al rebedor i cadires de potes enlaire i tasses per terra a punt d'embolicar amb paper i ficar en una capsa amb palla i el somier i el llit desfet contra la paret i tot desordenat. (174)

> [I'd wake up at night and all my insides were like a house when the moving men come and shift everything around. That's what I felt like inside: with wardrobes in the front hall and chairs with their legs sticking up and cups on the floor waiting to be wrapped in paper and packed in straw in boxes and the mattress and the bed taken apart and leaning against the wall and everything all messed up.] (139)

According to Sandra Gilbert and Susan Gubar, women writers of the nineteenth and twentieth centuries often use this "paraphernalia of 'woman's place'" to dramatize their imprisonment and their efforts of escape.[21] The image of the chair with its legs in the air recalls the dead dove with his belly up, his feet folded toward him, at the end of the previous chapter. Both images seem to be associated with the dead Quimet, who loved doves, who made furniture and who imprisoned Natàlia. On a more universal level, they represent the death and destruction caused by the Civil War.

In the desperation of wartime deprivation, Natàlia decides to kill her children and herself rather than allow them to starve to death. In her nightmares, her murder of the doves becomes the murder of her children. She sees her children as helpless eggs:

> I les mans agafaven els nens tots fets de closca i amb rovell a dintre, i els aixecaven amb molt de compte i els començaven a sacsejar: de primer sense pressa i aviat amb ràbia, com si tota la ràbia dels coloms i de la guerra i d'haver perdut s'hagués ficat en aquelles mans que sacsejaven els meus fills. (182)

> [And those hands picked up the children who were shells with yolks inside them and lifted them up very carefully and started shaking them. First slowly and then furiously, as if all the fury of the doves and the war and losing was inside those hands that were shaking my children.] (145)

In the murderous space between the hands, Natàlia sees the evils that have beset her life—the doves, the war and its losses—as the real murderers of her children. The funnel that she plans to use to pour acid into their mouths is, as Frances Wyers indicates, an "image of forced enclosure," which is linked to the doves because Quimet bought the funnel on the day the first dove came.[22]

As if she were trapped at the bottom of the funnel, the "forced enclosure" of her life, Natàlia is pressed upon to make another choice. What society sees as immoral becomes a moral choice for Natàlia: "i així hauríem acabat i tothom estaria content, que no fèiem cap mal a ningú i ningú no ens estimava" (182) [and that way we'd put an end to it all and everyone would be happy since we wouldn't have done anybody any harm and no one loved us. (146)] Carol Gilligan discusses this type of moral choice as particular to women:

> The essence of moral decision is the exercise of choice and the willingness to accept responsibility for that choice. To the extent that women perceive themselves as having no choice, they correspondingly excuse themselves from the responsibility that decision entails.[23]

According to Gilligan, society equates femininity, moral goodness, and self-sacrifice.[24] Women thus attempt to solve moral problems "in such a way that no one is hurt."[25] Here Natàlia is ready to sacrifice herself and her children, who are a part of her self since they, like her, have no one to provide for them or to love them.

At first Natàlia cannot bring herself to carry out her decision. Taking a walk, she follows a woman into a church. Inside, Natàlia imagines that she sees red balls of evil and death spilling off the altar and threatening to suffocate the worshipers. As she flees from the church and its smell of blood and death, Natàlia imagines herself as the dove of her name, Colometa, able to fly above the world's sorrow:

> . . . amunt, Colometa, que darrera teu hi ha tota la pena del món, desfes-te de la pena del món, Colometa. Corre, de pressa. Corre més de pressa, que les boletes de sang no et parin el caminar, que no t'atrapin, vola amunt, escales amunt, cap al teu terrat, cap al teu colomar . . . vola, Colometa. Vola, vola, amb els ulls rodonets i el bec amb els foradets per nas al capdamunt . . . i corria cap a casa meva i tothom era mort. (187)

> [. . . higher, Colometa, all the world's sorrow is behind you, get free of the world's sorrow, Colometa. Hurry, run. Run faster, don't let those bloody balls cut you off, don't let them trap you, fly, fly up the stairs, to the roof, to your dovecote . . . fly, Colometa. Fly, fly with your little round eyes and your beak with little nose-holes on top . . . and I ran home and everyone was dead.] (151)

Natàlia's hallucination of flying expresses her desire to escape entrapment by death: "que no t'atrapin, vola amunt." Her vision is another illusion of freedom, linked with her only open space, the roof: "cap al teu terrat." The use of second person here and the repetitions and the rhythm of the short, intense phrases reflect the desperation that the protagonist feels, faced with her decision to end her life and her children's. An ellipsis separates the hallucination from the final cause, the reality of death that surrounds Natàlia.

Rodoreda saves her narrator from tragic self-destruction by the agency of Antoni, the birdseed grocer, who hires Natàlia as a housekeeper and then offers marriage. Despite the fact that the union offers no physical fulfillment because of Antoni's war wounds, Natàlia accepts. She chooses the security and companionship the grocer offers her and her children. Antoni's house, too, has enclosures. The living room and bedroom balcony doors cannot be left open too long because of the rats.[26] The house is dark, the hallway "com un budell fosc" (210) [like a dark intestine (166)]. Despite her dislike of the house, Natàlia tries to personalize her new space: "i que més m'estimaria no portar a la casa nova ni una trista cosa de la casa vella: ni roba" (211) [and I'd rather not bring even one wretched thing from my old apartment to the new one: not even clothes. (167)] Natàlia wishes to leave the old unhappiness behind. Her desire for new furnishings and new clothes indicates that she hopes to find a new self. As Joan Ramon Resina explains, Natàlia's relationship with objects shows that she is not docile: "She relates to things, humanizes them and is in turn given meaning by them."[27]

The new house is at first a protective cocoon where Natàlia feels safe. The horror of her wartime experiences has left her with a kind of agoraphobia: "Vivia tancada a casa. El carrer em feia por. Així que treia el nas a fora, m'esverava la gent, els automòbils, els autobusos, les motos . . ." (217) [I stayed at home. I was scared of the street. As soon as I stuck my nose out the door the crowds and cars and buses and motorcycles made me dizzy. . . . (169)] The enumeration and the ellipsis not only reflect the narrator's dizziness but also indicate her obsession with threatening forces outside her confined space. Eventually she chooses to go outside when another fear—the fear that Quimet may return and spoil her new life—haunts her. She makes an effort to go out for fresh air, taking walks to parks but avoiding the streets, which make her dizzy.

After her daughter's wedding, Natàlia goes alone, late at night, to her old neighborhood. With great effort she is able to cross the street without fainting, without seeing the "blue lights" of the war years: "Era com si anés damunt del buit, amb els ulls sense mirar, pensant a cada segon que m'enfonsaria, i vaig travessar agafant fort el ganivet i sense veure els llums blaus . . ." (248) [I felt like a tightrope walker, not daring to look down and thinking every second I was going to fall, and I got to the other side gripping the knife and without seeing the blue lights. . . . (196)] After crossing what seems to her an abyss, Natàlia is amazed at her triumph. She continues walking until she reaches the old apartment. Unable to open the door with the kitchen knife she has brought, Natàlia carves the name "Colometa" on the door. By leaving, on the site of her old life, the name that had robbed her of her self, Natàlia confirms her desire to turn her back on the bitter—even bittersweet—memories of the past. As Joan Ramon Resina points out,

> Only this act of inscription in and from one's being can guarantee permanence. If it can also be read as a liberating action by which the hold of the past is broken (literally cut out), inscription is, nonetheless, avowal and preservation. By such means, the experienced past takes precedence over the interpreted, objectified past, the past that seems dead because it has been detached from the experience of those who lived it.[28]

Natàlia's inscription of her name on the door is also symbolic of Rodoreda's writing Natàlia's story in colloquial Catalan as a memorial to the suffering of the people of Catalonia.[29] While historical markers often indicate places of battles, the inscription with a kitchen knife is a tribute to the everyday suffering and anguish the war caused ordinary people who stayed home while their soldiers fought on the front lines.

The silence that her submissive existence has imposed on Natàlia is finally broken when she arrives in the Plaça del Diamant and the novel achieves its full circle. She has a frightening vision as the buildings of the square appear to lean toward each other, becoming a funnel. Natàlia feels Mateu's hand in hers and hears a storm coming up through the funnel. Again the extreme enclosure—this one hallucinatory—presses upon Natàlia. While her reaction seems involuntary, it is symbolic. Suddenly she lets out a scream, and with it a bit of nothing trickles out of her mouth, "i aquella mica de cosa de no-res que havia viscut tant de temps tancada a dintre, era la meva joventut que fugia amb un crit que no sabia ben bé què era . . . abandonament?" (250) [and that bit of nothing that had lived so long trapped inside me was my youth and it flew off with a scream of I don't know what . . . letting go? (197)]. In physical, organic terms, Natàlia defines her "inner space," which contains the whole of her youth. The narrator's past is released through her mouth, as it is released in the telling of her story, the novel itself.

The liberation of her voice allows Natàlia to free herself from the obsession with the past that has been haunting her. People around her are alive and concerned about her. Realizing that she is not alone, Natàlia seems to regain some of the self that Quimet and the war had taken from her. As her "inner space" is freed of the obstruction of the past, Natàlia makes a new choice to live in the present, to love Antoni: " . . . Gràcies. Gràcies. Gràcies. L'Antoni s'havia passat anys dient gràcies i jo mai no li havia donat les gràcies de res. Gràcies . . . " (250) [. . . Thanks. Thanks. Thanks. Antoni had spent years thanking me and I'd never thanked him for anything. Thanks . . . (198)] The repetition and the ellipses indicate the narrator's realization that she can now give of her newly born self to Antoni, the man who calls her "Natàlia." She begins to think of Antoni as a person who needs her tenderness and warmth, despite the physical limitations of their marriage.

At the end of her narrative Natàlia sees herself in the image of the birds drinking in the puddle of the park—"Contents . . ." (253) [Happy . . . (201)]. Like the puddle where the birds swim and drink happily, the rest of Natàlia's life is a limited space, reflecting its piece of shattered sky but promising happiness. Perhaps the final ellipsis suggests that such happiness is limited; nevertheless it is a happiness that Natàlia creates herself by a rejection of solitude and death, by acceptance of the love Antoni is able to give her and by her commitment to give him the love, companionship and family life he needs.

Natàlia's first-person narrative of her survival is evidence of Mercè Rodoreda's mastery of language. Using the spatial imagery of enclosure—both real and hallucinatory—the author has her narrator re-create through memory a tragic time of life. Natàlia's account of the loss of her youth to a time in history over which she has no control exemplifies a type of alienation which Annis Pratt finds characteristic of women's fiction:

> Women's fiction manifests alienation from normal concepts of time and space precisely because the presentation of time by persons on the margins of day-to-day life inevitably deviates from ordinary chronology and because those excluded from the *agora* are likely to perceive normal settings from phobic perspectives. Since women are alienated from time and space, their plots take on cyclical, rather than linear, form and their houses and landscapes surreal properties.[30]

Not only does the plot of this novel have cyclical characteristics—a series of illusions of freedom, escape or security followed by new enclosures and entrapments—but the paratactic style contributes to a cyclical rather than linear flow of language that is colloquial, non-analytical, and poetic. The use of ellipsis allows the reader to make the analyses or judgments that the narrator is unable to express.

The tight structure of *La plaça del Diamant* gives unity to the chapter-episodes in Natàlia's life. Indeed, the individual chapters may be considered spaces or chambers of Natàlia's mind. They have interconnecting doors that the author opens one by one with her transitions as she allows Natàlia to break her silence through the narrative. While Natàlia does not analyze or philosophize, Rodoreda's art of juxtaposition enables the reader to determine causality, to imagine the horror of physical and psychological suffering endured by the people of Spain in the 1930s and to judge man's inhumanity to man . . . and to woman.

Notes

I wish to express my appreciation to Dr. Frances Wyers for introducing me to Mercè Rodoreda's *La plaça del Diamant.*

1. Enric Bou, "Exile in the City: Mercè Rodoreda's *La plaça del Diamant,*" in Kathleen McNerney and Nancy Vosburg, eds., *The Garden Across the Border: Mercè Rodoreda's Fiction,* (Selinsgrove, Pa.: Susquehanna University Press, 1994), 32.

2. Ibid.
3. Ibid., 33.
4. Gaston Bachelard, *La Poétique de l'espace* (Paris: Presses Universitaires de France, 1957), 28. My translation.
5. Frances Wyers, "A Woman's Voices: Mercè Rodoreda's *La plaça del diamant*," *Kentucky Romance Quarterly* 30 (1983): 301.
6. Ibid., 302.
7. Ibid.
8. Mercè Rodoreda, *La plaça del Diamant*, 4th ed. (Barcelona: Club, 1966), 19. Further quotations from *La plaça del Diamant* are from this edition. Mercè Rodoreda, *The Time of the Doves*, trans. David Rosenthal (New York: Taplinger, 1980), 15. Further translations of citations from *La plaça del Diamant* are from this version. Subsequent quotations from this work, with translations, are cited by page numbers within parentheses.
9. This use of the word *choice* is, of course, relative. Natàlia's choices are extremely limited by the patriarchal society in which she lives and by her socio-economic status as a member of the working class. Needless to say, her choices are even more limited by the wartime conditions that surround her.
10. Unless otherwise indicated, the ellipses in citations from *La plaça del Diamant* and *The Time of the Doves* are those of the author or the translator.
11. Ellipses here are mine.
12. The waltz is reminiscent of Emma Bovary's waltz with the Viscount at the Château de Vaubyessard. Flaubert's prose also imitates the circular movement. See Gustave Flaubert, *Madame Bovary* (Paris: Garnier Frères, 1961), 49–50.
13. Gene Forrest, "El diálogo circunstancial en *La plaza del Diamante*," *Revista de estudios hispánicos* 12 (1978): 18.
14. Carol Gilligan, *In a Different Voice: Psychological Theory and Women's Development* (Cambridge: Harvard University Press, 1982), 12.
15. Joan Triadú, "*La plaça del Diamant* de Mercè Rodoreda," *Guia de Literatura catalana contemporània*, ed. Jordi Castellanos (Barcelona: Edicions 62 s/a, 1973), 405. (My translation.) Neus Carbonell also associates Natàlia's alienation with Quimet's new name for her. See Neus Carbonell, "In the Name of the Mother and the Daughter," in *The Garden Across the Border*, ed. Kathleen McNerney and Nancy Vosburg, 22.
16. Wyers, "A Woman's Voices," 303.
17. Forrest, "El diálogo circunstancial," 21.
18. Ibid., 20. In addition to the scales, objects such as the dolls in the oilcloth shop, the bedpost she breaks in childbirth, and later, the seashell in Antoni's house not only symbolize time passing but also provide something solid or consoling for Natàlia to grasp in the disorienting solitude she experiences. Forrest cites also Francisco Lucio, who sees such objects as a kind of circle of confidants providing warm companionship for Natàlia. See Francisco Lucio, "La soledad, tema central en los últimos relatos de Mercè Rodoreda," *Cuadernos Hispanoamericanos* 242 (1970): 458.
19. Sandra Gilbert and Susan Gubar, *The Madwoman in the Attic* (New Haven: Yale University Press, 1979), 79.
20. Ibid.
21. Ibid., 85.
22. Wyers, "A Woman's Voices," 305.
23. Gilligan, *In a Different Voice*, 67.

24. Ibid., 70.

25. Ibid., 71.

26. Enric Bou points out the similarity between animals that invade Natàlia's spaces, her first apartment and then Antoni's house: "doves are considered 'flying rats' in Barcelona." Enric Bou, "Exile in the City," 35.

27. Joan Ramon Resina, "The Link in Consciousness: Time and Community in Rodoreda's *La plaça del Diamant*," *Catalan Review* 2, no. 2 (1987): 235. Resina's comparison of the role of objects in *La plaça del Diamant* to that of objects in the New Novel is worth noting. See Resina, 234.

28. Ibid., 241.

29. Resina notes also that an important aim of Rodoreda's in writing this novel was "to honor the Catalan language." Resina, "The Link in Consciousness," 226.

30. Annis Pratt, *Archetypal Patterns in Women's Fiction* (Bloomington: Indiana University Press, 1981), 11.

The Question of Space in *La plaça del Diamant*

Adela Robles

The use of space as a literary technique in *La plaça del Diamant* is important in two ways. First, there is a constant description of physical spaces that may enhance or restrict a character's worldview; and, second, a character's relation to her physical space is directly related to that character's struggle to find her identity.[1]

It would not be completely accurate to say that *La plaça del Diamant* takes place in Barcelona before, during, and after the Civil War, since the city itself is hardly ever the setting in which Natàlia moves. In fact, the few descriptions she gives present a fragmentary vision of the city which is reduced to some streets and parks. Barcelona is a separate entity and it never acts as an abstraction of Natàlia on an allegoric level. Quite on the contrary, the streets and parks—the open spaces—are hostile towards Natàlia.[2] Most of the novel takes place indoors. Actually, Natàlia identifies herself with closed spaces, and especially with Quimet's apartment, the house she cleans, and Antoni's apartment. These form the real settings in which Natàlia struggles to develop her personality. The number of pages dedicated to the description of closed spaces shows clearly that these are more important than open spaces.

Open Spaces

All open spaces mentioned in the book act violently towards Natàlia in one way or another. These spaces are La plaça del Diamant, several parks—especially Parc Güell—, and several streets—especially Carrer Gran and its streetcars.

Natàlia expresses her alienation for the first time in La plaça del Diamant. Here she meets Quimet, who does his best to annihilate her personality. In a very allegoric scene at the end of the novel, this town square turns into a box that tries to trap Natàlia. This scene is a summation of what her contact with the open spaces has been like throughout the book. There are no lengthy descriptions of the square. Natàlia focuses on the festive decoration in Chapter 1, and she briefly mentions the square's houses in the last chapter.

Nor is there is a formal description of Parc Güell. Throughout Chapter 2 the reader gathers negative information about it: a man makes some indecent proposals to Natàlia, Quimet is an hour late, she feels cold and her feet hurt. Also, Quimet hits her and lectures to her about the place of woman in the world. And their first kiss, a romantic experience that should anticipate future pleasures, becomes a mysterious act by which Quimet threatens Natàlia with his own sexuality, and even God, who is watching them from the sky, hides behind some clouds to avoid seeing the kiss. In Parc Güell Natàlia can only identify herself with a little girl who is picking her nose and smearing mucus on a bench.

Streets are not any friendlier. In them she is compared to a bowl of soup, and there she fights with Quimet. One of the most torturing arguments with Quimet happens in the street because he claims to have seen her with Pere "pel carrer. Per quin carrer? Pel carrer." [in the street. What street? In the street.][3] Her punishment is to kneel down "¿al mig del carrer?" [32; "In the middle of the street?" 32]. She has to leave her children on the street with Senyora Enriqueta when she starts working, and Mateu dies in a nameless square. Being able to cross Carrer Gran is crucial, as are the streetcars that run along this street. Toward the end of the novel some quiet parks and streets become friendly spaces. These open spaces are not aggressive because they have been virtually invaded by private lives. The neighbors take out the plants and leave the windows open for Natàlia to peek inside.

We can conclude that the city is not a character in the novel nor does it help create analogies between the city and the protagonist. Natàlia does not dominate the city so much that she can talk about it as a feature of her personality.

Closed Spaces

Conversely, Natàlia feels perfectly comfortable in the various closed spaces. She dominates them and is able to offer minute, structured descriptions. She starts describing her first apartment, Quimet's apartment, in Chapter 4, and she never stops adding details until she moves out. She also dedicates two chapters—17 and 18—to the description of the house in which she works, and two more chapters to Antoni's house. When she is talking about closed spaces, she provides the reader with exhaustive descriptions of details that could seem unnecessary to the development of the narration. For example, she describes the internal side of the garden gate she has to cross when entering the house, since she cannot use the main door:

> I, abans d'anar-me'n, em va ensenyar com s'obria la porteta del jardí des de la banda del carrer. La porteta tenia una planxa de ferro a la part de baix i barrots de ferro a la part de dalt, però com que les criatures els tiraven porqueries al jardí, una vegada un conill mort i tot, el gendre, o sigui el senyor del guardapols, va tapar el reixat amb fustes per la banda de dintre: els barrots i el pany havien quedat a la banda del carrer; i a la banda del jardí, del pany només es veia el forat. Aquesta porta s'havia d'obrir, per la banda del carrer, quan no la tenien tancada amb clau, que només la tancaven amb clau a la nit, estirant el pany, passant després la mà per l'escletxa que s'havia fet i traient l'anella d'una cadena que estava passada en un ganxo clavat a la paret. (94–5)

> [Before I had left she showed me how to open the garden gate from the street. The gate had a sheet of iron along the bottom and iron bars at the top but since some kids had kept throwing garbage in the garden—one time they even threw a dead rabbit—her son-in-law, the gentleman in the smock, that is, boarded it up on the inside. The bars and the lock were on the outside and all you could see from the garden side was the keyhole. They only locked it at night, and to open it from the street during the day you had to tug on the lock and stick your hand through the crack and unhook the chain that was attached to a hook on the wall.] (87)

The length of this description in relation to its importance within the book seems somehow disproportionate. However, this is the rule rather than the exception. The reason that Natàlia favors closed spaces over open spaces, the reason that she describes the garden gate instead of praising Gaudí's architecture, is that she has to deal with closed spaces and the gate every day. And this *disproportion* leads us to the second consideration about space: that a character's relation to space is directly connected with her struggle to develop her personality.[4]

The Need for a Balanced Space

During the nineteenth century, a theory was developed that considered men and women as completely separate species that were fit for tasks that had no point of intersection. As Johanna Smith says in her article "Cooped Up: Feminine Domesticity in Frankenstein," this ideology "split off the (woman's) domestic sphere from the (man's) public world and strictly defined the feminine and the masculine traits appropriated to each sphere."[5] The domestic sphere is basically the underlying structure that prepares and helps men to perform in the public sphere. All characters in *La plaça del Diamant* suffer in one way or another from this radical separation. They are forced to live in only one of the spheres, being denied the possibility of having a balanced space. After trying to live in separated spheres, some the characters see the need of combining both spheres to create a space where they can find their identities and express their personalities.

"Les coses que jo duia per dintre": Natàlia's Own Space

At the beginning of the novel Natàlia lacks any space that she can call her own. She tries to solve her problem by marrying Quimet, but he relegates her to the private sphere from which her voice cannot be heard. The war and Quimet's death force her to go out to the public world, but this world is hostile to her. It is a traumatic experience. Her second marriage allows her to have a space without restrictions where she can exercise her own will. After a period of struggle in which she goes from agoraphobia to claustrophobia, she finally reconciles both spheres and achieves a balanced space.[6] When the novel starts she is living at her father's house:

> Vivia com deu viure un gat: amunt i avall amb la cua baixa, amb la cua dreta, ara és l'hora de la gana, ara és l'hora de la son; amb la diferència que un gat no ha de treballar per viure. A casa vivíem sense paraules i les coses que jo duia per dintre em feien por perquè no sabia si eren meves . . . (28)

> [I felt like a cat must feel, running around with the tail between his legs or sticking out. Now it's time to eat, now it's time to sleep. With the difference that a cat doesn't have to work for a living.

> We lived without words in my house and the things that I felt inside scared me because I didn't know where they came from (I didn't know whether they were mine)] . . . (28)[7]

Here we have the first association of space with fear. Not having her own space makes her feel that she does not have her own identity. Apparently, she had one before her mother died. She says that her mother's only joy was "tenir-me atencions" (16) [to fuss over me (16)] that thanks to her she had been able to walk through the streets "com una persona al costat de les altres persones" (170) [like a human being surrounded by other human beings (153)]. Her problems seem to have started when her mother died and her father married a woman who took over her space. However, there is a little hint that the problems might have started earlier with her mother's own dissatisfaction about her marriage. Her parents had many arguments after which they did not talk to each other for a long time. Natàlia was scared and could not sleep "com quan era petita i els meus pares es barallaven i després ma mare es quedava trista i sense esma, asseguda pels racons" (124) [when I was little and my parents had quarreled and afterwards my mother would be sad and tired and sat in corners (112)]. She connects these arguments with the fact that her mother never taught her anything about men. Maybe Natàlia could see her own future as a wife in her mother's negative experience. The conclusion is that lack of space results in fear. Not having a space makes her feel that she does not have an identity, and she feels an enormous gap between the things she feels inside and the things she is allowed to express.

Quimet comes along, and offers her a space to appropriate right away, and perhaps an acceptable identity to develop. This identity is Colometa: the perfect wife-maid-mother who serves as an underlying structure for Quimet's activities in the public sphere. Different people push her to accept this role. Senyora Enriqueta says that "trobo que fas ben fet de casar-te jove. Necessites un marit i un sostre." (29) [I think you're sensible to get married young. You need a husband and a roof over your head. (29)] Her stepmother makes her feel unwanted at home: "Però la senyora del meu pare va dir que més valia que la joventut s'anés a divertir i a les tres ja erem al carrer amb un sol que tot ho negava." (36) [But my stepmother said it was better for young people to go out and have a good time and there we were, out in the street with the sun beating down on us. (36)] Her father also urges her to marry, reminding Quimet that he is already the third suitor, and taking a sudden interest in the repair work at the apartment. On top of that, while living with her father she cannot control her own money, since "el meu pare m'administrava els cèntims que em quedaven després que la seva senyora havia retirat el que valia el menjar" (39) [my father took care of the little bit of money I had left over after his wife had taken some out for food (38)]. Marrying Quimet is a socially acceptable solution. After all, public spaces have never been friendly to her. At least with Quimet she will have her own space where she can express those things that she has inside and that scare her. That is why she is so obsessed about the repair work in the apartment.

After getting married she realizes that this space does not belong to her, either. As a matter of fact, she is only in charge of the maintenance. Quimet decides on colors, furniture, and everything else. Quimet does not allow Natàlia to express her personality; on the contrary, he tries to annihilate it to create Colometa. There are numerous examples of Quimet imposing his will around the house and using physical and mental violence to annihilate Natàlia's.

The only place where she finds delight is the roof. Here she can carry on with her life without feeling any pressure. All the images connected with the roof talk about clean, open air, and freedom. After all, the roof is an *open closed space,* that is, an illusion of open space that is sheltered within the apartment. She also loses this space when the doves move in: "a la Colometa la traiem de casa" (73) [we are evicting Colometa (67)], says Mateu. The process of losing and recovering the roof parallels losing and recovering her own personality during the years she lives with Quimet. The doves—symbols of freedom and peace otherwise—act in the novel as the symbol of this process. The day the doves get their freedom she loses hers: "I des d'aquell dia no vaig poder estendre la roba al terrat perquè els coloms me l'empastifaven. L'havia d'estendre a la galeria. I gràcies." (78) [From then on I couldn't hang the clothes on the roof because the doves would make them dirty. I had to hang them on the balcony. And be grateful for that. (73)] As things go progressively wrong the doves gain more and more space and Natàlia shows more and more the devastating effects of her seclusion in the private sphere: "La casa ja no era com abans; no era com quan em vaig casar." (87) [The house wasn't like before; it wasn't like when we'd gotten married.

(79)] She still needs a space in which to exorcise the things that she has inside, and the traditional formula of the separate spheres does not help. Right before she says these words she complains about her stressful life, the doves taking over the house, her children growing wildly, and about her husband not helping her at all. And right after those words she decides to take a part-time job. The fact that she makes the decision by herself is a step along her way to finding her own identity. This decision, unlike her decision to get married, takes her to the public arena. However, she does not master it because she is overwhelmed by the circumstances. Her situation is even worse now: her opinion is not respected at home by Quimet, or at work by the boss, who takes advantage of her because her lack of experience makes her an easy target. She is aware that she gets the worst part of both spheres but she does not have the tools to fight this situation.

Her incursion into the public space gives her the awareness that men and women are not two different species which inhabit different worlds. She is able to cross to the masculine sphere to help her family, and she reproaches Quimet because he does not deign to do the same: "En Quimet no veia que necessitava una mica d'ajuda en comptes de passar-me la vida ajudant, i ningú no s'adonava de mi." (119) [Quimet didn't see that I needed a little help instead of spending all my time helping others and no one cared how I felt. (107)] With these words she is urging Quimet to work and to stay at home instead of playing soldier. On the contrary, Quimet is delighted with his situation. His family serves him as infrastructure so that he can dedicate his time completely to being a hero of public life—the ultimate expression of manhood. By this time the doves have taken over the house, which means that Natàlia has completely lost her identity. "En Quimet ho va trobar molt bonic." (108) [Quimet thought it was all very cute. (97)] For him this is the perfect situation. For everyone else, including his own mother, it is a monstrosity:

> Quan va sentir el parrupeig que venia de l'habitació petita, es va esgarrifar. Va dir que allò només s'ho podia haver empescat el seu fill. I va dir que no sabia que els tinguéssim tan ficats a dintre de casa. I la vaig fer pujar al terrat i des de la golfa del terrat la vaig fer abocar a mirar baix, pel forat de la trapa, i li va venir un rodament de cap. (112)

> [She (Quimet's mother) was shocked when she heard the doves cooing in the little room. She said only her son could have cooked up something like that. And she said she hadn't realized we kept them right inside the apartment. And I took her up to the roof and had her bend over in the shed and look down through the trap door and she got dizzy.] (102)

Now that Natàlia knows that Quimet is not her superior and yet he is not willing to be her equal, she makes another decision to match her new awareness: "I va ser aquell dia que vaig dir-me que s'havia acabat." (123) [And that was the day I told myself I'd had it. (110)] She wants to recover the space that she was looking for when she married Quimet, the space that was going to allow her to express the things she had inside. She wants to break the spell of the doves that has eaten up her personality, and recover her house. And, of course, the first thing she vindicates is the roof: "La golfa del terrat per mi, la trapa tapada, les cadires a dintre de la golfa, la volta dels coloms aturada, el cove de la roba al terrat, la roba estesa al terrat." (124) [The roof shed mine, the trap door shut, the chairs in the shed, no more circling doves, the hamper on the roof, the clothes hung out to dry on the roof. (111)] She misses very much that area that should allow her to have some balance between open and closed spaces.

The Civil War makes her life—and the lives of many other women—more public than ever before. However, this appropriation is not permanent or satisfactory, because the public sphere does not recognize their work. Natàlia cleans the city hall for very little money, Senyora Enriqueta sells buttons and men's garters, sitting on the sidewalk on Pelayo Street. Women who have little experience dealing with open spaces have been thrown into a public world that is collapsing, knowing that they will be sent back home when peace returns. This is symbolized by the fact that she cannot cross Carrer Gran anymore. This street and the streetcars summarize her relationship to the open spaces throughout the novel. Until the last chapter, when she learns how to dominate her space within the city, streetcars are evil. The streetcars are present when Quimet catches her in the first chapter, they are said to have killed Gaudí, and they keep popping up in any scene where the city rejects Natàlia. On page 75 they are described in a positive way for the last time: "Sortia del meu carrer, i travessava el carrer Gran, amb tramvies amunt i avall, grocs amb campaneta." [I'd come out of my street, across the Carrer Gran with yellow streetcars going up and down ringing their bells. (69)] This is obviously a premonition of what comes later. Soon, the city starts rejecting her overtly: "I, tot anant-hi, els carrers que eren com sempre, em semblaven estrets" (97) [The streets, which were the same size as ever, seemed narrower (88)]; and finally Natàlia is unable to deal with them: "i, quan vaig travessar el carrer Gran, de poc no vaig parar a sota d'un tramvia, però no sé quin àngel em va salvar d'aquell perill" (99) [and, when I was crossing the Carrer Gran I almost got run over by a streetcar and I don't know what angel saved my life. (91)] During the Civil War they are most aggressive: "Altra vegada un tramvia va haver de parar en sec mentre travessava el carrer Gran; el conductor em va renyar i vaig veure gent que reia." (159) [Another streetcar had to stop short and let me cross the Carrer Gran. The driver yelled at me and I saw people laughing. (142)] On page 171 she crosses Carrer Gran only to buy poison, and once she has it she has to concentrate really hard not to fall when crossing: "Havia de mirar de no caure, de no fer-me atropellar, d'anar amb compte amb els tramvies, sobretot amb els que baixaven, de conservar el cap damunt del coll i anar ben de dret cap a casa: sense veure els llums blaus. Sobretot sense veure els llums blaus." [I had to avoid falling, or being run over, and to be careful with the streetcars, especially the ones coming down, I had to keep cool and go straight home: not seeing the blue lights. Above all not to see the blue lights.][8]

She never gets across. Antoni offers her a respectable job and she does not need to kill her children and herself anymore. Thanks to this job she will be able to start organizing her private life as well. She seems to be on her way to recovering her stability and to finding a decent balance between the private and the public sphere. And at this time, she visits the roof with her children very often, even sleeping there when the weather allows it. By the time Antoni offers to marry her she is able to make her own decisions, because she has taken much control over her own personality. She has come a long way from Quimet's proposal (imposition), when she needed her family and friends to reassure her because she was scared to use her will. Now she is aware that she is making important decisions: "Vaig estar uns quants dies rumiant i el dia que em vaig decidir, després d'haver sospesat molt el pro i el contra, vaig dir a l'adroguer que sí, que ens casaríem." (183) [I thought it over for a few days and the day I finally decided, after weighing all the pros and cons very carefully, I told the grocer yes, I'd marry him. (165–66)] The "con" is that she has to give up the fragile spatial balance that she was starting to achieve. For her this is like going back to the time when Quimet offered her an apartment. She risks undergoing the same process of annihilation of personality that she underwent with her first husband. The "pros" are a faster recovery for her and for her children, and the possibility of being finally sheltered and away from all the places that have hurt her so badly. Antoni offers her a new space that she disliked at first: "Perquè d'ençà que havia dit que sí, m'havien vingut ganes de dir que no. No m'agradava res: ni la botiga ni el passadís com un budell fosc ni allò de les rates que venien de la claveguera." (184) [Because as soon as I'd said yes I'd started feeling like I should have said no. Nothing pleased me: not the shop, or the hallway like a dark intestine, or the rats from the sewer. (166)] She fears being caged, but luckily, this does not happen. On the contrary, Antoni offers her a space to appropriate, as she had always wanted. She does not have to work outside anymore, and she does not have to work inside, either. Antoni does not impose his will on her, but rather encourages her to express her own personality and decorate the house to match it. Now she can finally express all those things that she had inside and that scared her. But she does not know how to go about it because she is out of practice. First, she tries to remain in the private space, far from everything that has hurt her, trying to make the old model work. She goes through a stage of agoraphobia: "Vivia tancada a casa. El carrer em feia por. Així que treia el nas a fora, m'esverava la gent, els automòbils, els autobusos, les motos. . . . Tenia el cor petit. Només estava bé a casa." (187) [I stayed at home. I was scared of the street. As soon as I stuck my nose out the door the crowds and cars and buses and motocycles made me dizzy. . . . I was scared of everything. I only felt good at home. (169)] She stays indoors only because she is scared of going outdoors. Life inside is not very balanced and satisfactory, as we can see in the following example: "Anava amunt i avall del passadís com si l'haguessin fet especial per mi tota sola molt abans de saber que el necessitaria per anar amunt i avall. . . . Parets i parets i passadís i paret i passadís i jo amunt i avall." (188) [I'd pace up and down the hallway like they'd made it just for me long before I knew I'd need it to pace up and down. . . . Walls and walls and the hallway and me pacing up and down. (170–71)] The allegory of not being able to cross the street is also a sign that her life is not at all balanced and that her staying indoors is more reclusion than a conscious choice: "Perquè viva com si visqués tancada en una presó." (189) [Because I lived like I was shut up in jail. (172)] She goes out with Rita, tries to cross the Carrer Gran, and she faints.

This uneasiness goes hand in hand with the fear that Quimet may be alive. Only when she gets rid of his obsessive memory is she able to go out again. It was the memory of the social system of the separated spheres carried to extremes. By getting rid of his memory, she is opening her mind to new possibilities. Now she is able to go out without fainting, although at first she avoids busy streets—especially Carrer Gran—and walks through quiet streets to get to quiet parks. These streets are the equivalent of her old roof. They are sheltered open spaces where the presence of the private is so tangible that they are not perceived as being dangerous. There is always an open window that makes an apartment merge with the street, where indoor plants are brought out to be watered. There is a constant blending of the private into the open. When she realizes that the open space is something delightful and harmless, she tries to make up for all those years of reclusion. Her agoraphobia turns into claustrophobia and her obsession will be reversed: "Però els dies que plovia em quedava a casa i no m'hi sabia estar i a l'últim també vaig sortir els dies de pluja." (193) [But on rainy days I'd stayed at home and I'd get restless and finally I started going out on rainy days too. (176)]

The final, balanced, and durable appropriation of a space that includes both the private and the public sphere, and that allows her to express the things she had inside and that scared her, comes through Rita's wedding. We will see that Rita represents what Natàlia never had: the option to choose and the will to decide. On page 203, Natàlia realizes that her future will be lived through Rita:

> . . . em vaig adonar que jo estava damunt de l'ombra del cap de la Rita; més ben dit, l'ombra del cap de la Rita em pujava una mica damunt dels peus, però així i tot, el que em va semblar va ser que l'ombra de la Rita, a terra, era una palanca, i que a qualsevol moment jo podria anar enlaire perquè feien més pes el sol i la Rita a fora que l'ombra i jo a dintre.

> [I realized I was standing on Rita's shadow's head; or more precisely the shadow of her head fell a little above my feet, but even so I felt that Rita's shadow was a seesaw and I could go flying through the air any minute because Rita and the sun outside were heavier than me and the shadow inside.] (183)

Natàlia passes on her life to Rita. It is worthwhile to stress the terms of the comparison: Natàlia and Rita's shadow—a dark, weightless imitation of person—are inside. The strong part is Rita and the sun—the real person and the light—who are outside and heavier. When Rita marries, combining perfectly both spheres, Natàlia finds her own balance. After the wedding, Natàlia tours the places where once she lived. She starts by crossing Carrer Gran, an important fact that merits a whole paragraph on pages 218–19. She gets to the curb and stays there, petrified. A streetcar goes by and nothing happens. She finally perceives it as an old faded thing, so different from the streetcar on page 75. Being aware that there is nothing to be afraid of because people dominate space and not the other way around, she crosses the street and feels proud of it. Her quest for a space ends in La plaça del Diamant, where it had started. The plaça tries to cage her again, but she breaks the spell, screaming out loud and letting out all those things that she had inside and which had scared her.

> i vaig ficar-me a La plaça del Diamant: una capsa buida feta de cases velles amb el cel per tapadora. I al mig d'aquella tapadora hi vaig veure volar unes ombres petites i totes les cases van començar a gronxar com si tot ho haguessin ficat a dintre d'aigua i algú fes bellugar l'aigua a poc a poc i les parets de les cases es van estirar amunt i es van començar a decantar les unes contra les altres i el forat de la tapadora s'anava estrenyent i començava a fer embut. . . . i vaig sentir un vent de tempesta que s'arremolinava per dintre de l'embut que ja estava gaire bé clos i, amb els braços davant de la cara per salvar-me de no sabia què, vaig fer un crit d'infer. Un crit que devia fer molts anys que duia a dintre, i amb aquell crit, tan ample que li havia costat de passar-me pel coll, em va sortir de la boca una mica de cosa de no res, com un escarabat de saliva . . . i aquella mica de cosa de no res que havia viscut tant de temps tancada a dintre era la meva joventut que fugia amb un crit que no sabia ben bé què era . . . (219)

> [I turned into the Plaça del Diamant: an empty box made of old buildings with the sky for a top. And I saw some little shadows fly across the top and all the buildings started rippling like they were

> in a pool and someone was slowly stirring it and the walls on the buildings stretched upward and leaned towards each other and the hole at the top got smaller and started turning into a funnel . . . and I heard a noise coming up like a whirlwind inside the funnel which was almost closed now and I covered my face with my arms to protect myself from I don't know what and I let out a hellish scream. A scream I must have been carrying around inside me for many years, so thick it was hard to get it through my throat, and with that scream a little bit of nothing trickled out of my mouth, like a cockroach made of spit . . . and that bit of nothing that had lived so long trapped inside me was my youth and it flew off with a scream of I don't know what.] (197)

In the course of the morning she has appropriated all the spaces that were hers in the past, so when the Plaça tries to lock her up indoors she is able to break the spell and get rid of all the things that were preventing her from expressing her identity freely. She runs back home, crossing the Carrer Gran in a hurry and not paying attention to this fact, because its symbolic meaning has died.[9]

The New Woman: Rita

Rita's relationship to space starts taking on importance in Chapter 42 when Natàlia realizes that Rita takes after Quimet. The fact that she is a woman pushes her to seclusion in the private sphere through marriage, but her strong character—Quimet's heritage—protects her from domination. Rita dominates the public space. She is the one who takes her mother out of the house and who cannot understand Natàlia's weakness: "No sé com ho farem, perquè quan ha de travessar el carrer es desmaia." (189) [I don't know what we are going to do. When she is about to cross the street she faints. (172)] Rita wants to be a flight attendant and study languages because her ambition is to see the world. No man is going to turn her into a housewife. Rita has a will and the strength to argue for her right to make decisions: "el trobava [Toni] cridant amb la Rita perquè tenia gana quan arrivaba de fer el soldat i la Rita no li volia preparar berenar." (208–09) [I'd find him [Toni] and Rita yelling at each other because he was hungry when he got back from the army and Rita didn't want to make him something. (188)]

Vicenç comes along and offers her the most traditional space one can think of. Everybody is amazed that she rejects him specifically because of that. As the coffee shop owner's wife, she would have to remain in the neighborhood and forget all her ambitions to see the world. She already knows what the private world has to offer women and, not rejecting it completely, she does not find it challenging. The role of the traditional wife means the death of the woman: "¿vostè es pensa que tinc ganes de casar-me i d'enterrar-me i ser la senyora del cafeter de la cantonada?" (200) [You think I want to get married and bury myself being the corner coffee-seller's wife? (182)] "Li va dir que no es volia casar, que volia veure món, i que no es volia casar." (201) [She told him she didn't want to get married, she wanted to travel. (182)] Vicenç tries to close her in the private space by creating a family circle around her. He wants her parents to urge her to get married, and he wants her brother to be on his side. But, unlike Natàlia, Rita does not listen to any opinion but her own, so she confronts him in his territory, the coffee shop:

> Em va dir que venia de veure en Vicenç i que s'hi havia barallat, perquè ella li havia dit que la primera cosa que ha de fer un noi que es vol casar amb una noia és conquistar-la i no anar a secretejar amb la família. . . . I va començar el festeig. Un festeig com una guerra. (204)
>
> [Her cheeks were burning and she said she'd just seen Vicenç and given him a piece of her mind because she told him the first thing a boy who wants to marry a girl has to do is to win her heart and not hold secret conferences with her family. . . . And their courtship began. A courtship like a war.] (184)

The courtship is a war between his intentions to keep her in the private sphere and her will to stay free. During the periods when she breaks the courtship, she only leaves her room to take the bus and go to class. She is very conscious that only through study does she have the chance to be independent from men, and she dedicates her time entirely to this end. It is noteworthy to recall that some twenty years before, it was Quimet who had the right to break up his courtship. Unlike Quimet, who dominated the street, Vicenç moans for Rita at Antoni's house while she is out in the street. Rita shows her strong will as the one who sets the day for the wedding and decides on almost everything. She wants everybody to believe that she only likes Vicenç because of his weakness. And he is really portrayed as a weak person who is always spying on her from a secondary position instead of confronting her.

Their courtship ends in a compromise:

> ella tenia ganes, ja que no podia fer el que s'havia proposat de servir en un avió, d'entrar en un cine o un teatre, molt ben vestida i amb un home que fes goig al seu costat, i en Vicenç, ella ja ho reconeixia, feia goig. L'única cosa que la molestava, i era el que la molestava més de tot, era que en Vicenç fos del barri i que tingués l'establiment tan a prop de casa. Li vam preguntar per què la molestava i va dir que no ho sabia explicar ben bé, però que li feia una mena d'angúnia, que casar-se amb un que visqués tan a prop de casa era com si es casés amb algú de la família i que això li matava moltes il.lusions. (207)

> [now that she [Rita] couldn't work on an airplane like she'd planned she wanted to be able to walk into a theater or a movie house all dressed up and with a handsome guy beside her and she realized that Vicenç was handsome. The only thing that bothered her, and it bothered her more than anything else, was that Vicenç was from the neighborhood and had his place so near where we lived. We asked why that bothered her and she said she really didn't know how to explain it but it upset her to marry someone who lived so close because it was like marrying someone in the family and it killed a lot of her dreams.] (186)

Rita has very different expectations of marriage than Natàlia did. Rather than an opportunity to create her own little private world, it is an opportunity to legally take over the public space. With her husband, she is allowed to act more freely than a single woman: "volia tenir-ho tot llest i no haver de donar ni un punt més mai més i en el moment d'haver-se casat començar a viure només per divertir-se." (209) [She (Rita) wanted everything to be finished so she'd never have to sew another stitch and could start just having fun as soon as she married. (188)]

As we can see, Rita ends up having all that Natàlia has ever fought for: her own space that is a mixture of private and public spheres, where she can explore her personality.

Com el corc dins de la fusta: The Men

Men's relation to space also travels a long distance. The novel starts with Quimet as the king of the public sphere, not leaving any space in it for Natàlia, and it finishes with Vicenç intruding into Rita's house, practically begging Rita to come back home. Natàlia's narration shows clearly the devastating effect that the theory of the separate spheres has on women and their need to get a balanced space. But, indirectly, it also shows that this theory also has negative effects for men, who likewise need a balanced space that must include a private side.

Quimet lives his life completely outdoors. His attributes include the use of motorcycles, bars, and flying doves. Of course, he is deeply involved in politics, the ultimate expression of public affairs, and he fights for the republic, the *res publica*. He forces Natàlia to be hermetically closed in the private sphere as a complement to his activities in the public one. His sexist behavior is directed at proving at all times that he is the essence of manhood. Since the accepted attributes of a man correspond to the public sphere, he tries to adopt all the qualities of this sphere. Perhaps his interest in demonstrating his manhood comes from the fact that his mother dressed him as a girl when he was young because she wanted to have a daughter.

However, during the course of the novel, his involvement in public affairs results in wounds that end up killing him. As he realizes that the open life is not enough, and starts to covet the private sphere, the metaphor of the worm in the wood acquires more and more importance.

As long as he believes in separate spheres, termites are destructive animals that have to be brought out from the wood, and their holes plugged, "tot el dematí encerant i tapant forats de corc i arribo a casa i en comptes de trobar-hi la pau i l'alegria, trobo plors i drama" (123) [all morning long waxing furniture and plugging termite holes and when I come back home instead of finding peace and happiness I find tears and drama and the pots still cold. (110)] In Quimet's own opinion, he has fulfilled his duty in the public sphere, and he is therefore entitled to come back home where his wife should have prepared everything for the hero to rest. We should note that at this stage termites must stay outside the wood.

Later on, Natàlia and Quimet discuss their opinion of termites. At this point, Quimet has realized that the public sphere can also be hostile and that a person needs a private space in which to retire and feel sheltered every once in a while. At the same time, Natàlia is tired of being secluded in a hole with no contact with exterior life and declares everybody's right to have an impact on the public life of society:

> Perquè tot era així: carreteres i carrers i passadissos i cases per ficar-se a dins com un corc dins d'una fusta. Parets i parets. Una vegada, tot passant, en Quimet em va dir que els corcs eren la desgràcia i jo li vaig dir que no podia entendre com s'ho feien per respirar, sempre foradant i foradant i que com més foradaven menys devien poder respirar i ell em va dir que ja estaven fets a viure d'aquesta manera, sempre de nassos a la fusta i bons treballadors perquè sí. . . . I vaig dir a en Quimet que potser els corcs, en comptes de treballar de fora endintre, treballaven de dins enfora i pel foradet rodó treien el cap i pensaven en les maleses que estaven fent. (216)

> [Because everything was like that: roads and streets and hallways and houses you could burrow into like a termite in a trunk. Walls and more walls. Once in passing Quimet had said that termites were a great misfortune, and I said I didn't understand how they could go on breathing always burrowing and burrowing and the more they burrowed the less they must have been able to breathe, and he said they were made to live with their noses in the wood and they were naturally hard workers. . . . And I told Quimet that maybe instead of working from the outside in, the termites worked from the inside out and stuck their heads out those little round holes and thought of the damage they'd done.] (193–94)

It is obvious that, for Natàlia, closed spaces are choking and destructive. She talks about people suffocating in a world that resembles a maze with no exit, just like termites choking as they dig deeper and deeper. Maybe people need to stick their heads out of their houses every so often to put things in perspective. Quimet, for his part, does not see why termites can choke when digging in. For him, it is positive to be a hard worker and to fight to have a snug home in which to be safe from the outside world. What is choking for Natàlia is sheltering for Quimet.

The Civil War is the ultimate expression of the public space. However, instead of bringing happiness to the men who reach this ultimate stage of *publicness,* it makes them collapse, just like Natàlia at the moment of absolute *privateness.* Quimet is not an exception, "en Quimet no parava de dir que enlloc del món no s'estava tan bé com a casa i que quan hauria acabat la guerra es ficaria a casa com un corc a dintre de la fusta i ningú no l'en trauria mai més." (148) [Quimet never stopped talking about how there was no place in the world a person felt as good as he did at home and when the war was over he'd burrow into his house like a termite in a tree and they'd never get him out. (132–33)]

Nevertheless, it is too late for him. He never has the opportunity to carve a hole in the wood. The only place in which he gets holes is his lungs, and the only worm he ever produces is a tapeworm. He dies together with the dove he brought home, along with his efforts to annihilate Natàlia's personality by secluding her in a closed space. Natàlia buries the dove "a casa seva" (153) [in what has been his home (138)], but this is a symbolic shelter, because his real corpse lies in the open field. She doesn't even know

> ni si encara s'estava damunt de la terra i de l'herba seca del desert d'Aragó amb els ossos al vent; i que el vent els colgava la pols, fora dels de les barnilles de les costelles com una gabia buida fent bomba que havia estat plena de pulmó de color de rosa amb forats que anaven lluny i bestioles. (197)

> [if he was still lying on the ground among the dried grass of the Aragonese desert with his bones in the wind and the wind covering them with dust except for his ribs like an empty cage that had been an airpump full of pink lungs with deep holes in them and germs.] (179)

The devastating effect of the public sphere on Quimet could not be more obvious. Even later, Natàlia describes herself like one of his ribs, that has, after all, been the only one that has escaped from the cage and is not lying in the fields.

The same fate falls upon all those men who fought for the *res publica;* the public sphere swallowed them. Mateu dies in the middle of a nameless square, like many nameless men. And those who do not die in the middle of a nameless square, like Antoni, are mutilated—castrated—by the war, and they retire to dark houses that resemble bowels and never leave their families again.

Toni

Toni was born to be the king of the open air. Even in his fetal stage, his father wanted him to get used to feeling the air and freedom: "I Quimet deia que el nen, tan avesat amb la moto mentre s'anava fent, guanyaria carreres de gran, 'ell no ho sap que va en la moto, però ho sent i s'en recordarà.'" (63) [And Quimet said that the child was getting so used to motorcycles when he was still being formed that he'd grow up to win races. "He doesn't know he's on a motorcycle, but he feels it and he'll remember it." (58)] Once he is born, Quimet does not let him get used to closed spaces: "En Quimet va dir que el nen necessitava aire i carretera: prou de terrat i prou galeria i prou jardinet de la iaia." (79) [Quimet said the boy needed fresh air and the open road. Enough hanging around the roof and the balcony and grandma's little garden. (73)] He definitely thinks that open spaces are making Toni grow healthy: "Té, va ple de salut i vent. Dormirà viut dies seguits sense parar." (79) [Take him, full of health and fresh air. He'll sleep for a week straight. (74)]

But Toni seems to grow roots in the house. When his mother has to go out to work, he insists that he wants to stay at home rather than in the street with Senyora Enriqueta. There are many times when little Toni cries to stay indoors:

> El nen estava ensopit i deia sense parar que volia estar a casa. Que no volia estar al carrer. Que el deixés estar al pis i que volia estar al pis. (104)
>
> [The boy got restless and said he wanted to go home. That he didn't like to be out in the street. That I should let him be in the apartment and that he wanted to be in the apartment.] (95)
>
> [Toni] va dir que no es volia moure de casa encara que no pogués menjar res. (150)
>
> [And the boy . . . said he didn't want to leave (home) even if we had nothing to eat.] (134)

When he grows up, he is pressured to leave home to endeavor in the open sphere, either to study or enter the military service far from home. But he politely refuses: "[Toni] no es volia moure de casa" (195) [(Toni) didn't want to leave home. (177)]; and he does not want to go because "quan era petit, durant la guerra, per culpa de no tenir menjar, havia tingut de passar una temporada fora de casa, i que li havia quedat com una mena de deliri d'estar sempre a casa, com el corc dintre d'una fusta" (205) [when he was little during the war and we didn't have anything to eat he'd had to leave home for a while and it had left him a kind of mad craving to be at home, to stay at home forever like a termite in a tree (185)]. And Antoni understands, because he felt the same way during the war.

Space plays a very important role in the creation and resolution of conflicts in *La plaça del Diamant*. In the internal structure of the novel there is a sharp distinction between closed and open spaces. The former occupy the majority of the text and are the places from which the language, tone, symbolism, and even events are born. The latter are vague, fragmentary, and short descriptions of a city that disregards Natàlia and excludes her from social activities. We can also see how all the characters in the book position themselves along these two axes, and how they are endowed with a certain personality according to the space in which they perform in their daily lives. Quimet chooses to live public life fully and marries Natàlia in the hope of making her embrace private life. He does so by torturing her physically and mentally until she forgets she ever had a will and complies with everything Quimet commands. Of all the characters, Rita and Toni are the ones who learn the importance of maintaining a balance between the public and the private sphere by watching what separate spheres do to other people. They are the only ones who reach their goal without suffering the wounds and carrying the scars that everybody around them has. In this sense Natàlia feels hopeful, and she tells her story in the hope that future generations will not have to suffer and be mutilated to have the space necessary to express what they have inside.

Notes

1. My approach to the use of space is based on that of Susan S. Lanser in her article "Towards a Feminist Narratology" in *Feminisms: An Anthology of Literary Theory and Criticism*, ed. Robyn R. Warhol and Diane Price Herndl (New Brunswick, N.J.: Rutgers University Press, 1991), 354–70. In this article she explains the need for feminist literary analysis to combine psychoanalytical and gender theories with classical narratology. In doing so, we avoid looking at literature as a mere copy of real life while still taking into account its connections with it, and we focus on the literary mechanisms that render the text feminist.

2. Guiomar Fages i Canals developed the idea of Barcelona's hostility towards the female characters in many novels written by Catalan women at the eighth colloquium of the North American Catalan Society in Bloomington, In., in 1995. Also see Enric Bou's "Exile in the City: Merçè Rodoreda's *La plaça del Diamant*" in *The Garden Across the Border*, ed. Kathleen McNerney and Nancy Vosburg (Selinsgrove, Pa.: Susquehanna University Press, 1994), 31–41.

3. Mercè Rodoreda, *La plaça del Diamant* (Barcelona: Club, 1993), 31; Merçè Rodoreda, *The Time of the Doves,* trans. David H. Rosenthal (New York: Taplinger, 1980), 32. All the translations, cited in brackets, unless otherwise indicated, are from this English version.

4. For questions related to the construction of the female subject in the text, see Catherine Belsey, "Constructing the Subject: Deconstructing the Text," and Gayatri Chakravorty Spivak, "Feminism and Critical Theory," in *Contemporary Literary Criticism: Literature and Cultural Studies,* ed. Robert Con Davis and Ronald Shleifer (New York: Longman, 1994), 354–70 and 519–34; also see Ann Rosalind Jones, "Writing the Body: Toward an Understanding of *l'Ecriture féminine,*" in *Feminisms: An Anthology of Literary Theory and Criticism,* ed. Robyn R. Warhol, and Diane Price Herndl (New Brunswick, N.J.: Rutgers University Press, 1991), 357–70.

5. Johanna M. Smith, "Cooped up: Feminine Domesticity in Frankenstein," in *Frankenstein, by Mary Shelley: Case Studies in Contemporary Criticism* ed. Ross C. Murfin (Boston: St. Martin's Press, 1992), 270–97.

6. This struggle for identity has been studied from different points of view. See Jaume Martí-Olivella, "Paseo crítico e intertextual por el jardín edípico del cine español," *Letras Peninsulares* (Spring 1994), 93–118.

7. " . . . no sabia si eren meves . . ." My translation: I didn't know whether they were mine.

8. I give my own translation, which is a literal one, to support my case. David Rosenthal translates: "above all not to see the blue lights and to cross the street without hurrying . . . not to see the blue lights" (154).

9. There are some other works that study Nàtalia's development in relation to her surroundings. Among these, see Leah Ball, "El lenguaje de la división y el silencio en Rodoreda," *Cine-Lit: Essays on Peninsular Film and Fiction,* ed. George Cabello-Castellet, Jaume Martí-Olivella, and Guy Wood (Corvallis: Oregon State University Press, 1992), 92–99; and Margaret E. W. Jones, "Las novelistas españolas contemporáneas ante la crítica," *Letras Femeninas,* 9, no. 1 (1983): 22–34. Patricia Hart describes very well the structural mechanisms that constitute the novel in her article "More Heaven and Less Mud: The Precedence of Catalan Unity over Feminism in Francesc Betriu's Filmic Version of Mercè Rodoreda's *La plaça del Diamant,*" in *The Garden Across The Border: Mercè Rodoreda's Fiction,* ed. Kathleen McNerney and Nancy Vosburg, (Selinsgrove, Pa.: Susquehanna University Press, 1994), 42–60. This article discusses the main differences between the book and Betriu's film.

Linguistic and Cultural Insights in Two English Translations of Mercè Rodoreda's *La plaça del Diamant*

J.-Vicente Andreu-Besó

Mercè Rodoreda's *La plaça del Diamant*[1] portrays a cultural world that, in some instances, may be lost through translation. This paper will attempt to compare the two published translations into English from the original Catalan: *The Pigeon Girl,* by Eda O'Shiel in 1967; and *The Time of the Doves,* by David H. Rosenthal in 1981.[2] Each version is coherent with the original work. However, several differences in vocabulary, expression, idioms, and cultural concepts account for the variety of techniques used by the translators: the names, situations, and cultural idiosyncrasies are depicted differently through language transfer, resulting in a limited spectrum of the cultural environment.

Three aspects will show whether a second translation was necessary: the accuracy of the language, the inter-and intra-linguistic and inter-and intra-cultural concepts, and, finally, the intended audience.

Accuracy is an important factor, especially in culturally bound expressions. The term "descriptive translation" coined by Gideon Toury may serve as a tool to set the parameters when transferring to a completely different language and culture.[3] The analysis of these translations will be based on his theory of translation about cultural terms.

Translations have been identified as being *inter-linguistic* (translating from one language to a different one), and *intra-linguistic* (translations that account for changes within the same language). The multiple versions of the Bible through history, each with its own perspective and interpretation of the Sacred Scriptures, are translated some from the originals, some through an older version in the same language.[4] Other portrayals of literary translation are the several versions of classical literature (Greek and Latin writings) throughout history, in which the original text was translated by comparison to previous versions.[5]

The next terminology that may cover our range of study is *inter-cultural,* and *intra-cultural* settings.[6] *Inter-cultural* may be defined as the differences and similarities between two languages and two cultures; *intra-cultural* as differences and similarities between the same idiolects or dialects and the array of subdivisions within the same culture.

The very nature of cultural concepts implies that they cannot always be identified when using a different language. This is partly due to the fact that culture is intrinsic to the language structure. Consequently, the translator must transpose the intended cultural meaning as accurately as possible in order to capture the reality of the work. The depiction of terms and words, names and expressions, should be as exact as possible in order to transfer not only words and expressions but also the force of the original.

La plaça del Diamant is one of the most important novels in the postwar period, and the boom of Catalan studies in the United States in the late 1970s and early 1980s accounts for the necessity of a second, American translation.

When a second translation of a work into the same language is published, the questions that come immediately to mind are whether the first translation did not have the impact it should have had on the audience; if it was adequately transferred into the cultural sphere; and if the language used is no longer natural. The colloquial language used in the British version does not seem natural to an American readership: expressions and colloquialisms seem stiff or outdated. Besides, the intended audience that the translator has in mind will determine the vocabulary and techniques used in order to depict the cultural spectrum. This may be one of the reasons that *La plaça del Diamant* was twice translated within a short period of time into the same language.[7]

Comparisons of translations into the same language emphasize differences rather than similarities. Nonetheless, it will be useful to regard the translations from their translators' point of view and background.

In theory of translation through history, there is an emphasis on the capabilities of the translator as a writer, in order to show his/her ability to express the content in a different language with the original force: each translated version should cause the same impression that it would to a hypothetical native speaker of the same culture. Therefore, there must be a very high degree of equivalence in most of the aspects to cover: grammatical, social, cultural, etc. It is necessary to strive for true equivalence between texts.[8]

La plaça del Diamant is written in seemingly simple, colloquial language that makes it a powerful stylistic tool for communicating deep feelings. This informal style, contrary to what may be believed, makes the art of translating a more difficult enterprise, since the transfer of the vocabulary and expressions to a different language varies within the stages of a language, both synchronically and diachronically. The mobility of the language in use is so rapid at the idiolectal/dialectal/jargon level that, within a decade, most of the expressions will be no longer used by the same speakers. These differences are greater within the English language, if British and American varieties are taken into account.

The comparison of these translations strives to show the differences in vocabulary and expressions, but also the changes of the language at a colloquial level, because they are socially structured. The translator must face non-standard language in a literary text, struggling for linguistic equivalence and also stylistic correspondence between the source-language text (SL) and the target-language text (TL). The social and cultural aspects are offered to the reader, who must decode the translator's understanding and transformation of the text.

First, the vocabulary used in most instances reflects a change in the language, since the rhythm and speech are rather colloquial, and the differences in such idiolects are greater than in formal registers. Second, the transfer of names, festivities, and historical and truly cultural events may identify some hidden interpretation in the original. And third, the portrayal of the introspective character of "Colometa" may be very distinctive due to subtle cultural idiosyncrasies.

The British version is more formal in language, using a more complex lexical density; the American counterpart, on the contrary, offers a steadier and smoother transfer of expression.

The title in the Castilian version is a direct translation of the original.[9] However, in the English versions, the titles are strikingly different: they could have remained as in the original, or translated word-for-word, as "The Diamond Square," as the phrase appears in O'Shiel's version, since it is the recurrent central place where Natalia starts her life over and where she is truly reborn, as her name indicates. The rebirth is also a reflection of the nationalistic values of a renewed culture, especially after it was oppressed for so long after the Spanish Civil War.

In *The Pigeon Girl,* the protagonist takes the personality of the birds, and fights her internal war against them, as a symbol of the political circumstances. After the war, when she marries Antoni, the sexually crippled shopkeeper, she becomes an equal in decision-making, and her struggle is symbolized by her touching the carved scales on the staircase. It is striking that O'Shiel concentrates on the main character's given name, "Colometa," (especially since she was given that name by husband-to-be Quimet the first day they met), thus giving a new identity to the novel.

However, in the American version, Rosenthal opts for a new title, emphasizing the order of Columbiformes, family Columbidae. In this version, *The Time of the Doves,* the birds are the central point of focus. Therefore, a close look should be taken at the names applied to birds of this family. There is not a strict concept or denomination, as this definition implies:

> Taxonomically, pigeons and doves are the same. Both are members of the order Columbiformes, family Columbidae. The term dove is generally used for smaller species with pointed tails. "Pigeon" refers to larger species with square or rounded tails. . . . Members of the subfamily Columbinae are considered typical, or true, pigeons. . . . Most species are predominantly white or drab colored . . . Homing pigeons are a variety of rock dove (Columba livia) . . . The mourning dove (Zenaida macroura) lives in urban areas.[10]

Although pigeons and doves are from the same bird family, doves are the white kind usually referred to as the symbol of peace, and pigeons are other colors. Pigeons, within the standard American concept, are dirty and have a bad reputation for taking over squares and main streets in big cities. They are even compared sometimes to rats. The use of the word pigeon is restricted to the British version, and dove to the American one.

At the symbolic level, a pigeon is a meek or gentle person, as in "pigeon-livered," or cowardly or timid as in the expression "pigeon-hearted." But the definition of a pigeon related to a person that best describes the character Colometa is "a girl or young woman . . . and (slang) a person easily deceived or gulled; dupe." *Dove,* on the other hand, refers to a person who is "regarded as gentle, innocent, or beloved."[11] In our interpretation of the novel, both *pigeon* and *dove* describe Colometa's personality. Therefore, the use of either depends on the translator's point of view.

Translators resort to different techniques when transferring proper nouns, such as names of people or places. Proper names are translated in various ways in both versions. O'Shiel is inconsistent in the transfer of the main square where the action starts. She translates the name as "the Square of the Diamond" (O'Shiel, 8, 9, 10, 11, 13) in the first chapters, but later on in the book she uses "Diamond Square" (O'Shiel, 71, 201, 204). Rosenthal, on the other hand, just keeps the name in its original form, "Plaça del Diamant" (Rosenthal, 16, 17, 18, 19, 21, 53, 74, 194, 196, 197). O'Shiel tries to translate several names, but keeps others as such; therefore, there are several inconsistencies: "We went towards the High Street by the Rambla del Prat" (O'Shiel, 18). Rosenthal, on the other hand, keeps names unchanged: "Rambla del Prat toward the Carrer Gran" (Rosenthal, 25). However, when a not-so-known street name is given, both translators translate "carrer" into "street," as "Montseny Street" (O'Shiel, 20; Rosenthal, 27), "Bertran Street" (O'Shiel, 38; Rosenthal, 44), "Pelayo Street" (O'Shiel, 119; Rosenthal, 118), etc. Referring to names of places, O'Shiel writes "Hotel Colon" (O'Shiel, 8, 9), while Rosenthal writes it with an accent mark "Hotel Colón" (Rosenthal, 16). O'Shiel uses the original "Café Monumental" (O'Shiel, 20) and later on it is referred to as just "Monumental", (O'Shiel, 31, 34), while Rosenthal transfers it as "Monumental Bar" (Rosenthal, 27), and later on also uses "Monumental" (Rosenthal, 37, 41).

Some names remain the same in both versions" Senyora Natalia (O'Shiel, 175, 186, 197, 198, 200; Rosenthal, 171, 180, 189, 190, 192, 193), Senyora Enriqueta (O'Shiel, 22, 23, etc.; Rosenthal, 29, 40, etc.), instead of Miss Natalia or Miss Enriqueta. This may arise from a cultural perspective: using *Mrs.* may require a last name, not a given or first name. On the other hand, *Miss,* with the first name, is typically used in the southern states of the United States. O'Shiel translates the name Father John (O'Shiel, 32, 33, 34, 36, 119, 143, 148, 149, 199), while Rosenthal keeps the original Father Joan (Rosenthal, 38, 39, 40, 43, 119, 141, 146, 147, 192). Both try to keep the original names, but when a distinction is to be made between the stepfather Antoni and his stepson, O'Shiel translates them as "Antoni-father" and "Antoni-son": "Antoni and I got married, and from that day he became Antoni-father and my son Antoni-son until we got into the way of calling him Toni" (O'Shiel, 170); while Rosenthal says "Antoni Sr." and "Antoni Jr.": "Antoni and I got married, and from that day on it was Antoni Sr. and Antoni Jr. till we got the idea of calling the boy "Toni" (Rosenthal, 166). However, O'Shiel translates Vincent (O'Shiel, 187, 189, 190, 191, 193, 194, etc.) but Rosenthal uses the original Vicenç (Rosenthal, 181, 182, 184, 185, 186, 189, 190).

The translator may resort to an explanation of a cultural term either within the text or in a footnote. Another way is to define the term in context by transliterating rather than translating.

Eda O'Shiel resorts to footnotes to identify several names and circumstances that cannot be translated, but which she thinks are necessary for the cultural background to be depicted and understood correctly. David Rosenthal, on the other hand, does not use any kind of explanatory notes outside the text, but sometimes tries to explain some terms within the text. O'Shiel openly explains the cultural concepts that may be necessary in order to understand fully the plot by using footnotes. There is one referring to a poster that appears in the novel: "At the beginning of the Civil War, the Government issued a poster saying: 'Make tanks, tanks, tanks', which amused everyone at the time as being nonsensical." (O'Shiel, 143). She signs the footnote as 'Tr' at the end. Some other cultural concepts that need to be explained are just translated in a different way: *escamots* translated as "shock groups of the Party" (O'Shiel, 106) or "street patrols" (Rosenthal, 106).

Several expressions and idioms are expressed differently. At the end of the first chapter, O'Shiel translates ". . . the elastic band broke and she ran like a hare," (O'Shiel, 11) and Rosenthal says: " . . . Her waistband broke and she ran like the wind . . ." (Rosenthal, 19). Several similar examples demonstrate that Rosenthal tried to use different expressions.

One of the most interesting aspects of translation is the transfer of onomatopoeic sounds. Four approaches can be identified: to leave them as in the original SL (source language), to delete them from the TL (target language), to transfer them as they would be in the TL, and to modify the original form so as to adapt them to the TL.

O'Shiel examples	**Rosenthal examples**
"And he was dribbling" (onomatopoeic transcription deleted from text) (O'Shiel, 60)	"And he puckered up his lips and started spitting: 'Brrrr . . . Brrrr . . .'" (Rosenthal, 64)
* * *	* * *
"tra-la-la-tra-la-la!" (O'Shiel, 10)	"'TararI TararI!'" (Rosentahl, 18)
* * *	* * *
"I struggled free and off with me down the passage and Quimet after me, uuuuuuuu . . . Into our bedroom I ran and he following me and he threw me on to the ground and kicked me under the bed and then he started jumping on the bed. When I'd be trying to come out, he'd be hitting me from above: punished! he'd shout. And no matter which side I'd try to get out: bang! with his hand on my head, punished! He played the joke lots of times on me after that." (O'Shiel, 38)	"I started running down the hall with Quimet behind me going "Oooooo . . . Oooooo . . ." I made it to the bedroom and he followed me in and threw me on the floor and pushed me under the bed with his feet and jumped on top of the bed. When I tried to get out he'd slap my head from above. "Bad girl!" he shouted. And no matter where I tried to get out, whack! his hand would hit my head. "Bad girl!" From then on he played that joke a lot." (Rosenthal, 44)
* * *	* * *
"we'd get on to the motorbike. Ruuuuuuuu . . . ruuuuuuuuu. Like a dash of lightning." (O'Shiel, 40)	"And we'd get on the motorcycle, Rruuum . . . Rruuum. Like thunder." (Rosenthal, 47).
* * *	* * *
"Meeee-kie . . . Meeeekie . . ." (O'Shiel, 12)	"Meki Meki . . . " (Rosenthal, 19)
* * *	* * *
"and the bum . . . bum . . ." (O'Shiel, 198)	"Booom . . . booom . . . " (Rosenthal, 192)
* * *	* * *
"hé" (O'Shiel, 8, 9)	"Hey!" (Rosenthal, 16, 17)

The differences in the techniques used account for most of the intracultural varieties. The translator's task demands a steady homogeneity throughout his/her work. The expressions and onomatopoeic registration of sounds are some of the best criteria to describe a translation, and especially to compare it to another in the same language.

Both translators succeed in portraying literarily and culturally the events in the novel. As more and more differences at the colloquial level are invading the jargon used by a certain set of speakers, there will be a need to reconstruct the language and unify and standardize the similarities.

Notes

1. Mercè Rodoreda, *La plaça del Diamant* (Barcelona: Club, 1962).
2. *The Pigeon Girl,* trans. Eda O'Shiel (London: Andre Deutsch, 1967) and *The Time of the Doves,* trans. David H. Rosenthal (St. Paul, Mn.: Graywolf, 1981).
3. Gideon Toury, *Descriptive Translation Studies* (Amsterdam and Philadelphia: John Benjamins, 1995).
4. Eugene A. Nida, *Toward a Science of Translating, with Special Reference to Principles and Procedures involved in Bible Translating* (Leiden: E. J. Brill, 1964).
5. George Steiner, *After Babel: Aspects of Language and Translation* (London: Oxford University Press, 1975). That postulate is a maxim in the history of translation, especially in eighteenth-century England and France: speak as if you were a contemporary writer. But this idea comes from translating the classics.
6. See Rolf Kloepfer, "Intra-and Intercultural Translation," *Poetics Today* 2, no. 4 (1981): 29–37 and Karsten Lomholt, "Problems of Intercultural Translation," *Babel* 37, no. 1 (1991): 28–35.
7. Rodoreda commented on the lack of enthusiasm for the English translation in an interview: see Sempronio [pseud.], "Cuatro cuartillas: mis mujeres," *Tele/expres* (Barcelona), 10 October 1970, 6.
8. Karsten Lomholt, "Problems of Intercultural Translation," *Babel,* no. 37, 1 (1991): 29.
9. *La plaza del Diamante,* trans. Enrique Sordo (Barcelona: Edhasa, 1965).
10. Compton's Interactive Encyclopedia, 1993.
11. Compton's Interactive Encyclopedia, 1993.

Exchanging Terms: Toward the Feminist Fantastic in *Mirall trencat*

LISA VOLLENDORF

> Women's imaginary is inexhaustible, like music, painting, writing: their stream of phantasms is incredible.
> —Hélène Cixous, "The Laugh of the Medusa"

FOCUSING ON THE INFINITELY RICH POTENTIAL OF THE FEMALE imagination to transcend reality, Hélène Cixous celebrates women's creativity in her moving essay, "The Laugh of the Medusa," in which she encourages women, all women, to write in order to break through the limits that confine them in all aspects of their lives. Cixous thus lays claims on space and redefines intellectual, cultural, and physical territories connected with women's writing and thinking. And, in a telling turn of phrase related to this idea of territory, Catalan critic Joan Ramon Resina protests feminist readings of women's literature, and particularly of Mercè Rodoreda's literature, by remarking on the erasure of cultural specificity enacted by criticism that remains at the symbolic or archetypal level since "(s)uch interpretative strategies effect a *deterritorialization* of the text."[1] These quite disparate thinkers share a concern for the dialectical notions of creativity and place, of writing and space, that occupy a central place in Rodoreda's writing.

When dealing with works by Rodoreda, we must pause to ask what indeed constitutes this author's 'territory'? She lived much of her life, including most of her productive writing years, in exile. Nevertheless, since the publication of *La plaça del Diamant* in 1962, she enjoyed literary fame in the country from which she was exiled. She was a mother who gave her son to her own mother to be raised; a Catalan who made a concerted effort to write in her native tongue even as this language was censored by the Franco regime; a writer who often detailed women's struggles, yet decidedly distanced herself from feminism. The well-known complexities of Rodoreda's life and *oeuvre* show that it is not enough to discuss her 'territory' in the geographical terms of Barcelona or in the temporal terms of twentieth-century Catalonia. Throughout her life, she crossed many borders and refused to be contained by restrictions relating to the politics of gender and language. In this light, we can see that Rodoreda spent a lifetime challenging and transgressing limits, defining and redefining her psychic, geographical, and literary territory in a way that underscores Cixous' assertion that "women's imaginary is inexhaustible."

Mirall trencat (1974), a three-part novel that narrates the rise and fall of one woman's matriarchy within the context of pre- and post-Civil war Catalonia, challenges limits regarding gender and genre at every turn. An intergenerational, realist novel, *Mirall trencat* presents the family dynasty of Teresa Goday as an experiment in matriarchal power. The matriarchy's failure is marked by the incest, death, and dissension that tear the family apart, leaving the survivors feeling ostracized from each other and from their family history. The pessimistic ending of the novel, which finds as its final image a rat who dies as the chalet tumbles to the ground, has led several critics to remark that *Mirall trencat* is a novel that closes in on itself, leaving no doubt that the matriarchy has come to an end.[2] In spite of the physical destruction of the house at the end of the novel, I would suggest that the fantastic represents a novelistic space that opens the possibility for a feminist future: crossing the borders that define realism, in the last part of *Mirall trencat* Rodoreda posits the fantastic as a liminal space in which feminine subjectivity and solidarity might be realized free from the patriarchal constraints that originally led to the downfall of the Goday matriarchy.[3] The use of the fantastic in the novel, which coincides with the definitive decline of the matriarchy, can thus be read as an attempt to liberate the feminine subject, to deterritorialize the feminine from the patriarchy.

Analyzing the failed matriarchy, we will see that *Mirall trencat* documents the processes that frustrate feminine subjectivity and then offers a vision for a feminist future by relocating the feminine in a fantastic borderland wherein these processes might be transcended. In this study, I draw upon the analyses of commodification articulated by Gayle Rubin and Luce Irigaray in the 1970s in order to explore the critique of the patriarchy and of the institutionalization of female power in *Mirall trencat*. The use of feminist theory contemporary to the novel itself also forges an intellectual link between Rodoreda and feminist contemporaries: in spite of Rodoreda's lack of allegiance with the feminist cause, this analysis reveals that many of the author's critiques of the patriarchy were also being explored by feminist theorists of the same period.

The Matriarchal Economy

Published in 1974, *Mirall trencat* participates in the quest for the maternal found not only in Rodoreda's own novelistic production,[4] but also in much of western women's fiction and feminist theory of the 1970s. The chronicle of Teresa Goday's life in *Mirall trencat* can be read as a search for feminine subjectivity, with the woman cast as mother at the center of the novel. This search for subjectivity in the maternal subject coincides with Marianne Hirsch's observations in *The Mother/Daughter Plot*. Discussing the seventies as a transitional period for feminist writers, Hirsch asks,

> At this particular moment of women's writing—at the moment of an emerging political feminist movement, of a feminist literary consciousness and at the moment of a scholarship which explores gender difference in a number of academic disciplines—what plots become speakable between mothers and daughters, what developmental paradigms emerge for fictional heroines and for women writers, and how is female subject-formation represented?[5]

In spite of Rodoreda's lack of sympathy for feminism, her texts clearly focus on a struggle for feminine subjectivity and protest the patriarchal practices that hinder the realization of women's potential for autonomy and power. Women as mothers, daughters, and in nurturing roles are at the heart of *Mirall trencat,* and we can turn to these characters, and to the relationship among them, in order to understand the flaws of Teresa's matriarchy and thus come to the core of Rodoreda's criticism of patriarchal systems.

At the beginning of the novel, we encounter Teresa Goday as she embarks upon an odyssey of social ascent that will lead her from her own lower-class background to bourgeois status. Teresa accomplishes this ascent through marriage, that is, through her complicity with the system of exchange in which women are commodified. After examining the pattern of commodification, we will see that Rodoreda depicts the consequences of Teresa's acceptance of this system as irretrievably detrimental to the matriarchy. The ramifications of the unquestioning acceptance of self-commodification become manifest in the devaluation of the maternal, the repression of female sexuality, and in divisiveness among women, all of which converge to frustrate and eventually destroy the matriarchy.

In her ground-breaking essay, "The Traffic in Women: Notes on the 'Political Economy' of Sex" (1975), Gayle Rubin identifies and criticizes the commodification of women which is a fundamental aspect of western kinship systems:

> 'Exchange of women' is a shorthand for expressing that the social relations of a kinship system specify that men have certain rights in their female kin, and that women do not have the same rights either to themselves or to their male kin.[6]

Soon thereafter, Luce Irigaray incorporated this same crucial insight into her thinking about women's identity and position in society. In "Women on the Market," Irigaray identifies the use of women as a commodity within patriarchy:

> Why are men not objects of exchange among women? It is because women's bodies—through their use, consumption, and circulation—provide for the condition making social life and culture possible, although they remain an unknown "infrastructure" of the elaboration of that social life and culture.[7]

Indeed, the basis for Teresa's matriarchy is precisely this type of commodification of women which Irigaray describes as "their use, consumption, and circulation." *Mirall trencat* begins with an economic transaction which sets into motion a series of exchanges that serve to link both women and children with a monetary value. As Teresa is willingly co-opted by a system that defines women as merchandise to be bought and sold, she unwittingly assimilates and propagates the objectification and commodification of human beings.

In fact, the novel opens with a series of economic exchanges that support this reading. In the first chapter, *Una joia de valor* [A valuable jewel], the human merchandising that lies at the center of the matriarchy is laid out. While one would suppose that the 'jewel' referred to is the brooch presented to Teresa by her new husband Nicolau Rovira, it is the very ambiguity of this term that captures the instability of the matriarchal base: by the end of the chapter we are unsure if the title refers to the actual jewel purchased, to Teresa herself, or to her son. The reading of Teresa as jewel merges not only from her depiction as youthful and beautiful (she is described as "una daina" a deer [27], for example)[8] in striking contrast to the elderly Nicolau, but also from the very terms of their marriage: "El senyor Nicolau Rovira preguntà a la Teresa si es volia casar amb ell: tot el que podia oferir-li era la seva fortuna; sabia de sobres que era vell i que cap noia no se'n podia enamorar" (30) [Mr. Nicolau Rovira asked Teresa if she wanted to marry him: all that he could offer her was his fortune and he knew all too well that he was old and that no young woman could fall in love with him]. With a marriage thus based on material worth, that Nicolau wants to please Teresa with material goods comes as no surprise, and it is with this intention that he takes her shopping for something that will truly please her.

The purchase of the brooch, the supposed "joia de valor" of the title, enables Teresa to secure her own "independence." By reselling the jewel, she is able to free herself of the burden of raising her son, who is a product of her union with Miquel Masdéu, a married man whom she truly loved. The son, to whom Teresa refers as "una relliscada com una casa" (30) [a monumental mistake], presents the single obstacle to her marriage with Nicolau, and only when she devises the solution of the jewel can she permanently solve this problem by using the money to pay the child's father, who takes the child Jesús in as his own. Maryellen Bieder describes the blanket suppression of Teresa's past in terms of exchange: "Teresa exchanged her true identity and her true emotion for a life of material wealth and beauty."[9] Significantly, the repression of the past (of motherhood, sexuality, and love that pre-date her marriage) is underscored textually by the omission of the child's name from this first chapter. With a value placed on him, the child is, like his mother, an object of exchange.

From the beginning, then, we see that the commodification of women and children lies at the center of the marriage that provides Teresa with an opportunity to escape her mother's fate as a fish-seller. Moreover, the brooch, the son, and Teresa herself function as objects of exchange, each one bearing witness to man's economic power and to one woman's (initially successful) attempts to gain access to this power.[10] But in seeking access to this power through marriage, the young Teresa also ironically compromises her own future as a feminine subject. The devaluation of self, marked by placing a fixed price on herself and her son, signifies Teresa's collusion in the exchange of women; her tacit acceptance of the dictum, as Irigaray summarizes it, that "woman thus has value only in that she can be exchanged."[11] This devaluation also requires the sacrifice of her son, which must be made in order to insure Teresa's viability as a marriageable woman. In the prologue to *Mirall trencat,* Rodoreda comments on the ingenuity of Teresa's resolution to the problem of Jesús and says, "Ja tenim una persona amb un secret per sempre" (12) [We already have a person with a secret forever]. Like many secrets in the novel, Teresa's are loaded with implications, for they represent the repression of the maternal role and of sexual identity. The assimilation of these patriarchal characteristics into Teresa's matriarchy are choices that will weigh heavily on future generations.

Even though Nicolau Rovira dies within a short period after the marriage, this relationship serves to catapult Teresa into the upper class. When Salvador Valldaura begins to court her a year after Nicolau's death, Teresa analyzes the prospects of this marriage in the same calculating way that she thought about the first. She analyzes her financial situation, for example, mentioning that Nicolau left part of his fortune to his widowed sister, and worrying about her own tendency to overspend: "Les rendes de la Teresa no eren il.limitades i ella era malgastadora; més aviat s'endarreria" (42) [Teresa's income was not without limits and she was a spendthrift; more likely than not to be behind in her payments]. The self-conscious way in which she presents herself to Valldaura (e.g. decorating her body with the violets he sends her) eventually pays off when he asks her to marry him. While Valldaura proposes that they support each other in their lives and does not mention money as a binding factor in the union, he does so on their honeymoon: "'Tot és teu: aquestes vinyes, aquesta terra i jo'" (46) [Everything is yours: these vineyards, this land, and me]. Once again, the notion of property and ownership is introduced, as Teresa fashions herself as a saleable commodity in the marriage economy. In this marriage, as in the first, the man's fortune seduces Teresa, impelling her to marry for money not once but twice. It is as though once she became part of the economy of exchange, Teresa self-identifies as a commodity and responds as such when the second marriage "opportunity" is presented to her.[12] With this second union, Teresa stakes out her claim as a successful bourgeois matriarch. Yet, in spite of the apparent power she wields in the family, Teresa's matriarchy will rapidly blossom and then slowly wither, leaving the reader to search for the causes of its long decline.

To understand the negative consequences of commodification within the matriarchy, it is helpful to turn to the central role of the maternal and to the politics at play with Teresa's dynasty. The initial commodification of women represents a fragile base for, as Irigaray argues, such commodification results in a denial of women's pleasure and causes women to relate to each other as objects of male desire.[13] The repression of female sexuality, rejection of the maternal, and competition among women abundantly manifested in *Mirall trencat* suggest that Teresa's matriarchy constitutes a mere inversion of terms. As Monique Wittig states in "One Is Not Born Woman," the same categories of sex that inform and define patriarchy also constrain matriarchy.[14] So, in spite of the attention paid to female characters and their private world within the chalet at Sant Gervasi, we seem to be facing an inversion of terms, a substitution of female for male, and thus to be looking at a matriarchy that operates within the same cultural system and the same cultural practices as the patriarchy. Rather than opposing or challenging patriarchal cultural codes, Teresa's matriarchy assimilates and expresses them in the dynamics surrounding women's sexual and maternal identities throughout the novel.

The quest for the maternal, mentioned by Hirsch as well as by Rodoredan critics, gives shape to *Mirall trencat,* as most of the plots and subplots can be traced to either a search for or rejection of the mother. In the prologue to the novel, for example, Rodoreda describes Teresa Goday as she first imagined her:

> Una bellesa que ajudava la seva mare a vendre peix però preparada interiorment a elevar-se de nivell amb aquella facilitat que té sovint una persona, sobretot una dona, arrencada al seu ambient per un destí. (6–7)
>
> [A beautiful woman who helped her mother sell fish but who was prepared to rise socially with that ease that a person, especially a woman stuck in her environment because of destiny, has.]

With this explanation that defines Teresa as a daughter who works side by side with her mother, Rodoreda links the protagonist's literary birth with her matrilineage and thus foregrounds the maternal as a primary source of identity in the novel.

Yet, as has been mentioned, in order to begin her journey towards her position as matriarch, Teresa somewhat paradoxically feels that she must de-materialize herself so that she can marry Nicolau. This exchange of the integrity of the self for an economically secure future confirms what Elizabeth Scarlett has suggested with regard to most of Rodoreda's fiction: "It is the Father's law that functions in Rodoreda's writing to destroy maternal relations."[15] The father's laws at play here involve not only the exchange of women, but also the implicit connection between motherhood and sexuality, for what Teresa must erase is not only a child but a sexual past that might frighten her future husband away. Beginning with this repression of the maternal and sexual identities, the stage is set for similar negative responses to these aspects of female subjectivity.

Just as she continues to view Jesús, with whom she maintains a primarily financial relationship as his godmother, as "objectification of a guilt she would like to erase from her memory,"[16] Teresa's negative response to motherhood continues throughout the novel. When she remarries and becomes pregnant, for example, she is said to suffer. Then, immediately after the birth of Sofia she follows the advice of the midwife and places three folded sheets on her stomach for several days: once again she seems anxious to erase the marks of motherhood from her life. Given these attitudes toward motherhood, it is not surprising that future generations of Teresa's family react similarly to the maternal.[17] The only child born to Salvador and Teresa (and thus the family heir), Sofia rejects all aspects of the maternal from birth. Not only does the baby refuse to allow Teresa to touch her, but she also rejects the wet nurse's breast milk. As one would expect from this pattern of maternal rejection and repression, no significant maternal bond is ever forged between Teresa and Sofia.

With this lack of identification with her mother, Sofia in turn adopts a similarly negative attitude toward motherhood. Hit with the news of her husband Eladi's illegitimate child on the night of their wedding, Sofia insists on taking the baby Maria in as their own. Seemingly willing to take on motherhood, in fact Sofia herein makes her greatest stand against a traditionally nurturing maternal role: "Voldria aquella filla de l'Eladi a casa encara que no pogués estimar-la mai" (96) [She wanted that daughter of Eladi's in her house even though she could never love her]. Immediately thereafter, Sofia endures a difficult pregnancy and childbirth and, when she becomes pregnant three years later she reacts with ambivalence: "No li sabé gens de greu" (101) [She didn't mind]. With this final pregnancy, Sofia continues to view children as pawns (like Maria) rather than offspring in a more affective sense: what Sofia most desires is to give birth to a daughter who will supplant the "bastard" child Maria's role as Eladi's favorite. Sofia does not feel any maternal instinct and, rather, tends toward a rejection of her children. This is best exemplified in the success with which she alienates the young Maria, who at one point even asks for a knife with which to kill her mother.[18] These examples of unhappy pregnancies, difficult births, maternal apathy and disdain, and the repulsion for the maternally marked body abound in the novel, suggesting that both the body and the spirit resist the maternal. Such negative ideology of motherhood betrays a fundamental problematic within a system that seeks to secure power through matrilineage, as Teresa's does.

We only have to take the maternal one step further to understand what is at stake here: women's sexuality poses a threat to the status quo, and women constantly struggle to sublimate tautological signs of desire. Women's impulse to cover up signs of childbearing is shown to be rooted in a valid fear when Sofia's husband, repulsed by her pregnant body, initiates an affair with the servant Armanda during the pregnancy. Similarly, Teresa's desire seems to be legitimate only during courtship, but certainly not once she is a married woman, and a mother at that. Once married, Teresa frequently re-routes her sensuality and sexuality: she eats an entire flower and scandalizes her friend Eulàlia; she endlessly eats chocolates in the privacy of her room; and she comments that the paralysis of her legs is the result of the rejection of a lover. This last comment, made to Amadeu Riera, who previously had been her lover for many years, points to the abundance of Teresa's desire. When Riera asks what happened to her legs,

> La Teresa trigà a parlar. Havia tingut un amic, digué a l'últim, i quan havia començat a negligir-la la pena havia estat tan violenta que els nervis de les cames se li havien mort. (136)

[Teresa waited before speaking. She had had a "friend," she finally said, and when he began to neglect her the pain had been so violent that the nerves in her legs died.]

Transformed from a voluptuously sensuous young widow who attends a ball adorned with flowers into an overweight, practically cloistered woman with paralyzed legs, Teresa becomes, as Scarlett has noted, a marker for the rise and decline of the family.[19] Yet Teresa's body, the maternal body, signifies much more than this: it signifies the interiorization and stifling of feminine sexuality. Just as the secret of this longstanding affair with Riera must be kept throughout Teresa's life, the sublimation of female desire is required for the maintenance of order in this family dynasty that is, in the final analysis, a matriarchy substituting for patriarchy.

In contrast to the suppression of women's desire, male desire need not be hidden, and Eladi's exploits with the maids exemplify this sexual double standard. The acceptance of men's sexuality (even when it comes in excess) leads to a competition among women for men, thus taking us back to the participation in the exchange economy that undergirds the matriarchy. Competing for Eladi's attention, Sofia silently does battle with the maids as her husband flits from one affair to the next. For example, Sofia offhandedly decides to fire the maid Rosa; yet as readers we have already witnessed a sex scene between Eladi and Rosa that sets this maid up as the scapegoat for Sofia's ultimate lack of control over her husband's exploits. The trusted servant Armanda, who plays an important role in the third part of the novel, also secretly competes with the other maids by convincing herself that since Eladi gave her earrings, he did in fact hold her in special regard. Teresa provokes a similar sense of jealousy in her friend Eulàlia, who for years could not believe that a refined man like Salvador would marry a woman of lower-class background. Along with the repression of the maternal, this competition among women for men's attentions betrays a larger preoccupation with the control of women's sexuality.

Devalued by the very fact that she accepts the value placed on her body by her first husband, Teresa enters into an exchange economy in which women's worth can only be defined in terms of men's money and power. Irigaray stresses this devaluation through commodification when she says, "*Commodities, women, are a mirror of value of and for man.* In order to serve as such, they give up their bodies to men as the supporting material of specularization, of speculation."[20] Defining herself as a "mirror of value" for men, Teresa gives herself over to Nicolau and then to Salvador and, in doing so, puts into motion an assimilation of patriarchal practices regarding women's sexuality, motherhood, and commodification.

We have come full circle, then, and have seen that in spite of Teresa's successful rise in social status and in power, this matriarchal experiment fails because it reinscribes the same gendered roles prescribed to women in the larger patriarchal society, because it fails to question and challenge the rules governing familial relations. In the end, Teresa's household is as connected to and dependent upon divisions among women, among classes, and among the sexes as is the macrocosmic patriarchy that lies just beyond (or perhaps is superimposed upon) the chalet at Sant Gervasi. Based on the devaluation of the feminine through the original acts of commodification and of maternal repression, the matriarchy cannot possibly survive. The deaths of the husbands Salvador and Eladi, the murder of the grandchild Jaume, the estrangement of the other male grandchild Ramon, Maria's suicide, and, ultimately, Teresa's death and Sofia's flight to France during the Civil War, lead to and secure the matriarchy's downfall.

However, Rodoreda addresses the need for a new order of things through the use of the fantastic, which is made manifest here primarily through the apparition of ghosts and of visions. Commenting on the possibilities of this narrative technique, Geraldine Cleary Nichols has stated that it offers "a new and ultimately liberating vision of a world where the One is not enthroned at the expense of the Other."[21] Just as death, suicide, and supposed incest have torn the family apart in Part Two, throughout Part Three of the novel Rodoreda responds to the loss of matriarchal territory by opening up the fantastic as a space that truly surpasses the patriarchy.

The Feminist Fantastic

In the last chapter of Part Two, after all of the male characters have left or died, the novel definitively shifts away from its realistic mode. Entitled "Somnis" [Dreams], the chapter constitutes a step toward the unconscious as Teresa and Armanda's dreams are narrated in an intimate, revealing scene. Teresa's dream, to which the reader has direct access, incorporates the elements of sexuality, motherhood, and material worth that are fundamental to her identity. Teresa dreams that she loves and makes love with a soldier, becomes pregnant, and that a doctor performs a caesarean section only to find that a huge apple, which later will be covered with precious stones, has been gestating in her womb. The connection to the Edenic myth and its attendant prohibitions on sexuality becomes abundantly clear when Teresa does not enter the garden in her dream for fear she might never be able to leave. Upon awakening, Teresa impels Armanda to recount her own dreams, at which time we find out that Armanda constantly dreams about Eladi. Lying in her bed, Armanda's soul leaves her body through her navel (giving birth to a non-corporeal self) and she encounters Eladi in the form of an angel. This dream recalls the first fantastic moment in the novel: Eladi briefly believes he sees a siren in the garden (part 2, chapter 4), and this episode links him not only to the lusciousness of nature but also to the feminine realm of the fantastic, thus underscoring his sexual excess as well as his effeminacy. In an important step toward the feminization of the fantastic, Eladi does not believe what he sees: he rubs his eyes in disbelief and refrains from asking anybody else if they saw the same thing.

Teresa and Armanda's dreams, both involving issues of maternity, sexuality, and love, reveal the power of the unconscious to release contained desire. And, importantly, Teresa and Armanda bond through their dreams, for not only do similar issues emerge, but the theme of love is so strong in both that Teresa urges Armanda not to let "el seu somni d'amor" (206) [her dream of love] die. With this compelling scene of solidarity between women, the second part comes to a close and the third part of the novel begins with the ambiguous T.S. Eliot epigraph, "But time past is a time forgotten. We expect the rise of a new constellation" (208). Beginning with this chapter on dreams, then, the novel takes a definitive step away from its realistic mode and moves to stake out a new territory (perhaps the "new constellation" of Eliot's quote) in which the detrimental practices of commodification, maternal repression, and competition among women are broken down and an outline for a new woman-centered, maternally oriented ethos emerges. Irigaray captures the essence of the forces working against the realization of the feminine self and lays out a plan for alternative action:

> For women to undertake tactical strikes, to keep themselves apart from men long enough to learn to defend their desire, especially through speech, to discover the love of other women while sheltered from men's imperious choices that put them in the position of rival commodities, to forge for themselves a social status that compels recognition, to earn their living in order to escape from the condition of prostitute . . . these are certainly indispensable stages in the escape from their proletarization on the exchange market.[22]

Crossing from reality to fantasy in the last part of *Mirall trencat,* the female characters experience liberation from the constraints that doomed Teresa's matriarchy, finding validation in each other, in their own abilities to speak and love, just as Irigaray suggests.[23] Marked by the release from realism and constituted by visions, ghosts, and anthropomorphization of nature, the fantastic allows the maternal to supersede the patriarchal economy of exchange. In this context, the maternal emerges as a liberating and liberated model for interpersonal relations. Unlike the matriarchy, which was bound to patriarchal practices, in the fantastic realm a feminist future is envisioned that coincides with Irigaray's description of a social order. This order does not reproduce phallocratic models but, rather, offers new ways of socializing "the relation to nature, matter, the body, language, and desire."[24] In this nonphallogocentric world imagined in Part Three of *Mirall trencat,* intergenerational communication is realized, class disappears as a marker of difference, and biology no longer strictly defines familial bonds, all of which is cast in terms of the feminine and the maternal, bringing us closer to the integrity of the self so vigorously sought and so obviously compromised in Teresa's lifetime.

The challenge to the strict boundaries of life and death characterizes the fantastic as it appears throughout Part Three. As Nichols has observed with regard to Rodoreda, Ana María Matute, and Carme Riera, "In the fantasy world of these authors, it is death which slides into or out of life; both states are ranged along a continuum with no clear ends."[25] The specter of death looms over the three women, Teresa, Sofia, and Armanda, who inhabit the chalet at the outset of Part Three. In a state of rapid decline, Teresa indicates to her doctor, "el que jo tinc és la mort a dintre" (29) [what I have is death inside me]. That he cannot find her pulse at times points to the Teresa's resignation to her own death and to the borderland which she inhabits before dying. Like the sharing of dreams at the end of Part Two, Teresa's physical decline bespeaks a deconstruction of traditional boundaries between life and death, the conscious and the unconscious, fantasy and reality.

Once Teresa dies, Sofia is the first to come into contact with the fantastic realm. With a new perspective as the heiress to the family name and fortune, Sofia begins to admit her admiration for her own mother:

> Al capdavall, pensava, si sóc poderosa, ho dec a Teresa Goday. La mort li féu adonar-se que la seva mare havia estat una persona excepcional i ella, davant d'aquella esplendor desapareguda, se sentia disminuïda. (224)

> ["In the end," she thought, "if I am powerful, I owe it to Teresa Goday." Death made her realize that her mother had been an exceptional person, and, with that splendor now gone, she felt diminished.]

In spite of this recognition of debt to her mother, Sofia nevertheless upholds the pattern of maternal rejection seen throughout the novel. Frightened by feeling a presence and seeing a mysterious fluttering ruffle ("un volant") in Maria's room, Sofia reacts negatively and demands that Armanda leave all of the rooms unlocked in the future. Sofia thus misses an opportunity to make contact and repair her maternal relationship with her adopted daughter. In contrast, Armanda does accept the mysterious experiences that she has and thus steps in and definitively takes over the role of caretaker, of matriarch even, as she respects the dead and devotes herself to protecting the house and the family fortune.

With the outbreak the Civil War, Sofia leaves the house with a servant, fleeing to France for safety. In the nearly abandoned chalet, Armanda has an intense encounter with the dead family members. Gazing at the "mirall trencat" of the title, Armanda takes in the vision of a fragmented reality and, I would suggest, takes on the responsibility of redefining reality and repairing the integrity of the fractured family legacy. Having drunk almost an entire bottle of champagne and made the decision to bury the family fortune for protection, Armanda has a vision of being joined at the table by the skeletons of all the dead family members. Unperturbed by the scene, she demonstrates her ability to cross the boundaries between life and death as easily as Teresa did earlier. Another night Armanda will be visited by angels, and several times she will have contact with Maria's ghost which manifests itself as a spider web, caressing people's skin with a light, ghostly touch. Maria's unease in death is expressed in the chapter devoted to her ghost's voice and it is here that we learn that she wants to lay claim to the house and is upset by the fact that the movers, sent by Sofia after the war to clear everything away, are stealing her tombstone.[26]

Through the years, however, only Armanda will reach out to the dead, attempting to save the family both financially and psychically by guarding the house and, ultimately, bringing peace to Maria's ghost. Armanda's definitive moments come at the very end of the novel, where the alternative to biological maternal relations is put forth. Returning to the house after a long absence (during which time she continued to visit and throw flowers into the yard in a sort of offering to the dead), Armanda recognizes that she has had contact with Maria's ghost, knowing for sure this time that the caress was too strong to come from a spider. Leaving the house for good this time and having dug up the fortune and turned it over to Sofia and Ramon, she decides to talk to the dead. Armanda offers comfort as she says, "Si és un mort d'aquesta casa el qui pensa en mi, que Déu l'ajudi i li doni el repòs i la pau que necessita" (262) [If it is a dead person from this house who is thinking about me, may God help him and give him the rest and the peace that he needs]. With these final words of release,

> una cosa la fascinà: una boira petita, una mica de boira de no-res, indecisa, una ala transparent que s'anà allunyant i a l'útim es fongué com si la terra l'hagués xuclada. (262–63)

> [something fascinated her: a small, indecisive cloud of fog, of nothing, a transparent wing that went farther away and finally dissipated as if absorbed by the earth.]

In this final encounter with the house and its living and dead members, we see Armanda fulfilling multifarious roles that define her as the caretaker of the financial, spiritual, and material aspects of the family dynasty. The childless Armanda has become the mother *par excellence,* the mother that neither Teresa nor Sofia ever was: transcending the boundaries of biology, class, and reality, Armanda comes to embody the ideologies of a feminist future that Irigaray calls for and Rodoreda narrates. The fantastic, and Armanda's contact with the characters who populate this liminal space, facilitates a reconciliation with the past and a liberation from patriarchal constraints.

Those, like Sofia, who remain outside the fantastic realm are not privy to this revolutionary vision. Trapped in the economy of exchange that tainted her mother's matriarchy from the beginning, Sofia continues to believe in the ultimate signifier of money, believing herself capable of reconciling with the past and of repairing her estranged relationship with her son through economic exchange. In a gesture similar to a business deal, Sofia hands over a check to Ramon and promises him more money in the future. In fact, the future that Sofia imagines revolves around money, as she counts on the profit and security garnished through exchange: like the profit she is sure to gain by razing the chalet and constructing luxury condominiums in its place, she repairs her relationship with Ramon through money and then promises to meet her grandchildren at a later date. The fragility of this newly reestablished link between mother and son, forged through money if not through emotion, is reinforced when Ramon himself reacts in astonishment at his reconnection with the family, "Imaginin, un hereu!" (256) [Imagine, an heir!].

Again, it would seem, we have come full circle; back to the first moment of the exchange, of commodification of the self when Teresa accepted Nicolau's marriage proposal, compromising her integrity and suppressing her maternal self. If indeed Sofia, with her unceasing belief in the economies of exchange, is the "rise of the new constellation" announced in the epigraph to the third section of *Mirall trencat,* then the past is *not* "a time forgotten," for Sofia has absorbed the rules of the Goday matriarchy and, perhaps as unwittingly as her mother when she was young, participates in the exchange economies. Like her mother, Sofia understands how to exploit the system to get what she wants and, probably due to generational differences, she enjoys more autonomy than Teresa did. Still, she turns to money, to exchange, as a means by which to secure familial bonds and refuses, by rejecting Maria and razing the chalet, to reconcile fully with the past.

This complicated characterization of the heir to Teresa's legacy takes us once again to the territory of paradox, or perhaps of subversion, to Rodoreda herself and her lack of allegiance with feminism and feminists. For in fact Rodoreda produced a novel whose preoccupations and thematics coincide with the same ideas being theorized by women like Luce Irigaray who asked,

> How can we speak so as to escape from their compartments, their schemes, their distinctions and oppositions: virginal/deflowered, pure/impure, innocent/experienced . . . How can we shake off the chain of these terms, free ourselves from their categories, rid ourselves of their names? Disengage ourselves, *alive,* from their concepts?[27]

Rodoreda addresses these issues, turning us to the fantastic as a transitional and exploratory space in which women do "shake off the chain of (the) terms." If we turn to the fantastic, to that fluid borderland in which the young Maria finds a voice and the servant Armanda protects and heals in a way that no other women do, then we can see that Rodoreda has presented a clever critique of the patriarchy and, importantly, has offered a compelling vision for its revision. Placed at the heart of the family in Part Three, Armanda is portrayed in the realms of realism and fantasy as the true heir to Teresa's legacy. The positioning of such a character at the emotional center of the family functions to deconstruct and question oppressive patriarchal dynamics at play in the first two parts of the novel. The following negative characteristics of Teresa's matriarchy are transcended in the realm of the fantastic: the reliance on biological lineage and class distinctions as markers of difference, the commodification of and competition among women, and the repression of the maternal. The mere inversion of terms, of matriarch for patriarch, seen during Teresa's lifetime, is superseded here. No longer bound to the same set of terms proposed by the patriarchy, the fantastic liberates women from the binaries of the phallus and provides them with a new, women-oriented locus.

In terms of the narrative economy, the fantastic occupies a relatively small space in the long family saga that is *Mirall trencat.* Yet in a few brief scenes and chapters revolving around Maria's ghost and Armanda's encounters, the novel entices us to explore the feminist possibilities of this borderless space.

With the erasure of the economies of exchange and all of its attendant oppression, the fantastic opens up the possibility for the expression of women's desire, for positive relationships among women, and for a less lineage-anxious family structure. In sum, the inherently borderless fantastic realm acts as a liminal space in which women's psychic and sexual autonomy may be safely and successfully explored. Sofia might represent the immediate generation of women, but the fantastic invites us to look ahead, toward the new constellation that might be, could be, a feminist future.

Notes

1. Joan Ramon Resina, "The Link in Consciousness: Time and Community in Rodoreda's *La plaça del Diamant," Catalan Review* 2, no. 2 (December 1987): 226; emphasis added.

2. Carme Arnau describes the novel as portraying a vision of the world that is "la de la destrucción y de la muerte, y que, contrastando con las anteriores, es una novela cerrada" ("La obra de Mercè Rodoreda," *Cuadernos hispanoamericanos* 383 [May 1981]: 241). Also see Elizabeth Scarlett's *Under Construction: The Body in Spanish Novels* (Charlottesville: University of Virginia Press, 1994), 125.

3. Mercè Clarasó attributes the complexity and daring of *Mirall trencat* to the successful unification of realism with fantasy, saying Rodoreda "achieves in *Mirall trencat* a depth that none of the other novels approaches" ("The Two Worlds of Mercè Rodoreda," in *Women Writers in Twentieth-Century Spain and Spanish America,* ed. Catherine Davies, [Lewiston, Me.: Mellen Press, 1993], 53).

4. Critics as diverse as Elizabeth Scarlett and Jaume Martí-Olivella in "The Witches' Touch: Towards a Poetics of Double Articulation in Rodoreda," *Catalan Review* 2, no. 2 (December 1987): 159–70, and Joaquim Poch i Bullich and Conxa Planas i Planas in "El fet femení en els textos de Mercè Rodoreda," *Catalan Review* 2, no. 2 (December 1987): 199–224 have remarked on the integral role of the maternal in Rodoreda's *oeuvre.*

5. Marianne Hirsch, *The Mother/Daughter Plot* (Bloomington: Indiana University Press, 1989), 127. Also see Elaine Showalter's "Towards a Feminist Poetics," in *The New Feminist Criticism: Essays on Women, Literature, Theory* (New York: Pantheon Books, 1985), 125–43.

6. Gayle Rubin, "The Traffic in Women: Notes on the 'Political Economy' of Sex," in *Toward an Anthropology of Women,* ed. Rayna Reiter (New York: Monthly Review, 1975), 177.

7. Luce Irigaray, *This Sex Which Is Not One,* trans. Catherine Porter (Ithaca: Cornell University Press, 1985), 171. All Irigaray citations are from this text unless otherwise noted.

8. All quotations from *Mirall trencat* are taken from the edition published by Clàssics Catalans (Barcelona, 1991). Subsequent references are cited parenthetically by page number only. The English translations are my own.

9. Maryellen Bieder, "The Woman in the Garden," in *Actes del segon col.loqui d'estudis catalans a Nord-Amèrica*, ed. Manuel Duran et. al., (Montserrat: l'Abadia, 1982), 364.

10. As Scarlett has stated with regard to Rodoreda's work in general, "the significance of the female body in male-dominated exchange economies of money and power recurs constantly through the institutions of marriage and prostitution" (ibid., 100).

11. Irigaray, 176.

12. Equating Teresa's desirability with her relationship to another man, her longtime lover Amadeu Riera will later remark that he took pleasure in 'stealing' his friend's wife: "¿Podria jurar que, en algun moment fugaç com un llampec, no havia sentit satisfacció de robar la dona a un amic?" (239) [Could he swear that, in some moment as quick as a lightning bolt, he hadn't felt the satisfaction of stealing the wife of a friend?]. That Riera sees Teresa's worth primarily in terms of rivalry with another man, in terms of her value as a commodity of exchange, is confirmed when a telling rhetorical question is posed: "¿I si en morir Valldaura la seva passió per la Teresa hagués minvat perquè no hi havia ni rivalitat ni necessitat de fer-se preferir?" (239) [And what if upon Valldaura's death his passion for Teresa had diminished because he did not have a rivalry or a need to make her prefer him?].

13. Irigaray, 187–88.

14. Monique Wittig, *The Straight Mind and Other Essays* (Boston: Beacon Press, 1992), 10.

15. Scarlett, 106.

16. Loreto Busquets, "The Unconscious in the Novels of Mercè Rodoreda," *Catalan Review* 2, no. 2 (December 1987): 107.

17. Further underscoring the lack of maternal love in the novel, even Jesús Masdéu feels neglected by his stepmother, who is said to not love him very much (90).

18. *Mirall trencat*, 186.

19. Scarlett, 126.

20. Irigaray, 177. This quote leads us to the ideas developed in Irigaray's *Speculum of the Other Woman*, trans. Gillian Gill (Ithaca: Cornell University Press, 1985).

21. Geraldine Cleary Nichols, "Stranger than Fiction: Fantasy in Short Stories by Matute, Rodoreda, Riera," *Monographic Review* 4 (1988): 41–42.

22. Irigaray, 33.

23. Angeles Encinar's comments about the fantastic in Rodoreda's short story collection *La meva Cristina* are helpful inasmuch as they address the need for an alternative vision of the world: "La perfecta estructura del universo fantástico es el medio de expresión adecuado para proyectar la realidad de un mundo agobiante que atrapa a sus protagonistas" ("Mercè Rodoreda: hacia una fantasía liberadora," *Revista canadiense de estudios hispánicos* 11, no. 1 [fall 1986]: 10).

24. Irigaray, 191.

25. Nichols, 37.

26. Maria's close relationship with the laurel upon which she throws herself to commit suicide underscores the possibility within the fantastic for a new relationship with nature. Cf. Bieder and Scarlett for more on the role of nature in Rodoreda's fiction.

27. Irigaray, 212.

Verbal Absences and Visual Silences in *Quanta, quanta guerra . . ., La mort i la primavera,* and *Isabel i Maria*

JOSEFINA GONZÁLEZ

IN "*ALOMA*'S TWO FACES AND THE CHARACTER OF HER TRUE NATURE," Randolph D. Pope suspects Armand Obiols (Joan Prat) of having influenced Mercè Rodoreda to rewrite a less sensual and less controversial second version of her novel *Aloma.* Published in 1969, this second version differs from the 1938 *Aloma* in the decreased criticism of "the violence of society, the degrading routine of marriage, the dangers of romantic delusions, the repression of the body, and the exploitation and abuse of women."[1] The article examines efficiently the editorial collaboration of Obiols and Rodoreda in the revision, concluding that almost every line of the first version had been altered in the revised text to silence the passionate and sensual *Aloma* of 1938. This first version, adds Pope, had denounced masterfully the repression of women at a time when Rodoreda had not yet met Obiols in exile after the Spanish Civil War.[2] Obiols, her longtime companion, was well known for neglecting his own writing to edit his friends' creative work. Therefore, Rodoreda was accused of having rewritten *Aloma* and other books with his help, as evidenced by her self-defense in a conversation with J. M. Castellet: "M'han explicat que algú ha dit que era ell qui m'escrivia els llibres: una bestiesa, com pots comprendre, perquè els meus llibres són llibres de dona, i els homes no en saben res, del món de les dones."[3] [I have been told that someone has said that he is the one who wrote my books: a stupidity, as you can understand, since my books are women's books, and men don't know anything about the world of women.] And indeed, Obiols himself believed that Rodoreda was at her best with female protagonists, as quoted by her biographer Montserrat Casals i Couturier: "sempre t'expresses millor, i vas més a fons, quan el protagonista és una dona."[4] [You always express yourself better, and more profoundly, when the protagonist is a woman.] *Quanta, quanta guerra* . . . (1980) [So much War]), published after Obiols' death, does not represent a woman's world or a female protagonist, but it is a novel which introduces a change in sensibility that increases the uncertainty as to the influence of Obiols in the creative process of her work. *La mort i la primavera* (1986) [Death and Spring] and *Isabel i Maria* (1991) [Isabel and Maria], both posthumously published and unfinished, are contrasts that add to these doubts, with *Mirall trencat* (1974) [Broken Mirror] as the boundary marker of the change.

Even if Rodoreda denies any collaboration with Obiols in writing her work, it is significant that when he died in 1971 she interrupted *Mirall trencat,* her work in progress, and decided not to write any longer in his absence: "Jo escrivia només per a l'Obiols, i ara ja no hi és."[5] [I only wrote for Obiols, and he is not here anymore.] She later changed her mind and published *Mirall trencat* in 1974, followed by *Quanta, quanta guerra* . . ., not allowing Obiols' absence to silence her. Rodoreda also revealed that she wrote constantly in isolation while waiting for Obiols to return from his many business trips. On his return, Obiols would then give her intense feedback and criticism on her writing. It is not unexpected, therefore, that this activity would influence Rodoreda's novels with a trace of the masculine, and in Obiols' absence a change would be evident in the representation of a woman's world. Contrary to the conclusion in the comparison of the two versions of *Aloma,* this influence seems impossible according to another observation by Pope that Rodoreda's later works "would subsequently concentrate on love and life at home, while they would grow fuzzy and sound hollow when trying to describe the worlds of finance, commerce, or industry, a deficiency that contributed to the weakness of many of her male characters."[6] This is an accurate observation evidenced clearly in Rodoreda's work written after Obiols' death, *Quanta, quanta guerra* . . . and *La mort i la primavera,* in which the androgynous male protagonists are impervious to the worlds of finance, commerce, and industry. Only one novel before Obiols' death, *Jardí vora el mar* (1967) [Garden by the Sea]), has a male narrator. However, in contrast with the characteristic first-person monologue of the female narrator-protagonist of Rodoreda's novels, the role of the male narrator of *Jardí vora el mar* is limited to that of voyeur, and his actions do not betray a male representation. This novel, therefore, does not offer any clues as to the true nature of Rodoreda's authorship before Obiols' death: a gardener (a traditional male occupation) who observes the activities of the inhabitants of a house by the sea, does not confirm Obiols' presence or absence. An excellent reading of the Hollywood movie *The Women,* Debra Fried's "The Men in *The Women*" defines a space where this presence/absence can be detected and compared to the boundary between *Mirall trencat* on the one hand, and *Quanta, quanta guerra . . . , La mort i la primavera,* and *Isabel i Maria* on the other.

The Women is a 1939 comedy with an all-star female cast in which male actors neither appear nor are heard.[7] But men are the only subject of conversation by fashionable Manhattan women engaged in their daily chores in beauty salons, fitting rooms, and women's lounges, where they are constantly getting ready to be seen. Men's presence is only evident in the objects appearing in the movie and in the fact that the women are given a voice through the medium of film; it is a woman's world created by the men behind the camera acting as voyeurs:

> Men can make telephones ring and (we must presume) provide the unheard part of telephone conversations; their remarks are quoted, their opinions predicted, their arrivals awaited. But they are present only in what they have left behind them: clothes, gift bottles of perfume, notes, children, lonely wives, and photographs—not ones they appear in but ones they have taken, because, like the film itself, the snapshots shown in this film refuse to record men. The world of *The Women* may be littered with clues to the presence of men, but throughout men cannot be heard and they cannot be seen.[8]

Mirall trencat, although it depicts male characters subordinated to a domestic environment, is also full of what men leave behind: illegitimate children; a brooch of rubies given to Teresa Valldaura by her first husband; a pearl tiepin Teresa gives to her second husband Salvador Valldaura, and after his death, to her lover; violets given by Salvador to his first love and later to his wife. Rodoreda admits the importance these objects have in her fiction in the prologue to a late edition of her first successful novel *La plaça del Diamant* (1962) [*The Time of the Doves* (1980)]:

> Les coses tenen una gran importància en la narració i l'han tinguda sempre, molt abans que Robbe-Grillet escrivís *Le Voyeur.* A

> *La plaça del Diamant*, de coses n'hi ha moltes: l'embut, el cargol marí . . . I el ganivet, símbol sexual, amb què a l'acabament del llibre la Colometa escriu el seu nom a la porta de la casa on havia viscut.[9]
>
> [Objects are very important in narrative and have always been, even before Robbe-Grillet wrote *Le Voyeur*. In *La plaça del Diamant*, there are many things: the funnel, the seashell . . . And the knife, sexual symbol, with which at the end of the book Colometa writes her name on the door of the house in which she had lived.]

This symbol of the knife as sexual object is an indication of Rodoreda's treatment of visual images in her narrative to sublimate the repressions imposed, apparently, by Obiols' censorship. The visual quality of Rodoreda's narrative centered in the objects presented is, therefore, a means by which Rodoreda could express her sexuality and sensuality, as evidenced throughout her literary production.[10] With this technique Rodoreda mimics the manner in which men express their desire by representing women as silent visual objects, a reversal of roles created by Obiols' apparent censorship of her voice in narrative. This sublimation into the realm of visual imagery created by a silence imposed on her could perhaps explain Rodoreda's refusal to identify openly with feminism, as she clearly states in her conversation with Castellet: "ja saps que no sóc feminista."[11] [You already know that I'm not a feminist.] Rodoreda had also mentioned her belief in the fictionality of feminism when she said to Montserrat Roig that it was "una mica literatura"[12] [a little bit literature]. An unwillingness to censure men and a willingness to silence verbally her real feelings were also observed by Elizabeth Rhodes in an insightful and straightforward essay on Rodoreda's well-known short story "La salamandra" [The Salamander]: "That affection [for Obiols, with whom Rodoreda led an adulterous relationship] perhaps created a dependency which the protagonist of the story contemplates openly. (Rodoreda was probably controlled by the knowledge that Obiols would read "La Salamandra").[13] This short story is an excellent example of Rodoreda's customary use of imagery as an outlet for escape when the female protagonist metamorphoses into a salamander to prevent being burned to death as punishment for an adulterous affair. The same subversive undercurrent appears also in *Isabel i Maria* in the form of geckos, animals that closely resemble salamanders.

In *Isabel i Maria,* however, the object foregrounded is a bougainvillea. What is significant about this plant is the fact that its bracts mimic the petals of flowers in their color. The bougainvillea, absent from books on the language of flowers popular during the nineteenth century and thus without a standard symbolic tradition, is a silent visual object.[14] Other flowers in Rodoreda's work are not without meaning, as evidenced by the mimosa in the the short story "Aquella paret, aquella mimosa" [That Wall, that Mimosa], in which the shyness denoted by a mimosa describes the personality of Crisantema, a young maid in love with a soldier.[15] The lack of a symbolic tradition for the bougainvillea intensifies its status as a visual object in the novel. Even though the bougainvillea is silent in its symbolism, the artifice suggested by its leaves becomes a clever fictional device that represents the constant duplicity in the characters' relationships and in the ambiguity of a male representation. This relationship between the bougainvillea and the characters to suggest an uncertain condition is not unique to *Isabel i Maria.* Kathleen McNerney points out a similar relationship of deceit in "Carnaval" [Carnival], a short story published in *Vint-i-dos contes* (1958) [Twenty-Two Stories]: "Once again, things aren't what they seem: the flowers have no perfume, they're definitely not gardenias. . . ."[16] In *Isabel i Maria,* things are not what they seem either. Nor does the bougainvillea have a smell, a detail observed by Lluís, the stereotypical male character of the novel: "vaig collir una flor de buganvília i la vaig olorar mig d'esma: no tenia cap mena de perfum"[17] [I took a flower from the bougainvillaea and smelled it mechanically: it didn't have a fragrance, 71].

Isabel i Maria, divided in two parts, is a reconstruction of a woman's life using alternating monologues of the woman herself, Isabel; her lover/brother-in-law/husband, Lluís; and their maid Crisantema, characters whose voices appear only in the first part of the novel. The second part consists of the unfinished diary of Maria, Isabel's daughter. These monologues are interrupted occasionally by minor characters. Absent from this reconstruction is the point of view of Joaquim, first husband of Isabel and brother of Lluís. This is a significant detail, since Joaquim is the only character in the novel without a voice, dead in the fictional present of the novel, and speaking only as quoted by living characters. It is also significant that he is the male character in the novel repressed by the deceptions of Isabel and Lluís' adulterous affair. This affair forces him to abandon the home he had built for Isabel, taking with him Isabel's newborn child, Maria, as punishment for his wife's betrayal, even though it is not known which of the two brothers is the real father of the child.[18] Joaquim then establishes a new home with a new garden in which, interestingly, there is no bougainvillea as there was in the childhood garden where the brothers met Isabel and fell into a love triangle, with the red color of the plant indicating the passion surrounding them.

The bougainvillea reappears later when Isabel marries Joaquim out of spite for Lluís' departure to a foreign country. After the father of the brothers dies, Lluís returns to claim his inheritance and the love relationship with Isabel resumes, increasing the visual vividness of the bougainvillea that is greatly admired by Riera, the family doctor:

> No sé per què m'agradava anar a aquella casa. Potser per aquest dimoni de buganvília meravellosa, que a la florida sembla una onada de foc. M'he passat la vida plantant-ne a casa i mai no m'han fet res de bo. I si alguna ha arrelat, ha pujat escarransida i sense lluc. Es clar que el meu jardí no està tan ben orientat com el seu. . . . (88)
>
> [I don't know why I liked going to that house. Maybe because of that marvelous bougainvillea that seemed like a wave of fire when it bloomed. I've spent my life planting bougainvilleas at home and I've never been successful at it. And if one has taken root, it has grown weak and budless. Certainly, my garden is not as perfectly located as theirs . . .]

From this quote it is clear that the bougainvillea is much more than an object of beauty, since the doctor sees in the plant a metaphor for the passion taking place in the home of Isabel.[19] And for the inhabitants of the house as well, the bougainvillea is a representation of their unexpressed desires. Isabel clearly implies this hidden meaning in her description of two kinds of plants: "La meitat del mur quedava colgat per penjolls carmí de buganvília i per penjolls blaus d'aquella planta que en diuen llàgrimes de Sant Josep" (134) [The middle of the wall was hidden by hanging carmine clusters of bougainvillea and by hanging blue clusters of a plant called the tears of Saint Joseph]. In this quote the bougainvillea stands for something hidden, forbidden, while the blue flowers contrast with the red to suggest the sadness provoked by that desire. Another quote establishes this interpretation of the bougainvillea when Lluís perceives the plant as a curtain encroaching on the house: "La buganvília era una cortina de fulles" (70) [the bougainvillea was a curtain of leaves], in a "balcó envaït per la buganvília" (98) [porch invaded by the bougainvillia]. Crisantema—who seems to be the same maid of "Aquella paret, aquella mimosa" when she admits being in love with a soldier—notices this threatening force of the plant in the first sentences of the novel: "Avui que estic sola hauria de fer el que ja volia fer la meva mare: tirar una ampolla de salfumant a la buganvília . . . Si clavés un bon cop de destral a la soca, la planta no patiria tant." (37) [Now that I'm alone I would do what my mother had always wanted: throw a bottle of acid at the bougainvillea . . . If I struck the trunk with a hatchet, maybe the plant wouldn't suffer as much.] At times Crisantema also wants to sweep the leaves as if by doing so she could eradicate the atmosphere of deceit and forbidden desires that surrounds her: "escombrar i escombrar la fullaraca i empaitar els dragons que s'amaguen darrera d'aquest tou de fulles maleïdes" (38) [to sweep and sweep the dry leaves and scare away the geckos hidden behind this pile of damned leaves.]

Significantly, this bougainvillea does not reappear in Joachim's new home with Maria where a new garden is planted that "era una bogeria de perfum" (169) [was a madness of perfumes] with flowers of all colors, fruit trees, a fountain with statues of nymphs, and a cement mermaid with water spouting from her mouth into a pond with red fish. The fountain in the garden evokes the sensuality of the idyllic bliss of pastoral Arcadia, suggesting the peacefulness that exists in the new home with Joaquim and Maria. Here, Joaquim raises Maria with the belief that he is her uncle and that her mother died. The home is surrounded by an atmosphere of love devoid of sexual passion since Joaquim plays a motherly role, caring for Maria's every need, dressing her, and cooking with her. This happiness ends when the death of Joaquim forces Maria at age twelve to live with Isabel after it is revealed that she is her real mother, with the uncertainty as to the identity of the father remaining. Maria finds life difficult in her new home, mostly due to the hostility of Lluís' temperament and dictatorial repression. To escape the oppressive atmosphere of her new home, Maria frequently slips from her upstairs bedroom into the garden during summer nights by sliding down the bougainvillea, which she considers "la planta més preciosa de tot el jardí" (136) [the most beautiful plant in the whole garden]. Maria also regrets that Joaquim did not plant one in her previous garden, suggesting her entry into the passion of womanhood and the will to escape Lluís' constant censorship of her desires.

It is not difficult, then, with this reading of the bougainvillea in *Isabel i Maria,* to interpret Rodoreda's visual imagery in her fiction as an escape into the realm of the senses. The shift in Rodoreda's voice under Obiols' censorship documented by Pope is not unexpected since the writer had revealed the escapist nature of her interest in the visual. In her isolation in exile, Rodoreda often visited museums and movie theaters, and during the 1950s in Switzerland, she turned briefly to painting, apparently under the direct influence of encountering the art of Paul Klee: "Me instalé en Ginebra en 1954. Pinté mucho, entonces, digamos en el estilo de Paul Klee. Pinté como una desesperada. Hice cosas bonitas."[20] [I settled in Geneva in 1954. I painted a lot then, let's say in the style of Paul Klee. I painted desperately. I did a lot of pretty things.] She abandoned painting soon afterwards, and in her denial, expressed the escapist nature of this activity: "Pero no he vuelto a coger los pinceles. Pintar era como una evasión frente a cuanto tenía que hacer y no me gustaba . . . Necesito mucho tiempo para escribir, mucha tranquilidad."[21] [I haven't picked up the brushes since then. Painting was like an escape from what I had to do but didn't like . . . I need a lot of time to write, a lot of peace.] *La mort i la primavera* presents explicitly the influence of Klee's primitive painting, depicting childlike whimsical gardens, flowers, trees, and sprouting seeds in a primeval and springlike environment of rites practiced by an unknown civilization.[22]

Even though Rodoreda had abandoned the writing of *La mort i la primavera* because it made her feel "fàstic" [revulsion], of all her novels, this is the most visual and suggestive of painting.[23] In this novel the visual element that predominates is color—not objects—in the pink of the wisterias, plants that resemble botanically the bougainvillea in their climbing strength and shrub-like characteristics. These wisterias reflect the pink hue from the houses in contrast with the green of the vegetation as in an afterimage effect. Pink, a lighter shade of the red bougainvillea, foregrounds the visual field of the novel and distracts from the narration of the rituals: "Les cases del poble eren totes de color de rosa. A la primavera les pintàvem i potser per això la llum era diferent: perquè agafava el rosa de les cases com a vora del riu tot agafava color de fulles i de sol.[24] [The town's houses were all pink. We painted them in spring and perhaps for this reason the light was different: because it would catch the pink from the houses just as by the river bank everything would take on the color of the leaves and sun.] With this color the town becomes integrated with surrounding nature, since the paint was mixed from red dust found in a nearby cave as "vermella i molla com la boca d'un malalt" (18) [red and wet as the mouth of a sick person], a paint applied with brushes made from the tails of the horses they ate in their rituals. This is the cave where they sacrifice victims by throwing them into a river that runs underneath the town, a ritual believed to prevent the town from being washed away by the uncontrollable forces of nature. The wisterias, from which pomade is made to help form "miques de pell damunt de la sang" (74) [pieces of skin on top of the blood], are also threatening to the inhabitants, creating a resistance in their relationship with nature: "Havien dit que les glicines decantaven les cases . . ." (98) [they said that wisterias tore houses apart], and "les glicines . . . feien la nit carregada . . ." (13) [the wisterias . . . made the night oppressive . . .]

The color effect of *La mort i la primavera* is very similar to that of color field painters of the mid 50s to late 60s who tried to eliminate any distinction between a subject and its background in order to be faithful to painting's two-dimensional nature rather than to create an illusion of three-dimensionality. It is clear that by using the color pink, with the wisteria as mediator, Rodoreda intended to merge the subject with the background to integrate the town with surrounding nature. The intention is evident in the ritual tree burials practiced by the society depicted in the novel. Both the protagonist, and previously his father, experience desire for and fear of burial in a tree. This wish to blend two worlds, animal and plant, is also a constant fear throughout the novel:

> I no ens en vam anar fins que ens va semblar que érem arbres, perquè a les plantes dels peus hi sentíem créixer i néixer arrels de fred de gebre que ens anaven lligant on érem. (63)

> [And we didn't leave until it seemed to us that we were trees, because we felt cold roots of frost grow from the soles of our feet, which tied us down where we were.]

> Tot s'està acabant . . . la llum i el meu viure que encara em lliga a la terra com la terra lliga i volta les arrels." (110)
>
> [Everything is ending . . . the light and my life that is still tied down to the earth like the earth ties and surrounds the roots.]

The novel ends with his suicide inside a tree in a moment of epiphany when the reader realizes that the narrator has been speaking from the realm of the dead. A similar situation appears in *Mirall trencat* with a laurel tree that marks the full entry of the fantastic in the novel when Maria's voice narrates after her death. In this instance, the laurel tree is the conjunction of the real with the fantastic and of life with death.[25] But in *La mort i la primavera,* there is not a difference between life and death from the perspective of the protagonist who felt himself already rotting alive, as the leaves of the forest floor: "els sentiments que em lligaven eren herbes podrides . . ." (155) [the feelings that bounded me were as rotted grasses]. Merged with the world of plants in his death, the subject of *La mort i la primavera* finally becomes one with the background. This blending resembles the objectives of the genre of ekphrasis, which W. J. T. Mitchell equates with the desire to merge with the Other.[26]

A frequent model of comparison between the visual arts and literature is the notion inherited from the Renaissance that the visual arts are inherently spatial and that literature is limited to the realm of time. This is an inaccurate notion denounced by Mitchell, since painting as well as literature "can tell stories, make arguments, and signify abstract ideas." Communicative acts of painting and literature are not medium-specific: "narration, argument, description, exposition, and other so-called 'speech acts' are not medium-specific, are not 'proper' to some medium or other."[27] One of the objectives of modernist art was to liberate itself from this relationship with the verbal by taking refuge in the silence of abstract painting. But this objective was not an ideal accomplished outside an elitist milieu, since it was very common for this kind of painting to evoke a reaction like the one Harold Rosenberg describes in *The De-Definition of Art:* "When Theodore Roosevelt observed at the 1913 Armory Show that Duchamp's 'Nude Descending a Staircase' reminded him of a 'Navajo rug,' he committed the archetypal critical *faux pas.*"[28] To avoid this constant referentiality to reality extraneous to their medium, artists felt the need to explain their work, and fell again into the trap of the verbal in a new relationship, which Tom Wolfe summarizes in *The Painted Word:* "these days, without a theory to go with it, I can't see a painting."[29] Mitchell has named this new relationship with the verbal *ut pictura theoria* to differentiate it from the Renaissance tradition of *ut pictura poesis* that established a parallel between art and poetry in which the visual subordinated to the verbal was considered to be mute poetry. In *ut pictura theoria,* as defined by Mitchell, a new relationship of subordination is established:

> the wall erected against language and literature by the grid of abstraction only kept out a certain kind of verbal contamination, but it absolutely depended, at the same time, on the collaboration of painting with another kind of discourse . . . the discourse of theory.[30]

In this exchange, the visual found a new relationship with the verbal by rejecting literary narrative in an interaction with theory, which Mitchell reminds the reader is:

> that curious hybrid of mainly prose discourse compounded from aesthetics and other branches of philosophy, as well as from literary criticism, linguistics, the natural and social sciences, psychology, history, political thought, and religion . . . characterized, generally, by a refusal of disciplinary identity.[31]

La mort i la primavera is also characterized by this refusal to be identified merely as narrative in the resistance of the protagonist to perceive himself as separate from his environment. A similar attitude can be found in the writings of Paul Klee, a painter chronologically classified within modernist art and singular for his rejection of art as a pure medium devoid of the verbal. This attitude is evidenced by his hieroglyphic paintings and in writings where he establishes a similar relationship with his environment as the protagonist of *La mort i la primavera:*

> From the root the sap flows to the artist, flows through him, flows to his eye.
> Thus he stands as the trunk of the tree.
> Battered and stirred by the strength of the flow, he moulds his vision into his work.[32]

La mort i la primavera's resistance to purity is in contrast with *Quanta, quanta guerra . . .* , a novel with which it shares, besides a male protagonist, an atmosphere of death and horror experienced during initiation into adulthood. Carme Arnau establishes this similarity in esoteric values believed to have been the result of Rodoreda's involvement with the Rosicrucian community in Girona during the last years of her life.[33] But in *Quanta, quanta guerra . . .* , *bildungsroman* experiences are clearly framed, as opposed to *La mort i la primavera,* by picaresque conventions.[34] Both novels also converge in the protagonist's desire to merge with the environment. There are several references in *Quanta, quanta guerra . . .* to this desire:

> Deprés de fer un sot molt fondo al peu de l'avellaner, m'hi vaig ficar i em vaig cobrir de terra fins als genolls. Havia dut la regadora plena d'aigua i em vaig regar. Volia que em sortissin arrels: ser tot branques i fulles. (31)
>
> [After digging a hole very deep at the foot of the hazelnut tree, I went in and covered myself with dirt to the knees. I had taken the full watering can with me and I watered myself. I wanted roots to sprout from me: to become all branches and leaves.]

> M'agradaría més ser una planta de les que broten i broten sense saber que viuen. (79)
>
> [I would rather be one of those plants that sprout and sprout without knowing they are alive.]

> per les arrels de l'arbre s'haurà encabit el seu fantasma soca amunt fins a respirar altra vegada tots els vents de la rosa. (116)
>
> [the ghost will have entered through the tree roots up its trunk far enough to breathe all the winds of the rose again.]

> poder ser arbre poder ser núvol poder ser vent (206)
>
> [to be able to be a tree to be a cloud to be wind]

> hauria volgut no ser jo . . . ser un arbre ben arrapat a la terra arrels endins branques enlaire" (223)[35]

> [I would have liked not to be me . . . to be a tree, roots well anchored deep in the earth, branches high above]

However, these images differ from those in *La mort i la primavera* in a lack of hallucinatory delusion, since in *Quanta, quanta guerra* . . . a certainty exists that the desired transformation will not occur.

Quanta, quanta guerra . . . was inspired by the cult movie directed by the Polish filmmaker Wojciech J. Has, *Rekopis Znaleziony w Saragossie* (1965) [The Saragossa Manuscript] as Rodoreda clearly reveals in the prologue to the novel: "*Quanta, quanta guerra* . . . va néixer una tarda al vestíbul de l'antic Publi Cinema on havia entrat a mirar les fotos de la pel.lícula que estaven passant: 'El manuscrit trobat a Saragossa' . . ." (13) [*Quanta, quanta guerra* . . . was born one afternoon in the lobby of the old Publi Cinema, which I had entered to look at the photographs of the movie being shown: *The Saragossa Manuscript* . . .] The influence of this movie on *Quanta, quanta guerra* . . . is significant in the opening scene of a fight between warring soldiers in Saragossa, Spain.[36] One of the soldiers, apparently from the soon-to-be-defeated invading faction, enters a damaged building, where he finds an old book. Delighted by the drawings illustrating the manuscript, he looks in ecstasy at a representation of two women lying next to each other, provocatively dressed. At that moment the Spaniards enter, and, taken prisoner, he convinces the arresting soldiers to sit down and translate the story which introduces the next frame of the movie. In the following frame, the story being read, of the adventures of a young soldier, appears visually. These adventures lead to encounters with characters who narrate stories within stories in a *mise en abîme*. This is definitely an invitation to view the movie as a text of *The Saragossa Manuscript*, the work of Count Jan Potocki (1761–1815), a Polish scholar, traveller, soldier and poet, on which the movie is based.

In the prologue to *Quanta, quanta guerra* . . . , Rodoreda expresses the desire to create a character who will look at the world as poets do, "tot el que veiés el deixés sorprès" (14) [surprised at everything seen]. And with this attitude, Adrià Guinart leaves home to join the war, encountering experiences and tales told by the people he meets in a structure very similar to that of the film. There are some images in conjunction with the movie: marks on foreheads, skulls as utensils, hanged men, and particularly, a constant awakening or lying next to rotting corpses left by the war in desolate landscapes. But just as in the movie Saragossa does not appear, in *Quanta, quanta guerra . . .* war scenes are not described, as Rodoreda clearly states in the prologue. What is most interesting is the fact that in the prologue, Rodoreda also laments that she could not see the movie again, as it was no longer playing. In *The Saragossa Manuscript,* the protagonist who connects the string of stories also complains that he is always afraid he will not see two charming girls who are always disappearing whenever he tries to kiss them. This preoccupation with sight is also evident in the novel in Adrià's constant remembering of a pair of violet eyes seen in his childhood, and later, in a nude girl he meets by the river with whom he falls in love. But aside from these few details, the movie bears no resemblance with *Quanta, quanta guerra . . .*—Rodoreda's least pictorial novel—since the images mentioned in conjunction with the movie are very few. Moreover, they do not function as memorable descriptions of objects, nor are they repeated as leitmotifs in the manner of the bougainvillea of *Isabel i Maria* and the wisteria of *La mort i la primavera.* Perhaps they only contain the esoteric symbolism of the Rosicrucians stated by Arnau in *Miralls màgics,* a concept Montserrat Casals i Couturier accurately refutes.[37] In any case, the pictorial images are few in *Quanta, quanta guerra. . . .* The most evident parallel between the novel and the film is the almost total absence of war scenes and the narrative structure of stories connected by a male protagonist who engages minimally in the action, narrating and limiting his presence as voyeur as does the gardener in *Jardí vora el mar.* The gaze is limited to actions and not objects. It is clear, therefore, that Rodoreda is playing a game in returning this movie into a literary text in *Quanta, quanta guerra. . . .* The movie as mediator delineates a space of pictorial and verbal exchanges in the manuscript by Potocki translated into a movie, only to be returned transformed, and in Catalan, to the near purity of narration.

A parallel with another book published by Rodoreda the same year, *Viatges i flors* (1980) [Travels and Flowers], confirms the predominance of the verbal in *Quanta, quanta guerra. . . .* Difficult to classify within a specific genre, *Viatges i flors* also has themes and leitmotifs similar to those found in *La mort i la primavera.* Nancy Vosburg has noted the similarity with *Quanta, guanta guerra . . .* in the structure of the first part of

Viatges i flors with a wandering narrator who observes communities encountered in his travels: "Self-referential statements are limited, and the narrator's presence seems to have a trivial effect on the villages he visits."[38] This narrator is also very similar to the male narrator of *Jardí vora el mar* in the limitation of self-referential statements. And again, in *Viatges i flors*, the predominance of narration is separated from the mostly visual second part of the book entitled "Flors de debò" [Real Flowers], which describes flowers associated with the female, as stated by Vosburg:

> "Flor Vergonya" ["Shame Flower," 106], who resents her status as a mere object of beauty, the "Flor Felicitat" ["Happiness Flower," 80–81], depicted as a type of siren who leads men to their death, and the "Flor Tendra" ["Tender Flower," 89], a grape-shaped flower whose strong odor of blood attracts a leech.[39]

The division of the verbal part of the book narrated by a male from the pictorial with images of the feminine is also very similar to the relationship of *Quanta, quanta guerra . . .* and *La mort i la primavera* described in this essay (in *Isabel i Maria* the narration is shared by male and females voices). Vosburg's comparison of the flower vignettes with the collection of stories *Vint-i-dos contes* (1958) [Twenty-Two Stories] illustrates the relationship between the two novels: "The 'Flors' collection is in fact very similar in tone and content to the longer narratives of *Vint-i-dos contes* . . . This is not surprising in light of Arnau's assertion that the *contes* and the more lyrical 'flors' were written at approximately the same time."[40] Vosburg adds that the first part of *Viatges i flors* was written at the same time as *Quanta, quanta guerra . . . :* "Although exact dates are difficult to pinpoint, Arnau's affirmation [is] that the 'Viatges' section was written shortly after Rodoreda's return from exile."[41] Both were written also after Obiols had died. In contrast, *La mort i la primavera* was written intermittently since 1961, as stated in the prologue to the Castilian translation, while Obiols was still alive.[42] Obiols' presence in this novel is documented in the prologue to the Catalan edition where he is quoted as saying in a letter:

> Tot i que considero que La Mort, tal com la vas enviar, no estava prou treballada, estic segur que és molt millor que qualsevol de les novel.les que han tingut més vots (. . .) [*sic*]. No crec que en

> tota la prosa catalana hi hagi un personatge tan vivent com Colometa, ni un poble tan al.lucinant i real com el de La Mort." (7)
>
> [Even though I consider *La Mort,* just as you sent it, not quite finished, I'm sure that it's much better than any of the novels that have had more votes . . . I don't think that in all of Catalan prose there has been a character so alive as Colometa, nor a town as hallucinatory and real as that of *La Mort.*

Rodoreda also started writing *Isabel i Maria* before Obiols' death. In the prologue to the novel, Carme Arnau claims, based on the paper of the manuscript and the typewriter used, that it was one of the first works that Rodoreda started after the Spanish Civil War when she resumed her writing in exile, which had been interrupted by the immediate need for survival. Arnau also quotes a 1967 letter from Obiols that leads her to believe that part of the existing material of *Isabel i Maria* was used to write *Mirall trencat:* "La gran sort d'haver pogut aprofitar 'Una mica d'història'—sort que té una mica de miraculós—t'omple perfectament tot aquest any i una bona part de l'any que ve. Aquesta novel.la pot ser *extraordinària* i més val no espatllar-la." (23) [The good luck of having been able to profit from "Una mica d'història"—miraculous luck—keeps you perfectly busy this year and a good part of next year. This novel can be *extraordinary* and it's better not to ruin it.] What Arnau questions in this quote is the title "Una mica d'història" [A Bit of History], considered to be the original title of *Jardí vora el mar.* However, Arnau reminds us that *Jardí vora el mar* was already published and she is certain that Obiols was referring to *Isabel i Maria,* a novel in which she finds many similarities with *Mirall trencat* in a comparison elaborated in the same prologue (24). Montserrat Casals i Couturier reiterates this publication history in her biography on Rodoreda.[43]

These facts confirm that Rodoreda's tendency to express the repression of the female condition in the pictorial dimension of her work waned in the only finished novel written and published after Obiols' death, *Quanta, quanta guerra. . . .* It is also interesting to notice, in the absence of Obiols' censorship, the lack of female desire represented in the visual, and of the constant rivalry of love triangles present in *La mort i la primavera, Isabel i Maria,* and much of Rodoreda's other literary production. In *Quanta, quanta guerra . . . ,* Rodoreda returns to the dominance of the verbal, which Mitchell suggests in an analysis of the genre of ekphrasis is the realm of the masculine:

> the relation of text and image in ekphrasis is frequently a political one, and more specifically a matter of gender. It is remarkable how many ekphrastic images . . . turn out to be doubled images of the female—feminized (silent, beautiful) images that represent silent, beautiful women.[44]

Unhindered by Obiols' censorship, it is possible that Rodoreda no longer needed to escape into the visual to express a sensuality accorded only to men, or as in *The Women,* forced into the visual paradoxically to find a voice. The return to the supremacy of the verbal, for the appropriation of male power in a reversal of roles, is hinted at in *Quanta, quanta guerra . . .* when the female character, significantly named Eva, wishes to be of the opposite sex: "Li hauria agradat ser un noi en comptes d'una noia." (54) [She would have liked to be a boy instead of a girl.]

Before *Quanta, quanta guerra . . .,* it is also possible that Obiols' presence in Rodoreda's work was the opposite of Laurie Anderson's multi-media performance, "spoken by a distinctly male voice (Anderson's own processed through a harmonizer, which dropped it an octave—a kind of electronic vocal transvestism)."[45] In the same manner, before Obiol's death, Rodoreda's writing seems to be the instrument through which a female and a male voice could be heard. After his death, the lack of images in *Quanta, quanta guerra . . .* documents the return of Rodoreda to a writing that is not a synthesis of a female and a male voice, of the visual and the verbal. *Quanta, quanta guerra . . .* does not need a visual filter for Rodoreda's true verbal voice. Or perhaps, as Rodoreda's powerful visual images suggest in her previous work, and if she had lived long enough, she would have found her other nature in a return to the pure medium of a painting, devoid of the verbal and of the presence of Obiols. A visit by Mariàngela Vilallonga to Rodoreda's house in Romanyà after the writer's death confirmed that possibility: an empty easel remained next to the typewriter.[46]

Notes

1. Randolph D. Pope, "*Aloma*'s Two Faces and the Character of Her True Nature," in *The Garden across the Border: Mercè Rodoreda's Fiction,* ed. Kath-

leen McNerney and Nancy Vosburg, (Selingsgrove: Susquehanna University Press, 1994), 144.

2. Ibid., 145–46.

3. J. M. Castellet, "Mercè Rodoreda," *Els escenaris de la memòria* (Barcelona: Edicions 62, 1988), 42. All translations from the Catalan and Castilian in this essay are my own.

4. Montserrat Casals i Couturier, *Mercè Rodoreda: Contra la vida, la literatura* (Barcelona: Edicions 62, 1991), 263.

5. Castellet, 41.

6. "Mercè Rodoreda's Subtle Greatness," in *Women Writers of Contemporary Spain: Exiles in the Homeland,* ed. Joan L. Brown (Newark: University of Delaware Press; London and Toronto: Associated University Presses, 1991), 117.

7. George Cukor, *The Women,* Metro-Goldwyn-Mayer, 1939. Norma Shearer, Joan Crawford, Rosalind Russell, Joan Fontaine and Paulette Goddard played leading roles.

8. Debra Fried, "The Men in *The Women,*" in *Women and Film,* ed. Janet Todd (New York and London: Holmes & Meier, 1988), 47.

9. *La plaça del Diamant* (Barcelona: Club, 1993), 10.

10. Elizabeth Scarlett has established this gynocentric quality of Rodoreda's visual imagery with the recurrent presence of flowers in "'Vinculada a les flors': Flowers and the Body in *Jardí vora el mar* and *Mirall trencat,*" in McNerney and Vosburg, 72–84.

11. Castellet, 41.

12. "L'alé poètic de Mercè Rodoreda," *Retrats Paral.lels* (Montserrat: l'Abadia, 1976), 174.

13. "The Salamander and the Butterfly," in McNerney and Vosburg, 177.

14. Beverly Seaton gives an excellent account of her comprehensive research on the genre of the language of flowers in *The Language of Flowers: A History* (Charlottesville and London: University Press of Virginia, 1995).

15. For a detailed description of the relationship between the mimosa tree and Crisantema, see my article "La mimesis en un cuento de Mercè Rodoreda: 'Aquella paret, aquella mimosa,'" *Romance Notes* 36, no. 1 (Fall 1995): 93–99.

16. "Masks and Metamorphosis, Dreams and Illusions in Mercè Rodoreda's 'Carnaval'," *Catalan Review* 7, no 1 (1993), 76.

17. Quotes are from: *Isabel i Maria* (València: Eliseu Climent, 1991), 71. Succeeding page numbers in parentheses refer to this edition.

18. Another deception in the novel is the abortion of Isabel masqueraded as an appendectomy.

19. This is an interesting attraction since Riera also appeared in *Mirall trencat,* but as a lawyer and lover of Teresa, the female protagonist.

20. Baltasar Porcel, "Mercè Rodoreda, Frente a los árboles," *Destino,* no. 1689 (14 February 1970): 15.

21. Ibid., 15.

22. Donna McGiboney gives an excellent detailed account of the nature of these rites in "Rituals and Sacrificial Rites in Mercè Rodoreda's *La mort i la primavera,*" in McNerney and Vosburg, 61–72. James S. Pierce examines in detail the primitive and childlike aspect of Paul Klee's work in *Paul Klee and Primitive Art* (New York: Garland, 1976).

23. Quoted by Casals i Couturier, 254.

24. Quotes are from *La mort i la primavera* (Barcelona: Club, 1986), 18.

25. A full description of this passage appears in my essay "*Mirall trencat:* Un umbral autobiográfico en la obra de Mercè Rodoreda," *Revista de Estudios Hispánicos* 30, no. 1 (January 1996): 103–19. It is through a laurel that Maria enters the realm of the dead to exist in the novel as a ghost. Since she doesn't change into the tree, the metamorphosis of the myth of Daphne has not occurred in this instance. Even though metamorphosis is a well-known device of Rodoreda's characters to escape the tragedy of their lives (as in "La salamandra"), in *La mort i la primavera,* a transformation of matter has not occurred in the burial, but rather a merging of animal and plant material. For an article on the subject of metamorphosis in Rodoreda's work, see Janet Pérez, "Metamorphosis as a Protest Device in Catalan Feminist Writing: Rodoreda and Oliver," *Catalan Review: Homage to Mercè Rodoreda* 2, no. 2 (1987): 181–89. In this essay I do not imply that *Mirall trencat* is the boundary of the fantastic in Rodoreda's work but rather of a change in Rodoreda's voice. The fantastic element in Rodoreda's work is constant in the collection of short stories *La meva Cristina i altres contes* (1967) [*My Christina and Other Stories* (1984)]. For an article dealing with an exception to this fantastic trend in the collection, see my essay on the short story "Aquella paret, aquella mimosa" cited earlier.

26. W. J. T. Mitchell, *Picture Theory* (Chicago: University of Chicago Press, 1994), 151–81.

27. Mitchell, 160.

28. Harold Rosenberg, *The De-definition of Art* (1972; Chicago: University of Chicago Press, 1983), 57.

29. Tom Wolfe, *The Painted Word* (New York: Bantam, 1976), 4.

30. Mitchell, 220.

31. Ibid., 220–21.

32. Paul Klee, *On Modern Art* (1948, London: Faber and Faber, 1974), 13.

33. Carne Arnau, *Miralls màgics: Aproximació a l'útima narrativa de Mercè Rodoreda* (Barcelona: Edicions 62, 1990).

34. For articles dealing with *bildungsroman* and picaresque conventions in *Quanta, quanta guerra . . .,* see Maryellen Bieder, "Cataclysm and Rebirth: Journey to the Edge of the Maelstrom: Mercè Rodoreda's *Quanta, quanta guerra . . .,*" *Actes del tercer Col.loqui d'Estudis Catalans a Nord-Amèrica* (Montserrat: l'Abadia, 1983): 227–37; Gene Steven Forrest, "Myth and Antimyth in Mercè Rodoreda's *Quanta, quanta guerra . . .,*" in *German and International Perspectives on the Spanish Civil War: The Aesthetics of Partisanship,* ed. Luis Costa, et al., (Columbia, S.C.: Camden House, 1992), 367–75; Janet Pérez, "Presence of the Picaresque and the Quest-Romance in Mercè Rodoreda's *Quanta, quanta guerra . . .,*" *Hispania* 76, no. 3 (September 1993): 428–38. These articles also note similarities between the two novels.

35. These quotes are from *Quanta, quanta guerra . . .* (Barcelona: Club Editor, 1986).

36. Wojciech J. Has, *Rekopis Znaleziony w Saragossie,* Zepoly Filmwe, 1965. Zbigniew Cybulski, Iga Cembrzynska, Joanna Jedryka, and Kazimierz Opalinski played leading roles.

37. Casals i Couturier, 256–57.

38. Nancy Vosburg, "The Roots of Alienation," in McNerney and Vosburg, 149.

39. Ibid., 157.

40. Ibid., 157.

41. Ibid., 150.

42. Pere Gimferrer, prologue to *La muerte y la primavera,* trans. Enrique Sordo (Barcelona: Seix Barral, 1989), 5.

43. Casals i Couturier, 248–66.

44. "Against Comparison: Teaching Literature and the Visual Arts," in *Teaching Literature and Other Arts,* ed. Jean-Pierre Barricelli, Joseph Gibaldi, and Estella Lauter (New York: The Modern Language Association of America, 1990), 35.

45. Craig Owens, "The Discourse of Others: Feminists and Postmodernism," in *The Anti-Aesthetic: Essays on Postmodern Culture,* ed. Hal Foster (Seattle: Bay, 1983), 61.

46. "Els arbres, Romanyà i Mercè Rodoreda," *Revista de Girona* 39, no. 157 (March-April 1983): 91.

Godless Religions in *La mort i la primavera*

Carles Cortés i Orts

> Comme l'eau avance dans le lit d'un fleuve, pareillement la musique avançait dans le lit de mon être, entrenant, entraînant ampleur, et aspiration à l'ampleur.
>
> —Henri Michaux, *Le jardin exalté*)

Mercè Rodoreda died in April 1983 of liver cancer. She had been working on what would be her last published novel, *La mort i la primavera.* Rewritten several times, its creation is parallel to that of *La plaça del Diamant,* in the late fifties. It was put forward for the Sant Jordi prize in 1961, but did not win.

La mort i la primavera is an elaborate reflection, an image of the inner evolution of the writer. With *Quanta, quanta guerra* . . . and the collection of brief narrations *Viatges i flors,* she tries to introduce an alienation from reality, through the creation of symbolic universes where the characters develop while they fight against the obstacles that surround them. Thus, to understand *La mort i la primavera,* one must decipher the complex and extensive imagery established by Mercè Rodoreda.

This process in the later works of the author has been pointed out by Carme Arnau, who finds that the symbolism is perceptible throughout the work of the author. Suggested in her novelistic origins, it is fully developed in the remarkable image of the garden that has roots in the early chapters of the latest published novels.

The re-creation of myths leads to the musicality of the words, and rhythm dominates the prose, making it all the more intimate and striking. The imaginary universes that she recreates are based directly upon the sources of our own civilization and even of distant civilizations.

My analysis presents a possible interpretation of some of the aspects of this novel. I will examine the following: first, the creation of the mythical world that is represented by the town where the action develops; second, the early relationships established between the characters; and finally, their attempts to overcome the difficulties of the re-created universe.

THE NATURAL SETTING IN *LA MORT I LA PRIMAVERA*: THE COSMOGONIC MYTH OF THE TOWN'S CREATION

The town was created by a "malestar de la terra" (the land's indisposition):[1] the "Sacred Mountain" cracks and water comes out. This creation pattern follows the cosmogonic myth described by anthropologist Mircea Eliade, according to which a territory suitable for human life emerges, and the story of origin is recorded and passed on from the beginning of the community.[2] The religious rites that we find within the narration remind us of the legendary principles of creation. In the novel, myth and cult merge with ritual to form a coherent framework.

The novel is set in a town limited by Maraldina, a mountain characterized by always being green. Carme Arnau sees a symbol of immortality in the constant green of the vegetation and in the name, so close to *maragda,* or emerald, associated with Hermes, the messenger of gods. Maraldina, physically and conceptually surrounding the town, is the empirical obstacle that brings about the spiritual enlightenment of the hero, but at the same time it increases, in some circumstances, the ideological paralysis of his society.

Maraldina is seen as sacred since it is the origin of life and of the town, having been split in two by the snake. The snake, according to Eliade,[3] within the myths of creation of many archaic cultures, symbolizes chaos, the original disorder before life began; to hurt the snake (dividing or decapitating it) is identified with the change from the amorphous to the formal, the beginning, therefore, of life. The mountain presents magical characteristics that highlight its sacredness: red powder is extracted from it to paint the houses in order to protect them from the bad spirits. Within Maraldina the cave man also lives, and one can find as well the cemetery-of-the-dead-without-cement, crucial points for a full interpretation of the novel.

The mountain represents everything that motivates the flight of the anonymous protagonist, the hero. In search of individuality, he has to flee the earthly world in order to gain, on the one hand, liberty, represented by the element air, and on the other hand, his state of equilibrium, symbolized by the figure of Hermes in the science of symbols.

According to Eliade, the cosmogonic myth generally becomes known through the revelations of the old townspeople to the heroes and the initiated, so that children can pass into the next phase of training.[4] In *La mort i la primavera* the blacksmith provides the ontological principles of the town religion to our initiated protagonist. This revelation creates an unconscious source within the initiated that enables him to break away from sacred nature. According to Eliade,[5] the rupture shows authentic reality and unmasks the other reality, whose function was to control the behavior patterns of the society.

Mircea Eliade[6] also points out the possibility of applying cosmogonic myths to different planes of reference within archaic societies: periodicity, religious sacraments, everyday work, festivals, social structure, etc. The myth of the creation of the town in *La mort i la primavera* also applies this theory, visible even in physical features such as the river, characterized by a zig-zag movement similar to the mythical snake.

A Possible Interpretation of the Oedipus Myth in *La Mort i la Primavera*

We have seen how the natural setting of the novel makes the personal progress of the hero difficult. It is interesting to analyze his development as parallel to that of Oedipus, with a basis in the connection that Freud made with the relationship in the Greek myth. According to Freud, it was the root of infantile development, that is, the cause of psychopathological evolution.[7] My interpretation is based on this perspective, on the idea of the personal progression of the protagonist in the novel. Thus, it will be useful to review the parallels and correspondences between the lives of Oedipus and our protagonist.

Oedipus murders Laius; this differs from our hero, who does not personally kill his father. However, he transgresses a social norm; as a witness of his father's suicide, he also collaborates in his father's death. In both cases, this development will be important in the hero's life: the social transgression that has taken place marks the progression to the adult world.

Very soon afterwards, Oedipus marries Jocasta—his mother, the widow of Laius—and they form a couple, playing infantile games. The juridical mother, for having married his father, will also become the hero's amorous partner.

Oedipus is punished for the double crime—parricide and incest—with the loss of his eyes. Jocasta kills herself. In *La mort i la primavera,* the hero is also punished for the double sin (having witnessed the death of his father and committed incest with his mother): first, his daughter dies, and then, his wife rejects him. Finally, he dies according to the customs of the town. Her fate is hardly satisfactory either: confined to her parents' house, she also loses the horizon of her existence. It is the punishment of a patriarchal society that rejects the incest and the seduction of a son. This interpretation of the myth is based on the investigation by Fromm of the ideas of Sigmund Freud; some interesting things arise from Fromm's words: "The patriarchal system has won, and the myth explains the fall of the matriarchy. The mother, having violated her own highest duty, has provoked her own destruction."[8] She represents a matriarchal reaction in an eminently patriarchal society. We again find ourselves at the root of the myth of creation that we have seen in the previous chapter.

This is a schematic synthesis of the parallels with the myth of Oedipus:

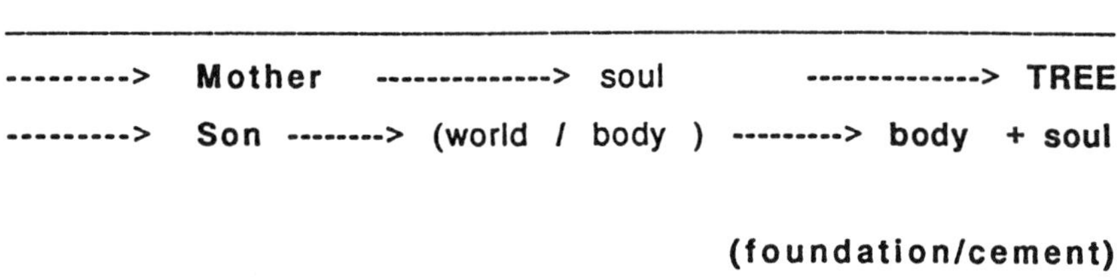

According to this hypothesis, the initiated hero never manages to separate from his feminine maternal principle because his life turns out to be parallel to a false companion, his own mother, his father's widow. In the novel, death is the only solution, in order to escape from the feminine principle and separate from the family environment. With death, the hero can freely make his own life. In this way, life and death bring about two consecutive realities.

Religion as an Attempt to Escape from the Earthly World

The origins of various images are present in the narrations of the author's childhood:

> The religion lived so intensely during that epoch, with images of kindly saints represented ingenuously by figures of ideal beauty and perfection, with miracles and supernatural happenings, must have helped Rodoreda to create a magical atmosphere: Guardian Angels, the Sacred Heart . . .[9]

In spite of this, according to Carme Arnau in the her biography of Rodoreda, it is not until *La mort i la primavera* that the religious aspect centers the literary development of the characters. The novel focuses the daily lives of the townspeople on the town's legendary origin, around which is placed a series of sacred rites: religious tribal manifestations that deny, as we will see, the existence of a specific god.

The religion in *La mort i la primavera* presents us a sacred central space from the moment of the first revelation: the mountain of Maraldina. In archaic religions we often find a sacred mountain,[10] center of the world, where the world of the living is connected with the world of the dead and spirits; for example, the Olympus of the Greek gods, the Hebrew Sinai, where Moses received the Ten Commandments,[11] or, within the religious tradition of our country, the peak of Randa, where the pious Ramon Llull was devoted to divine contemplation. *Quanta, quanta, guerra* . . . also presents the mountain as center of the world: the "mountain of the angels" of the final chapter where Adrià receives the last revelation.[12] The connotation of purity, stability, and immutability of mountains is seen in a great number of religions.[13] In Taoist mythology, for example, the "immortals" live in the sacred mountain called "the center of the earth" because they believe that the everlasting sun and moon go around it. In this mountain, Taoists believe that they achieve the desired state.

Thus, there is a great deal of precedent for the symbolism in the novel, and the magic mountain, Maraldina, is especially significant. The "cosmic mountain," as named by Mircea Eliade for its sacred quality, sanctifies the surrounding land.[14] On the hillside of Maraldina are the woods of the dead, the cemetery-of-the-dead-without-cement, and the well from which red powder is extracted in order to paint houses. This powder protects the houses; in not painting them because the adolescents have lost the paintbrushes, the fatal destiny of the novel's population begins. The map of the town (a drawing made by Mercè Rodoreda and her sentimental companion, Armand Obiols, and reproduced by Carme Arnau in *Miralls màgics*) shows a magic mountain and a replica of it in the center of town. The residence of the Lord, atop the hill, is separated from the houses by an ivy-covered hillside. A great number of the symbols denote verticality, the rising progression that represents the importance of the Lord in society.

The wooden bridge, a crossroad, is the center of the important events in the narration, and just like the conversations among the protagonists, it is of profound significance. It is also the path that leads to the sacred places: the cemetery, the woods of the dead, and Maraldina. The bridge is another sacred center for the society as a whole.

A literary precedent for this space can also be found in a previous novel by the same author. I refer to the mountain of the "Encantades" [Enchanted Women] in *Del que hom no pot fugir* [The Inevitable], where Cinta, the crazy miller, finds the "Encantades," marvelous beings.[15] A significant passage in *Del que hom no pot fugir* describes the voices of their victims: "quan fa vent se senten veus planyívoles . . . a les víctimes de les Encantades els pateix l'ànima. Són veus d'ànima que ploren pel cos que es deixà temptar . . ." (141) [when it's windy, wailing voices are heard . . . the souls of the victims of the Enchanted Women suffer. Soul voices who cry for their bodies that fell into temptation . . .] With the following passage in *La mort i la primavera* we can see the similarity of the images in the two novels:[16] "el vent de la Maraldina era un vent carregat d'ànimes que voltaven per la muntanya només per fer el vent més fort quan era l'hora d'anar a buscar la pols. I com que no tenien boca les ànimes ens ho deien amb la veu del vent." (19) [Maraldina's wind was full of souls from the mountain, and it only blew to strengthen the wind when it was time to collect sand. And since the souls didn't have mouths, they told us with the wind's voice.][17] In both cases, the author uses the legend as a source to rationalize strange things. The mountain, with its myths, has an essential role: the approximation between the profane and the sacred worlds.

The sacredness developed in the novel reminds us of a religion centered on the fate of the human being, in the belief in the perenniality of the soul. It is, at the same time, a tremendously primitive religion, full of superstitions that acquire "reality" through the sacramental belief of the town. The birth of a critical spirit—the reader—is a sign of empirical truth, far from the described religion, and it will destroy the configurative bases of the town's cosmogonical principles. Some children, some adolescent rebels, cause the rupture of the myth, which leads the community to wander lost and without a horizon because the bases of society have disappeared.

Religious Manifestations of a Religious Society: the "Death of God" in *La mort i la primavera*

An analysis of the conduct of the townspeople in *La mort i la primavera* shows it to be a direct result of established collective customs. A religion or a certain group of sacred activities forms a kind of religious sentiment. These collective activities control the individual wills of the components. In this way a firm and closed society that does not allow transgressions of the law is structured, and this provokes moments of cruelty and absurdity, since customs and conservatism drown out individual initiatives and the rational roots of the everyday life among the townsfolk.

On the other hand, *La mort i la primavera* offers us an interesting group of rites without any supreme ontological principle. There is no divinity present in the lives of these humans. Religion is simply an anthropological reality with no established point; it is a way of living based mostly on the beliefs of the collective society. It is in these terms that we can talk about "the death of god" in the novel: the supreme divinity does not exist. This term was put forward by Mircea Eliade after his anthropological investigation about archaic religions.

Lluís Duch, an expert on the work of the Rumanian anthropologist, describes to us the concept put forward by Eliade: the term "death of god" is used "when the supreme god becomes a 'deus otiosus,' that is, when he retreats from the world, when his transcendence is confused with his eclipse, it is at this point when the religion starts as a significant anthropological reality."[18]

In *La mort i la primavera,* there is a substitution for a possible supreme divinity by forms that are more concrete and therefore closer to life. The religion developed here is more materialized, more concentrated upon the resolution of problems and questions of everyday society. The only religious hierarchy present in the novel seems to be the figure of the blacksmith who has supreme responsibility for the rites.

In the societies where the "death of god" exists, the human being becomes a complete person. The inhabitants of the town in *La mort i la primavera* live far beyond the tragedies and vicissitudes of history, adopting an anthropological equilibrium between religious tragedies and historical vicissitudes; they live in the present and faithfully follow ritualized customs, with the intention of maintaining their belief in the myth of the creation and looking for the eternal return, the constant ontological preoccupation with survival after death.

Thus, we are left with only a series of rituals. In primitive societies and even later, in Oriental as well as in Occidental cultures, the sacred fact converts itself into the revelation of reality, and its symbols give meaning to human existence. The town of *La mort i la primavera* presents some sacred activities which support the meaning of life as a collective one, and these are the truths. But the group of religious rituals, these "truths," is denied by the reader. Herein lies the author's irony: religious manifestation, the truth of the town, is broken in the presence of the external reader, who is foreign to that civilization.

The discovery of truth by the protagonist in *La mort i la primavera* marks the arrival of the profane world. Doubt and indecision take hold of him. The acquisition of profane knowledge causes the protagonist's break with religion, and consequently his life loses the original meaning that he learned as a child. Death becomes a rediscovery of the beginning, of birth; thus, the physical death of the individual is the immediate consequence of the knowledge of the death of god.

The Desire for Immortality: The Myth of Osiris in *La mort i la primavera*

This society is without divinity, a society that aspires to achieve the "complete man" and to implement constantly the myth of creation in order to find its identity. Thus, it will also aspire to life after death. One of the most characteristic and surprising rites of the novel embodies these aspirations: the process of creating *arbres-taüts* [tree-coffins] in the *bosc dels morts* [woods of the dead].

When a person believes that he is close to the moment of death, the adults of the town go to the woods of the dead to take leave of the dying person. The person is put inside the tree that has been assigned to him since birth, so that the flora converts itself into the coffin. It is important to highlight a very strange fact: the future corpse is filled with cement because, according to belief, this prevents the loss of spirit in death. For this reason the act of cementing is carried out while the person is still alive, when the soul is still inside the human being. A psychological concept of death would explain this as a return to the mother's womb in order to be born again soon after. The cultural precedents of this passage are ancient. Carl Jung says of the Greek legend of the ash tree, mother of humanity in the bronze age: "When the world is destroyed, the universal ash tree becomes the preserving mother, the tree of life and death."[19]

According to some ancient Eastern traditions, as described by Jung, the human species was born from trees. Germanic cultures follow funeral customs that use hollow trees for tombs; in fact, in ancient German, coffin is "totenbaum," which in a literal sense is the "tree of the dead." Most interesting for the novel is the Celtic tradition in which the sacred tree was the oak.[20]

Moreover, *La mort i la primavera*[21] presents the development of a concrete myth, that of Osiris.[22] According to this legend, Set throws Osiris, inside a wooden chest, into the sea. The chest arrives at the land of Byblos, along with some branches of a bush. As the plant grows into a big tree, it wraps itself around Osiris' coffin. The king of Byblos makes a column for the palace from the bush. So the Egyptian god is freed in order to be born again in his son, Hor-Pi-Khaud. Thus, Osiris is obviously a symbol of mythical immortality.[23]

The title of the novel reflects the desire for immortality, a resurrection of life after death. The sacred trees—ash, the tree of the dead, and wisteria—evoke an imagery that was used by primitive peoples. It is, therefore, a cultural myth which has roots in diverse indirect sources.

Plato offers Timeus a similar concept. For Plato, the soul is the receptacle of the world in the form of a body, the image that reminds us of the mother. We can establish the parallels shown in the accompanying chart.

Therefore, if the tree, in symbolic tradition, is the receptacle of death (physical body) and of life (soul, breath), a quite similar use appears in *La mort i la primavera,* since the trees of the woods of the dead are the receptacle of death (with the bodies inside) and, at the same time, of life (the foundation/cement preserves the soul/breath).

Mercè Rodoreda overcomes death in this novel, since the dead body is not transformed, but converted into another human being (like Osiris); there is a wish for immortality, for conserving the physical and spiritual union of life and death, body and soul. But the author's irony is heightened as the narration advances and the reader realizes the terrible reality of the deception lived by this society, of the innocence of its suppositions. Once more, Rodoreda does not confine herself to the perennial principles put forward by the many Orientalist philosophies which might have influenced the culture of her day. The principle character, an image of the writer, discovers the fallacy of the society. This ruptures the myth of the tree. The immortality of the soul cannot be achieved by physical means: the raw materials destroy themselves in the process of regeneration. This explains the function of the cement in the novel: with it, Rodoreda creates the principle that supports the spiritual philosophies.

La mort i la primavera

Since it is a mythical novel, *La mort i la primavera* has become universal, formulating abstract worlds and allowing the author's message to be interpreted on many intellectual levels. A society without God, which constantly remembers its origins and strengthens its identity through rites, it is a closed society that drowns personal initiatives of its members. The cruelty of the human being, widespread in a repressive society, is ex-

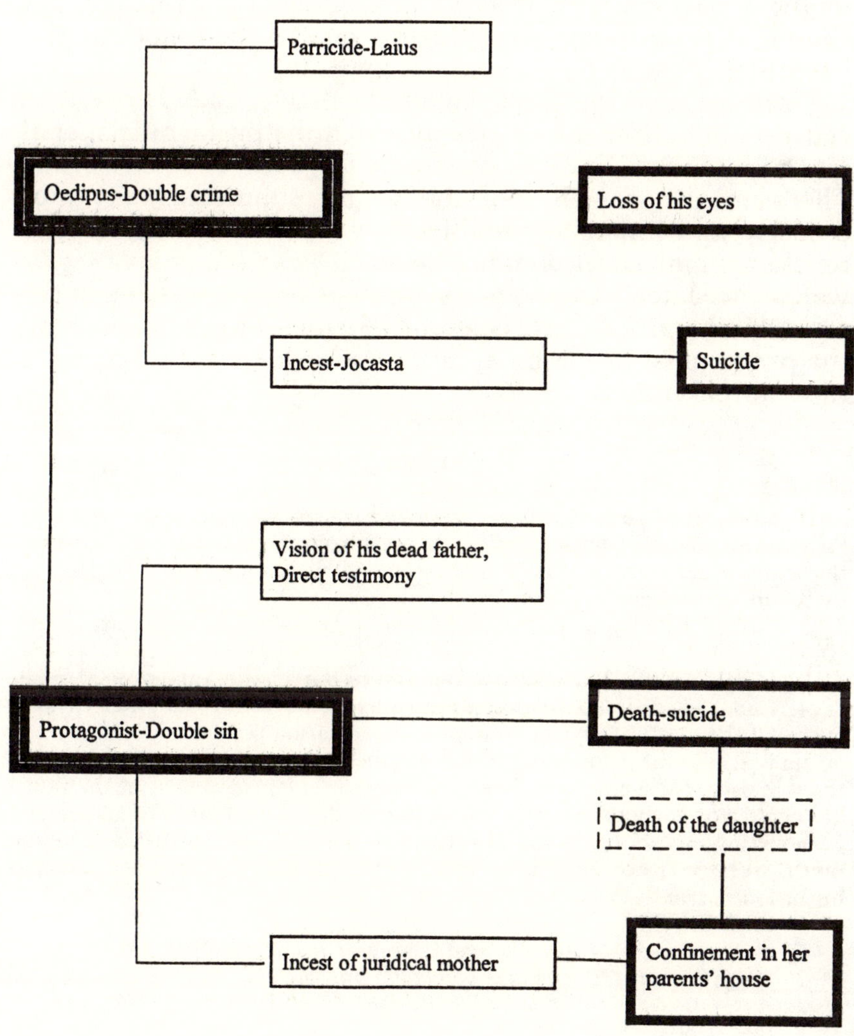
Parricide-Laius
Oedipus-Double crime
Loss of his eyes
Incest-Jocasta
Suicide
Vision of his dead father,
Direct testimony
Protagonist-Double sin
Death-suicide
Death of the daughter
Incest of juridical mother
Confinement in her
parents' house

pressed by myth on pages that without doubt draw the attention of the unsuspecting reader. Rodoreda's literature reaches in these pages a high level of interaction with readers, and she plays with them, very much aware of the functions that literature offers her.

This evolution in Mercè Rodoreda's style leads her to a recreation of fictitious societies in which the protagonists, challenged by nature, have to overcome the daily obstacles of life. The narrative capacity of the writer submerges us in repressive and imaginary ambients, where oneiric description reaches a high level of expression. *La mort i la primavera,* as well as her later narrations, exemplifies the progression of this style. Myths, rituals, and customs join forces to overcome man, the protagonist of these narrations, along with the passage of time unrelenting.

Notes

1. Mercè Rodoreda, *La mort i la primavera* (Barcelona: Club, 1986), 33. Page numbers for all subsequent quotations from the novel are given parenthetically in the text. Translations of essay and quoted material from Catalan by Kathleen McNerney.

2. Mircea Eliade, *Le mythe de l'éternel retour* (Paris: Gallimard, 1969), 20–25.

3. Mircia Eliade, *Lo sagrado y lo profano* (Barcelona: Labor, 1988), 53.

4. Ibid., 82. It could be that the protagonist's young daughter, who is aware of the cultural mysteries (due to information passed on from the son of the blacksmith) before anyone else, is the origin of his destruction, since the tribal law of secrecy has been challenged. The protagonist of the novel has access too early to the cosmogonic knowledge of the reality of his society, without having acquired the ability to understand and to assimilate the myth, so he will not be able to develop the already commenced personal initiation normally.

5. Ibid, 130–33.

6. Mircia Eliade, *Mito y realidad* (Barcelona: Labor, 1991), 38.

7. Erich Fromm, *El lenguage olvidado: Introducción a la comprensión de los sueños, mitos y cuentos de hadas* (Buenos Aires: Hachette, 1972), 148–72.

8. Ibid., 160.

9. Carme Arnau, *Mercè Rodoreda* (Barcelona: Edicions 62, 1992), 17. A similar image of the author's childhood appears in "Semblava de seda": "O bé parlava amb Jesús, que de seguida que el vaig veure a les estampes, vaig estimar." *Tots els contes* (Barcelona: Edicions 62, 1988), 330. [or I talked to Jesus, whom I loved from the moment I saw him on the holy cards.] In this narration, the first-person protagonist confesses to not practicing religion often: "Resava. No es pot dir ben bé que resés perquè mai no he pogut dir una oració sencera." (330) [I prayed, I can't say I prayed, exactly, since I've never been able to say a whole prayer.]

10. The sacredness of nature is not strange. In primitive religions, as Mircea Eliade points out (*Lo sagrado y lo profano,* 101), nature has an essential role in religious manifestations: gods gave life to human beings, but they also created the world. For this reason, nature stops representing chaos in order to become cosmos.

11. Another symbol of the elevation of the center of the world, within Christian tradition, is the parallel "tree of the world" identified as the cross of Jesus.

12. According to Judeo-Christian beliefs, the sacred mountain is the sign of surviving the universal flood, since it was not submerged. Thus the top of the cosmic mountain is the highest place on the earth, the navel, the place where creation began. Mircea Eliade, *Imágenes y símbolos* (Madrid: Taurus, 1983), 44–50.

13. J. Chevalier and A. Gheerbrant, *Diccionario de los símbolos* (Barcelona: Herder, 1991), 722.

14. Mircea Eliade, *Lo sagrado y lo profano,* 39; also Mircea Eliade, *Occultisme, sorcellerie et modes culturelles* (Paris: Gallimard, 1978), 34–40.

15. According to some African beliefs, mountains are very often frequented by fabulous beings, spirits, or hidden forces that don't want to be disturbed. Thus the noises and songs of the mountains are an incomprehensible mystery to the uninitiated. They are inaccessible without a guide. Chevalier, 726.

16. The above-mentioned parallels between *Del que hom no pot fugir* (Barcelona: Clarisme, 1934) and *La mort i la primavera* are clear, but in the former, the fictional universes don't have their own entity, they are simply products of a mentally disturbed imagination, of someone rejected by society. In *La mort i la primavera,* these universes cover external reality. In *Del que hom no pot fugir,* the protagonists refuse the possible concreteness of fiction: "Res. No crec res del que diuen. Quina llàstima que les fantasies no siguin veritat!" (142) [I don't believe any of what they say. What a shame the fantasies aren't real!]

17. For the symbolic concept of the wind, see Gaston Bachelard, *El aire y los sueños* (Mexico City: Fondo de Cultura Económica, 1986), 278–93.

18. Lluís Duch, *Mircea Eliade: El retorn d'Ulises a Itaca* (Montserrat: l'Abadia, 1986), 63.

19. Carl Jung, *Símbolos de transformación* (Barcelona: Paidós, 1982), 258.

20. Ibid., 249. The Celts planted a tree at the moment that a child was born and its wood would eventually be used to make the child's own coffin.

21. There is a contemporary parallel in Catalan literature. In the novel *Ducat d'ombres* by Joan M. Monjo (Valencia: Eliseu Climent, 1982), thirty youngsters fall into the hands of bewitched oaks and "little by little they metamorphose. The oaks surround them and end the lives of the prisoners." (143).

22. Osiris is one of the most important Egyptian divinities and has had a great influence on the formation of legends and local beliefs. Son of Geb and Nut, Set's brother and both husband and brother to Isis, he was enclosed in a chest and thrown into the river by the envious Set. Isis set him free, but he was imprisoned again by Set, who cut him up into little bits and scattered them out throughout the country. Isis, with the help of the gods Neftis and Anubis, gathered all the pieces and returned Osiris to life. Osiris symbolizes the immortality of the pharaohs and is the god of vegetation and, more concretely, he represents the seed that dies in order to sprout into a plant.

23. Ibid., 254.

A la Recherche d'*Isabel i Maria* (In the Garden of Childhood with Rodoreda and Proust)

ALEJANDRO VARDERI

> La torreta . . . [t]enia dos jardins: un de petit devant i un de más gran darrera. S'entrava per una reixa de ferro pintada de verd, es pujaven set o vuit graons i s'arribava al jardí.
>
> [the villa . . . (h)ad two gardens: a small one in front and a bigger one at the back. One entered through an iron gate painted green, climbed seven or eight steps and reached the garden.]
>
> —Maria *Isabel i Maria*

> *And then . . . it stood before our eyes, the backgate of our own garden . . . that garden where for so long my actions had ceased to require any control, or even attention, from my will.*
>
> —*Marcel*
>
> Marcel Proust *In Search of Time Lost. Swann's Way*

ON THE JACKET OF MERCÈ RODOREDA'S NOVEL *ISABEL I MARIA,* there is a picture of the author at an early age standing in front of the monument to Verdaguer that her grandfather had placed in the yard. She has flowers covering her dress and is unaware of the fact that, years later, the death of her grandfather, the Civil War, and the sentimental choices she made would steal that garden from her forever. In like manner, I imagine Proust as a child standing in the garden of his uncle Weil in Auteuil or in the garden of his uncle Amiot in Illiers, with his eyes wide open and looking at a landscape that writing would later transform into the gardens of Combray once asthma and the direction of his desire had expelled him from such a paradise.

Within the texts of Rodoreda and Proust the garden of childhood stands, therefore, as the symbol of a lost Eden. It is a lost Eden perceived, however, not as a playground or a melancholic retreat, but as an active component in the process of portraying the emotional and sexual shift toward the forbidden. Incest, adultery, and homosexuality hide behind the vegetation that encircles the lives of these writers and their characters: among the flowers of the bougainvillea Isabel gazes passionately toward Lluís, her brother-in-law, and half-hidden among the bushes of Montjuovain Marcel observes the female lover of Mlle. Vinteuil profaning the photograph of Mlle. Vinteuil's dead father.

With this vision of the garden as place for desire in mind, this essay will explore the image of the garden as it subverts social conventions and crossses gender boundaries, in light of Rodoreda's *Isabel i Maria* and Proust's *A la recherche du temps perdu*. Both novels seek to exorcise the feelings of loss rooted in the authors' childhoods, when they were suddenly deprived of those moments of happiness that their gardens sustained.

Certain Analogies in Time

Mercè Rodoreda was born in October 1908, the same year Marcel Proust undertook his *Recherche*. In July Proust disclosed the titles of certain "written pages"[1] to his friend Mme. Strauss—"Ma grand-mère au jardin" [My Grandmother in the Garden] among others—and in October, after a violent asthma attack, he elaborated on the scene of the mother's goodnight kiss while congratulating Mme. de Pierrebourgh on her new book called *Ciel rouge* [Red sky].[2] Hence, two visions of time lost and about to be recovered came to him as the setting and the subject of joy and of his worst fears: the goodnight kiss, refused and granted at the garden of Auteuil, "told him that love is doomed and happiness does not exist,"[3] at a time when the beloved obstacle to his writing was no longer alive and his illness had made more audible than ever the sound of the garden's bell, turning writing into an unavoidable task.

Fifty years later, Mercè Rodoreda felt a similar urge, once she had come to terms with her uncle-husband, her lover, and the war years. Self-exiled in Geneva, like Proust from the outside world in his apartment at the Boulevard Haussmann, Rodoreda undertook her own task, writing "[c]om si no hi fos a temps"[4] [as if she had no time left].[4] That is to say, she wrote as if the peal of the gate-bell in her garden of Sant Gervasi had rung, and would not cease ringing until her time lost had been regained. Consequently, writing became the instrument that granted Rodoreda the right to recover time, that opened into the world outside time when, at twelve, she forfeited the garden.

Proust and Rodoreda made up for the minuteness of their gardens by integrating into their fiction the splendor of the foliage framing the geography beyond the "torreta" and the "backgate" of their childhood: the Bois de Saint-Eman, the garden of the great-uncle Weil in Auteuil, and the Pré Catelan of Jules Amiot in *A la recherche,* and the Marquis of Can Brusi's park in *Isabel i Maria.* Gardens "with gravel paths and flower-beds, and lawns, and trees which had grown too tall for the garden"[5] foreshadow the reverse side of the authors' lives haunted by the obsession to write "la meva gran novel.la"[6] [my great novel]. It was obsession that made their everyday lives grow too tall for life itself, in the effort to collect through diaries, articles and letters the fertile soil where text would germinate.

For the novels to sprout from experience, both authors relied upon the skillful trimming of two gardeners: Rodoreda's grandfather Gurgí and Proust's grandmother Weil. Sitting on her grandfather's lap and clutching a bunch of flowers, Mercè listened attentively to Verdaguer, Víctor Català, and Ruyra; strolling with his grandmother along the Auteuil garden, Marcel learned of Musset, George Sand, and Rousseau. Thus, "cherchant à éliminer 'la banalité commerciale' au profit de la valeur esthétique"[7] [wanting to eliminate 'commercial banality' in favor of aesthetic values], those grandparents introduced their grandchildren to eclecticism in literature, (im)planting in their unconscious a craving for beauty, within a protected bohemian and bourgeois environment; one that would make Rodoreda and Proust despise vulgarity and share the same passion for grace and refinement. In this way, even during her precarious years in Bordeaux, Rodoreda's "ultimate happiness" would have been, indeed, to possess "un vestit de gasa negra amb estrelles brodades, *pailletées,* un braçalet bonic i moltes sabates esquisides"[8] [a chiffon black dress embroidered with sequined stars, a fine bracelet and many exquisite shoes.] In a like manner Proust, immersed in a somehow solid and solemn middle-class society, would have wanted to be considered more than a dilettante in the dazzling world of the French aristocracy that his *Recherche* captured from a rather bourgeois point of view, as he had predicted in a letter written in his youth to his own grandfather: "Puisque le genre sublime ne me va pas, j'essaierai du bourgeois"[9] [Since the sublime genre doesn't suit me, I will practice the bourgeois.]

The garden of childhood, with its camellias, roses, and lilies, was to Mercè an escape from the ordinary, an escape from the fights between her parents and grandfather because of their lack of money, along with the extravagant behavior of the latter. Furthermore, the garden was a refuge from the stinginess and despotism of her uncle-husband as a result of his forced emigration to Argentina in his youth and of the careless use that Rodoreda's family made in those years of the money he sent. Similarly, Proust would spend many mornings in his uncle's garden to avoid family squabbles and to preserve the fragrance of an uncontaminated time enclosed in the geraniums, pansies, and water lilies that memory would perpetuate inside him, in "a region in which beauty was real and eternal, uncontaminated by disappointment, sin and death."[10]

Grandfather Gurguí initiated Mercè into the passion for plants and trees, and the parish priest of Illiers taught Marcel the names of many flowers. Later, the combined aromas of their gardens accompanied both writers in certain moments of solitude, filling their secret places: an empty dovecote on the roof in Sant Gervasi where Rodoreda locked herself away in order to write letters to her uncle and future husband, and a lavatory at the top of the house in Illiers "scented by a festoon of irisroots,"[11] where Marcel released his emotions and felt the thrills of forbidden pleasures. In this way, they desacralized the sacredness of family and social conventions at a time when death and sickness had not yet deterritorialized them from their gardens.

During those long years that passed before Rodoreda and Proust could be territorialized again through writing, they carried their gardens to exile, enhancing the flora with new species skillfully scattered among the scenes of their writings, scenes that harsh and traumatic events ultimately brightened with fierce colors. Using this strategy the authors displaced innocence—which is always involuntary—replacing it with a conscious purity that conferred to *A la recherche* and *Isabel i Maria* their perverse power to subvert sexual and social practices, at a time when both authors had already freed themselves from life's impositions, gaining therefore their right to rebel. Consequently, if Rodoreda, on the one hand, had been obliged to invest in making a blouse before she could write the bulk of that uncompleted text, and Proust, on the other, had to endure many periods of physical weakness and mental turmoil before he could compose his novel also left unfinished; when time to regain time came at last, the childhood garden had become the final destination,[12] allowing them to recover what had been lost and to plant seeds collected from experience. "The seeds are flowers for the imagination,"[13] Marcel Proust said to Marie Nordlinger's symbolic offering of a two-penny packet of balsam seeds, as a way of expressing his love of the flowers that he could no longer smell. Similarly, Mercè Rodoreda kept *Isabel i Maria* next to her, working on the story long before she began her signature texts but without ever bringing herself to finish it: "com si anés plantant una sèrie de llavors i n'esperés la florida"[14] [as if she kept planting seeds and waiting for them to sprout.]

The Garden Blooms

Although Mercè Rodoreda did not fill out the famous Proustian questionnaire until 1979, giving as a feature of her personality "the desire to escape,"[15] it is possible that she read *A la recherche* in the Proa edition during the early thirties,[16] at a time when such desire was stronger than ever: a rapacious husband, an unwanted son, a growing popularity as writer and journalist, and a craving for personal freedom suddenly grasped when political circumstances forced her into exile. All these situations fueled the uprooting of the species enclosed in the garden of childhood.

In this sense, the Deleuze study of the rhizomes,[17] or systems of deterritorialized lines, constructed as a result of the powerful "feeling of uprootedness"[18] experienced by Rodoreda during the early years of her exile, is particularly interesting in *Isabel i Maria,* since the novel not only signals her return to writing,[19] but also becomes the most autobiographical text of her literary production. It is not surprising, then, that Rodoreda had written the final chapters—"La Partença. Paris," "Bordeus"—first, leaving the other sections to time as Proust would have it:

> The Méséglise way with its lilacs, its hawthorns, its cornflowers, its poppies, its apple-trees, the Guermantes way with its river full

of tadpoles, its water-lilies, and its buttercups constituted for me for all time the image of the landscape in which I should like to live . . .[20]

Shortly before her departure Maria seizes with one look all the trees of that garden in which, like Marcel, she should also have liked to live, "amb un desig violent de no oblidar-los mai més" (225) [with the strong desire to not forget them ever again]. This expression of desire opens the mechanism of deterritorialization where the repressive forces that chained her appetites disappeared, allowing desire to move freely outside the world of social conventions and emotional boundaries that have restricted her life since she was twelve. At this point, the death of the good uncle Joaquim took her away from the primal garden and into the garden of adulthood colored by the red flowers of the bougainvillea, the symbolic plant of the incestuous relationship between Isabel, her mother, and Lluís, her bad uncle.

Territorialized in the Sant Gervasi garden until her coming of age, Maria feels that her desires have been repressed and her productive energies tamed and confined. Nevertheless, the escape to Paris will not bring her the freedom she had been longing for, as one can deduce from the descriptions of her precarious life years later in a boarding house in Bordeaux, and from her yearning for a return—the reterritorialization, so to speak—to the gardens of her childhood and adolescence:

[E]ra com si veiés la meva casa de fa vint-i-cinc anys, amb la buganvília, amb les carolines florides i oloroses. . . . La meva casa i el meu jardí. (258)

[It was as if I had seen my home of twenty-five years ago, with the bougainvillaea, with the scented flowers in bloom. . . . My home and my garden.]

In this way, Maria opens the writing path to other Rodoredan heroines such as Natàlia, Cecília, and Armanda for whom experience could only blossom within the well-known territory of a house, a garden and an old neighborhood, that is to say, in the *casolà* [homey] environment of the Catalan *petite bourgeoisie* where, under other circumstances, Mercè Rodoreda would have probably spent most of her life. As a matter of fact, Rodoreda's finest works deal with the accounts of the time before the moment of uprootedness, and with the strategies that she used in order to regain such time. For these reasons, her "desire to escape" inscribed in the Proustian questionnaire becomes more symbolic than real, following once more the precursor works of Proust—who spent almost his entire life within the limits of the same Parisian neighborhood and died shortly after moving into a "foreign" *quartier*—and of Marcel in *A la recherche,* forever confined to his apartment or "caverne sensorielle" [sensory cavern][21] from where the outside world—"l'experience sénsible" [the sensitive experience]—was only perceived as in shadows.

> I torna tot. Tot tempestuós i barrejat com les fulles que empeny el vent. Torna tot com si només el que ha passat fos viu i jo fos morta; como si jo només fos viva en el record de totes les coses que han passat. (132)
>
> [And everything comes back. Everything comes tempestuous, and mixed like fallen leaves blown in the wind. Everything comes back, as if only the past were alive and I were dead. As if I were alive, only in the remembrance of things past.]

Halfway through the first part of Rodoreda's novel, titled "El carrer del desig" [Desire Street], the reader finds Isabel exhausted after a self-inflicted abortion and isolated in her cavern on the second floor of the Sant Gervasi house. She remains "a les fosques" (117) [in the dark], immersed in the "sommeil proustien"[22] [Proustian sleep] and "on the edge of the abyss of Time Lost."[23]

Detached from the outside world since her daughter Maria left the house and took the garden with her, Isabel retrieves the shadows of the night when her husband Joaquim announces her pregnancy, and the years when she was happy playing in that garden with him and his brother Lluís, who later becomes her lover. With this strategy, Rodoreda finally grants Isabel the right to explain her own side of the story for the purpose of no longer being "le désir incestueux"[24] [the incestuous desire] of the others but, rather, an active woman fighting against sexual repression and the "myths of motherhood"[25] that constrain her.

In this way, Isabel emerges as the "Modernist Madonna" willing to break the structure of male dominance, female submission that stripped her of her beauty, her child and, ultimately, her life. Following the "process of double articulation"[26] that constitutes Rodoreda's texts, Isabel's determination, however, will not fracture the patriarchal triangle of desire formed in her childhood, at a time when a wall divided her property from that of the two brothers, and she was still in possession of her side of the garden. But such conviction will sustain her in the "learning process of the wound"[27] that she undergoes while struggling in a Proustian sleep with the intensity of *things past.*

> [B]ut in vain did I make a screen with my hands, the better to concentrate upon the flowers, the feeling they aroused in me remained obscure and vague, struggling and failing to free itself, to float across and become one with them.[28]

"Tot s'havia buidat de mi . . ." (150) [Everything had emptied of myself . . .] acknowledges a motionless Isabel. The garden also remained immobile—"[a]l jardí no es movia una fulla" (147) [not even a leaf moved in the garden]—the day when Isabel admitted, under Maria's pressure, that she had never loved her. At that stage of life, Isabel's feelings toward her daughter and herself remained "obscure and vague" because she was, like Marcel in the last *soirée* at the house of Mme. de Guermantes, fusing all the past periods of her life,[29] before the bell in the garden ceased ringing. Unlike Marcel however, Isabel, although rich, was not in control of her financial situation and therefore she lacked the male power to rule the house and the garden. Consequently, Sant Gervasi turned into a prison and life became for Isabel-Mercè "dura i desagradable"[30] [hard and unpleasant].

Expelled from her paradise, Isabel feels "vella" [old], and in the hands of the others—Crisantema the maid, and Lluís—who perceive as "manies" (41) and "neurastenia" (46) the painful process of recovery that she undertakes with the intention of healing the wounds inflicted upon her body and psyche:

> Què voleu? que sigui una bona mare? Que enyori la Maria? Una Isabel per a en Lluís, una Isabel per a la Crisantema, una Isabel per a en Joaquim. A cadascú en regalo una. Sóc vella. Ells m'han fet vella, de mica en mica, amb una gran tenacitat. . . . Tots, tots m'han fet mal, casdascú a la seva manera, cadascú amb el seu estil: els uns amb més traça: els altres, amb menys. (148)

> [What do you want from me? To be a good mother? To miss Maria? One Isabel for Lluís, one Isabel for Crisantema, one Isabel for Joaquim. I granted one to each of them. I am old. They made me old,

little by little, with tremendous tenacity. . . . All of you, all of you hurt me, each of you in your own way, each of you with your own style: some of you more skillfully than others.]

Woman, once more, is seen as "the guilty one"[31] at the center of neurosis. Isabel is the madwoman in the cavern, in whom Rodoreda symbolically transposes her own resentment toward the intolerance of the patriarchal order that took her garden away and imposed upon her the bourgeois values of the time. Hence, Isabel's malady stands, in a larger picture, for the alienation of a period in Catalan life when women remained confined to the iron balconies and red geraniums of the medieval Barcelona, to the walled gardens in the "torretas" of the nearby towns, and to the back galleries with the palm trees and interior gardens of the growing Modernist city that Ildefons Cerdà had envisioned. Conversely, Marcel's "déséquilibres"[32] [instabilities] are seen as an expression of the author's power to punish his mother, grandmother, and female lovers every time they did not satisfy his wishes; thus, his malady becomes an active mechanism in the process of subverting the impositions of phallocentrism.

As if there were no time left, Isabel, willing to destroy the patriarchal order and to break away from the angelical image that Lluís and Joaquim created of her, remembers in a last effort the days when they played in the garden of childhood *vora del mar* [close to the sea] and the triangle was formed. In this section of *Isabel i Maria,* it is interesting to observe that although Rodoreda, employing Proust's techniques, re-created those episodes from a male perspective, Isabel remained the protagonist of Lluís and Joaquim's games and in control of the other's gaze, since she was still in possession of her own garden. Like Gilberte, whom Marcel perceives "across the heads of the stocks and jasmines,"[33] Isabel is first seen by Lluís in her father's garden. The boy's gaze, "eager to reach, touch, capture, bear off in triumph the body at which it is aimed, and the soul with the body,"[34] is fastened to a particular component of the girl's attire: "un llaç blau violent" (56) [a fierce blue ribbon.] This "descriptive element"[35] of Isabel's clothing remained—as the "vivid azure"[36] of Gilberte's eyes for Marcel—as one of the most powerful impressions in Lluís's mind. Aware of such effect Isabel, in the process of growing up, gradually mastered the discourse of clothing, fusing the powerful signs of ribbons, summer dresses, and formal gowns with the language of flowers.

The blend of garments and flowers, often present in Rodoreda's subsequent works, unfolds and flourishes indeed in *Isabel i Maria.* It is as if the author, by keeping this text always nearby and unfinished, had wanted to perpetuate the sentiment which they aroused, and that the violent uprootedness after the Civil War had threatened to destroy. A sentiment that was stimulated by that "desire to see" inscribed in the Proustian questionnaire.[37] In this way, if the blue ribbon signals the first encounter between Isabel and Lluís, the white clothes shape the triangle, drawing the two brothers and Isabel together on the afternoon when the girl all dressed in white and the boys in their first pairs of long pants, also white, walk along the beach "com si tots tres fóssim un retrat per sempre" (67) [as if the three of us were in a portrait forever]. In both scenes Isabel keeps Lluís under her spell, asking him to tie her loose ribbon or holding his hand long after they had finished walking.[38] Nevertheless, shortly after, the rivalry between the brothers for the girl's attention increases, and the garden of childhood becomes a battlefield, tearing them apart and precipitating the self-imposed exile of Lluís in Bordeaux.[39]

On his return to Barcelona seven years later, Lluís, aware of his brother's marriage to Isabel, would be met at Isabel's villa by some inhabitants of her garden of childhood: the magenta flowers of the bougainvillea. Before encountering her and after jealously admiring the lavish lifestyle of the couple, Lluís sees the plant as "una cortina de fulles [on] de tant en tant es veia una flor magenta oberta tardanament" (70) [a screen of leafage (where) here and there one could see a magenta flower tardily opened]. In the following scene, Lluís looks at Isabel standing in the dining room and wearing "un vestit de color de fum complicat i vaporós i una rosa de seda, una rosa de color de rosa, al pit" (70) [an elaborate and flowing dress the color of smoke and a silk rose, a rose the color of a rose, on her bosom].

This succession of events, connected by the Proustian gaze of Lluís, links the two gardens where the trio spent the years of childhood and adolescence. Under Lluís' scrutiny, aimed to touch Isabel's body and soul, the intricate dress that she wears signifies a disorder of the primal garden, reinforced by the erotic connotations of the unveiled flowers among the foliage. Thus, Lluís' examination acknowledges Isabel's success in turning the pubescent body into a "civilized body" to be deciphered, although on its own terms.[40] As an autonomous "floral construction,"[41] hers is a scented body, whereas the flower of the bougainvillea that Lluís smells the first night "no tenia cap mena de perfum" (71) [had no fragrance at all]. Consequently, Isabel grows for Lluís—like Mlle. Vinteuil for Marcel—as "a necessary and natural product of this particular soil."[42]

> I was suddenly aware of a bitter-sweet scent of almonds emanating from the hawthorn-blossom, and then I noticed on the flowers themselves little patches of a creamier colour, beneath which I imagined that this scent must lie concealed, as the taste of an almond cake lay beneath the burned parts, or that of Mlle. Vinteuil's cheeks beneath their freckles. Despite the motionless silence of the hawthorns, this intermittent odour came to me like the murmuring of an intense organic life . . .[43]

The strong blend of flowers and garments inscribed in Isabel's adult body revitalizes the triangle of desire and renews the sexual games. In this way, although Maria becomes once more "l'àngel" (73) [the angel] of Joaquim and Lluís, she is still in control of the garden. Therefore, her power to subvert "the body's total subordination to the spirit"[44] that her condition as a creature of light entails remains untamed, as can be seen in the scene at the breakfast table, a week after Lluís' arrival. Here, Rodoreda emphasized the Proustian method to regain time through the scene of flowers by retrieving certain elements of Isabel's former attire imprinted in Lluís' "remembrances of things past," the white dress and the ribbons:

> Quan vaig baixar a esmorzar, ella seia a taula esperant-me. Duia una bata de seda blanca, tota brodada de crisantems blancs, i els cabells lligats enlaire amb una cinta de vellut negre. (73)

> [When I went downstairs to have breakfast, Isabel sat at the table waiting for me. She was wearing a gown of white silk, embroidered with white chrysanthemums, and had her hair up, tied in a black velvet ribbon.]

With this tactic, the author momentarily grants Isabel the control of the Proustian women over Marcel, who was forever under the spell of certain details of the *toilettes* that Mme. de Guermantes or Mme. Swann once wore, which he grasped in his childhood when the ladies rode in their carriages along the Avenue du Bois.

The Garden Decays

The black dress with red roses to the waist that Isabel wears the night when Joaquim announces her pregnancy signals the peak of the heroine's power over the two men and, consequently, the maximum splendor of her garden. For a moment, in Lluís' mind this image of a triumphant Isabel merges with the one he kept of their first encounter in the garden of childhood, fusing again both spaces. Nevertheless, the birth of Maria would strip Isabel of her beauty, the garden, and of command over Joaquim and Lluís: "com si . . . l'hagués buidada d'ella mateixa" (89–90) [as if . . . it had emptied her of herself]. Only the red flowers of the bougainvillea, blooming like "una onada de foc" (88) [a wave of fire] retain the memory of Isabel's life, scattered among those flowers and certain objects such as "un ventall blanc amb una flor vermella . . . com si fos l'ala d'un ocell, tacada de sang" (88) [a white fan with a red rose . . . like the wing of a bird, stained with blood]. Isabel carries the fan when she asks her doctor for an abortion that he refuses to perform, leaving to time the two most destructive events in her life: the birth of Maria and the decadence of her garden.

Shortly after Maria's birth, Joaquim acknowledges the fact that she could have been his brother's daughter and moves immediately with the newborn baby into another house, abruptly annulling his wife's rights as mother and preventing her from seeing Maria again. With this gesture, Rodoreda—like Proust after the death of his own mother[45]—cancelled her past and transferred the garden of childhood into a new domain devoid of family burdens and restraints, unfolded in the second part of the novel as pages of the unfinished "Diari de Maria" [Maria's Journal].

In the Garden of Childhood with Maria and Marcel

By setting the second part of the novel in the villa at San Hermenegildo Street, Rodoreda regained the primal garden of childhood and consequently the moments of happiness that its vegetation preserved. Violently uprooted from the incestuous garden of adulthood, Mercè-Maria is reterritorialized "through time and space,"[46] into a place in which those "mythic narratives of maternity and codes of sexual difference" mentioned before are subverted as in the author's real life. With this shift, the good-uncle Joaquim assumes the maternal role of Rodoreda's grandfather Gurgí: dressing her when they go to Badalona to collect the rent money from their tenant and taking care of her education at home.

In addition, the "Two Ways" of Marcel's realm become the front garden and the back garden of Maria's Combray. Maria's "Guermantes Way," on the one hand, signifies the joyful journeys that she spent playing in the mythical Eden, prior to the death of her uncle Joaquim when she was twelve; whereas her "Méséglise Way," on the other, symbolizes the cruelty of the outside world, half-seen in the fights between the two uncles and in the uncanny encounters that she has with strangers, the day when for the first time she walks alone outside her garden. The forbidden connotations that Méséglise—Swann's Way—had for Marcel are transposed into Maria's garden in the open flowers "color de sang" (191) [the color of blood] of the eucalyptus at the house next door, and in the first rosebush that her uncle Joaquim gives to her, saying that, sometimes, a white flower would open showing a single petal "de color de foc" (192) [the color of fire].

> Damunt del meu cap, molt alta, hi ha la campaneta que dringa. I dringa, encara, mentre, de puntetes, miro al carrer. (195)
>
> [Very high up above my head, there is a bell ringing. And it still rings while I, standing on my toes, look at the street.]

The sound of the bell signals Maria's first step beyond the family garden and into the outside world. Not long after this episode, the good uncle dies and Maria returns, at twelve, to the incestuous garden in Sant Gervasi. The gate-bell, however, did not stop ringing for Mercè-Maria, and years later, when the events deterritorialized Rodoreda and her heroine from that garden forever, the sound became for Mercè Rodoreda an obsession—as it had become for Marcel Proust—until time had been regained through writing, and the "Two Ways" had also met at last.

Notes

1. Roger Duchêne, *L'impossible Marcel Proust* (Paris: Robert Lafont, 1994), 586. My translation.
2. Ibid.

3. George D. Painter, *Marcel Proust: A Biography,* 2 vols. (New York: Random House, 1987), 1:9.
4. Carme Arnau, *Mercè Rodoreda* (Barcelona: Edicions 62, 1992), 78.
5. Painter, *Proust,* 1:8.
6. Mercè Rodoreda, *Cartes a l'Anna Murià* 1939–1956, ed. Isabel Segura i Soriano (Barcelona: laSal, 1985), 95.
7. Duchêne, *L'impossible,* 82–83.
8. Mercè Rodoreda, *Cartes,* 59.
9. Duchêne, *L'impossible,* 85.
10. George Painter, *Marcel Proust,* 1:38.
11. Ibid., 1:24.
12. See my articles, "Los dos caminos de Marcel," *Anotaciones sobre el amor y el deseo* (Caracas: Academia Nacional de la Historia, 1986), 15–21; and "Mercè Rodoreda: Mès enllà del jardí," *Catalan Review* 2, no. 2 (1987): 263–71.
13. Painter, *Marcel Proust,* 2:3.
14. From the editor's prologue to Mercè Rodoreda, *Isabal i Maria,* ed. Carme Arnau (Balencia: Eliseu Climent, 1991), 18. This and all translations from Catalan are my own. All quotations from this novel are cited within the text, parenthetically, by page number.
15. Arnau, *Mercè Rodoreda,* 38.
16. Ibid., 35.
17. "The rhizome itself assumes very diverse forms, from ramified surface extension in all directions to concretion into bulbs and tubers [and] is made only of lines: . . . lines of segmentarity and stratification as its dimensions, and the line of flight or deterritorialization as the maximum dimension after which the multiplicity undergoes metamorphosis, changes in nature." Gilles Deleuze and Félix Guattari, *A Thousand Plateaus. Capitalism and Schizophrenia,* trans. Brian Massumi (Minneapolis: University of Minnesota Press, 1987), 7, 21.
18. "In exile, the feeling of uprootedness may become transmuted into narrative via heroines who are *arrencades*—uprooted from their environments by destiny and/or orphaned." Elizabeth Scarlett, "Vinculada a les flors: Flowers and the Body in *Jardí vora el mar* and *Mirall trencat,*" in *The Garden across the Border: Mercè Rodoreda's Fiction,* ed. Kathleen McNerney and Nancy Vosburg (Selinsgrove, PA.: Susquehanna University Press, 1994), 81.
19. Cf. Arnau, *Isabel i Maria,* 15.
20. Marcel Proust, *Swann's Way,* 1:260.
21. "Du monde extérieur, le prisonnier ne perçoit que des ombres mais, sortirait-il de la caverne, qu'il serait ébloui par le Soleil. Il lui faut donc accéder à une réalité intermédiaire, qui n-est ni illusion sensorielle ni invisible secret, mais construction mathématique de formes, permettant l'accès à la connaissance vraie." [From the outside world, the prisoner perceives nothing but shadows. However, as soon as he/she leaves the cavern, the Sun will dazzle him/her. He/she has, therefore, to reach an intermediate reality—neither sensorial illusion nor invisible secret—but a mathematical construction of forms, which allows him/her to gain access to real knowledge]. Julia Kristeva, *Le temps sensible: Proust et l'expérience littéraire* (Paris: Gallimard, 1994), 289. My translation.

22. "[C]e sommeil proustien profond s'installe lorsque le feu (de toute intelligibilité?) baisse. Aucune clarté, seule l'intensité des sensations baigne et bouleverse la dormeur. Plus qu'une 'autre scène,' ce sommeil-là est un espace fermé sans scène: un 'second appartement,' écrit Proust." [This Proustian deep sleep falls when the fire (of all things intelligible?) decreases. No clarity. Only the intensity of sensations bathes and disturbs the sleeper. More than 'another scene,' such sleep is a shut space without scene: a 'second apartment,' wrote Proust]. Ibid., 291. My translation.

23. George Painter, *Proust,* 1:336.

24. "Le désir incestueux mêlé à l'ambivalence agressive constitue, du meme mouvement, *l'object* du rêve (qui était jusqu'alors sans object), sa *pensée* et ses *signes.* Ils interrompent le plaisir et la douleur sensoriels, enclavés dans la partie profonde du rêve." [The incestuous desire mixed with an aggressive ambiguity constitutes, by the same force, *the object* of dreams—which has had no object until then—its *belief,* and its *signs.* They interrupt the feelings of pleasure and pain, rooted in the deepest zone of dreams.] Kristeva, *Le temps sensible,* 294. My translation.

25. "[I]t can be interpreted that mythic narratives of maternity and codes of sexual difference are structured by both repression and the splitting apart of the affectual links which carry sexual and emotional feelings between men and women and those which tie parents to their children (and the reverse.)" Jane Silverman Van Buren, *The Modernist Madonna: Semiotics of the Maternal Metaphor* (Bloomington: Indiana University Press, 1989), 2.

26. Jaume Martí-Olivella. "The Witches' Touch: Towards a Poetics of Double Articulation in Rodoreda," *Catalan Review* 2, no. 2 (1987): 163.

27. Ibid.

28. Marcel Proust, *In Search of Time Lost. Swann's Way,* vol. 1, trans. C. K. Scott Moncrieff and Terence Kilmartin, revised by D. J. Enright (New York: Random House, 1992), 1: 195.

29. Marcel Proust, *Remembrance of Things Past. Time Regained,* vol. 3, trans. C.K. Scott Moncrieff, Terence Kilmartin, and Andreas Mayor (New York: Random House, 1981), 1087.

30. Mercè Rodoreda, *Cartes a l'Anna Murià,* 71.

31. "The madmens' festival, the savages' wild celebrations, the children's parties: woman is the figure at the center to which the others refer, for she is, at the same time, both loss and cause, the ruin and the reason. She, once again, is the guilty one." Hélène Cixous and Catherine Clément, *The Newly Born Woman,* trans. Betsy Wing (Minneapolis: University of Minnesota Press, 1986), 24.

32. Roger Duchêne, *L'impossible Marcel Proust,* 87.

33. Marcel Proust, *Swann's Way,* 1:199.

34. Ibid., 1:198.

35. "[H]owever functional it may be, real clothing always includes a descriptive element, insofar as every function is at least a sign of itself . . ." Roland Barthes, *The Fashion System,* trans. Matthew Ward and Richard Howard (New York: Hill and Wang, 1983), 264.

36. Marcel Proust, *Swann's Way,* 198.

37. Carme Arnau, *Merçè Rodoreda,* 55.

38. It is important to notice that the association of flowers, women, and sexuality had also a preeminent role in *La recherche,* as has been observed by Kristeva: "Les catleyas vont devenir le mot fétiche d'Odette et de Swann,

l'expression intime de leur langage secret: 'faire catleya.'" [The cathleyas became a fetish word for Odette and Swann, the intimate expression of their secret language: "to make cathleya."] Julia Kristeva, *Le temps sensible,* 22. My translation.

39. As Nancy Vosburg has observed in reference to the image of the garden, "[a]cts of cruelty and indifference predominate, while happiness, compassion, and tenderness make brief and momentary appearances." "The Roots of Alienation," in *The Garden across the Border,* 157.

40. "By constructing a soul or psyche for itself, the 'civilized body' forms libidinal flows, sensations, experiences, and intensities into needs, wants, and commodified desires that can gain a calculable gratification. The body becomes a text, a system of signs to be deciphered, read, and read into." Elizabeth Grosz, *Space, Time, and Perversion: Essays on the Politics of Bodies* (New York: Routledge, 1995), 34.

41. "As for what Rodoredan floral constructions have to say about feminism, one must begin with the syllogism that emerges from *Jardí vora el mar:* women are flowering plants, and plants have something of the divine about them." Scarlett, 80.

42. Marcel Proust, *Swann's Way,* 1:221.

43. Ibid., 1:158.

44. "[I]n this concept of the celestial body . . . certain propositions remain in place: the body's total subordination to the spirit, its perfect agreement with the soul, and its affinity with the milieu that envelops it. This paradoxically open enclosure *(hortus conclusus)* contains creatures of light whose remoteness can be measured in terms both of spacetime and of dematerialization . . . winged things, difficult to identify, that encompass physical quintessence and blissful sublimity." Nadia Tazi, "Celestial Bodies: A Few Stops on the Way to Heaven" in Michel Feher, Ramona Naddaff and Nadia Tazi, eds., *Fragments for a History of the Human Body.* Part two (New York: Zone, 1989), 522.

45. A year after his mother's death, Proust moved from the apartment at 45 Rue de Courcelles, where he had spent most of his life, to 102 Boulevard Haussmann. Here he would undertake his *Recherche,* which lasted for the time of his lease: twelve and a half years. (Painter, *Marcel Proust,* 2:61.)

46. Marcel Proust, *Swann's Way,* 1:4.

Isabel i Maria: Mercè Rodoreda's Mother/ Daughter Plot

JAUME MARTÍ-OLIVELLA

FEMINISM, PSYCHOANALYSIS, AND MERCÈ RODOREDA

MORE OFTEN THAN NOT, MERCÈ RODOREDA'S WORK HAS BEEN INTERpreted from a psychoanalytical perspective that reinforces Freud's traditional Oedipal narrative. In recent years, however, several feminist readings have begun to unearth alternative desiring subjects in the extraordinary corpus of Catalonia's foremost twentieth-century novelist.[1] This essay springs from the latter tradition and considers Rodoreda's second posthumous novel, *Isabel i Maria,* as one of the author's clearest and strongest feminist and maternal narratives.[2] Indeed, despite Rodoreda's own words, "Jo crec que el feminisme és com un xarampió" [I think feminism is like the measles], or Anne Charlton's dismissal: "Mercè Rodoreda no ha manifestat cap interès per la problemàtica feminista" [Mercè Rodoreda has not shown any interest in feminist issues],[3] it seems obvious to me that Rodoreda's work captures a dramatic and universal sense of feminine experience while, at the same time, becoming a historical document that inscribes Rodoreda's own triple exile: as a Catalan woman who fought on the losing side of Spain's Civil War, as a member of a suppressed culture, and as a woman who was marginalized within her own culture because of her adulterous liaison with Joan Prat.[4] Rodoreda's feminism does not follow any specific agenda, it lies on the fact that she was able to create a historical subject that had until then been silent: Catalan middle-class women. In my view, Rodoreda's commitment to feminism springs from her aesthetics. She chose to incorporate traditional patriarchal narratives in order to subvert them subtly from within. This gesture is what constitutes Rodoreda's dialogical poetics: her double articulation of the literary sign which includes, at the same time, the reappropriation and the transgression of traditional patriarchal discourses.[5] Most prominent among these narratives is the myth of Eden. Most Rodoredian texts, in fact, tell of an original loss. This loss has been traditionally constructed following Freud's family romance as a means of recovering the lost paradise of a childish Oedipal plenitude. This interpretation is best exemplified by Carme Arnau, one of Rodoreda's foremost canonical critics, who writes, alluding to Cecília Ce, the protagonist of *El carrer de les Camèlies* [*Camellia Street*]:

> In this man Cecília may satisfy the Oedipal complex that has haunted her throughout her entire life and that has pushed her from one man to another . . . By his side, she reencounters a childhood that she hasn't been able to live fully until now.[6]

Arnau's reading is based on a teleological construction that presupposes the traditional master narrative of childhood as a (patriarchal) lost paradise Arnau analyzes Rodoreda's text as a gradual process of growing interiorization and spiritual ascension that culminates in the final access to a mythical garden of Eden. What this vision ignores is that childhood, from a post-Freudian and feminist perspective, can no longer be recovered only as paradise, as Catherine Clément reminds us in *The Newly Born Woman:*

> Freud, contributing the idea of polymorphous perversity, returns to this figure and cancels the image of childhood innocence. But also, by describing the tortures of a child who is cruelly trapped between the signifiers, Mother and Father, Freud overturns the image of childhood as paradise and transforms it into hell.[7]

Rodoreda's poetic dialogism consists precisely in her double articulation of the maternal and paternal signifiers and the creation of an uncertain subject whose desiring economy bespeaks a childish tension. This tension ultimately becomes Rodoreda's way of inscribing her own intense and problematic relationship with motherhood as a self-fulfilling role and as a patriarchal social imposition. Too little has been written about the importance, both at an existential and at a metaphorical level, that motherhood has had in Rodoreda's life and work. Let us hear it from Rodoreda herself: "A més, el paper de la dona, que, en definitiva, és la mare de l'home sí que és important en el món, molt més important que el de l'home."

(Oller/Arnau, 6) [Besides, the role of woman as, finally, the mother of man is very important, more important than that of man himself.] This clear consciousness of the fundamental function of the maternal in a universal sense is reflected in her private anxiety concerning the situation of her own mother: "El que cada cop la preocupa més a ella és la seva mare i demana insistentment al seu fill que l'atengui, que li faci alguna finesa." (Casals, 188) [What worries her more and more is her own mother so she always asks her son to take care of her, to do something nice for her.] In her rich and sometimes polemical biographical study, Montserrat Casals has consistently shown us Rodoreda's attempt to fulfill her maternal duties despite the difficulties of her exile. Such an effort becomes problematized, however, by the final dismissal of her son Jordi amidst the turmoil created by discussions over a family inheritance:

> Les últimes cartes de Jordi, escrites en castellà, trasllueixen una relació comercial. S'hi parla de béns i de vendes i hipoteques. A la darrera, el fill s'acomiada amb un simptomàtic parèntesi: "Besos de tu hijo que te quiere (ya sé que lo pones en duda)." Era a final de 1968 i no té resposta. Al cap de pocs mesos mare i fill van retrobar-se a Barcelona. Mercè va passar el vespre amb els seus quatre néts i, després d'un sopar agradable com ho havien estat sempre les taulades a casa dels Gurguí, mare i fill van iniciar una última conversa. Va ser una nit blanca. Van buidar una ampolla de Chartreuse i diversos paquets de cigarretes. Jordi no vol repetir què van dir-se. Al matí es van separar: mai més no es tornaren a veure. (Casals, 298)
>
> [Jordi's last letters, written in Spanish, reflect a commercial relationship. They speak of sales, mortgages and properties. In the last one, the son takes leave with a significant parenthesis: "Kisses from your son who loves you (I know that you doubt it)." This letter was written near the end of 1968 and does not have an answer. After a few months, mother and son met again in Barcelona. Mercè spent the night with her four grandchildren and after a pleasant dinner like most of those spent at the Gurguí's, mother and son began their last talk. It was a sleepless night. They emptied a bottle of Chartreuse and several packages of cigarettes. Jordi won't repeat what they said. In the morning they parted. They would not see each other again.]

Besides the dramatic mystery involving this separation, what I find particularly remarkable is that from now on Rodoreda will live her exile as a state that empties her of maternal feeling. That is why most of her texts become a gesture of maternal compensation. Despite his positioning as a Freudian orthodox, Joaquim Poch's analysis coincides with this view of the fundamental role of the maternal in Rodoreda's work. Thus, he writes about Natàlia, the protagonist of *La plaça del Diamant:*

> Obviously, Natàlia doesn't take into consideration the couple formed by her parents to conceive and raise her. She lives with the illusion that she and her mother share an idyllic relationship, with a cruel father disrupting this dream. Her mother's death leaves her in a precarious situation with nothing to hold on to . . . She has become empty. Thus, we see clearly illustrated the image of the mother as a dream, as illusion, but without any separate existence, capable of leaving her things. I could say that Natàlia hasn't in fact parted from the mother, hasn't been able to recognize her as somebody capable of having her own life and relationships beyond her daughter.[8]

What Poch criticizes as Natàlia's dysfunctional adjustment, her "illusion" or fixation with an ideal mother is what many feminist psychoanalysts have theorized as constituting the figure of the pre-Oedipal mother, the maternal metaphor, which, as a pre-discursive "illusion" may be constructed as an alternative to the male renditions of the imaginary processes involved in the subject's formation.[9] Elizabeth Scarlett is quite explicit concerning Natàlia's male attachments when she writes:

> Natàlia's subsequent attachments to the men in her life—first Quimet, then Antoni—bear the stamp of the sundered mother-daughter bond, in the first case because of this prolonged mourning period, and in the second because he also "lived only to take care of" Natàlia. Here as elsewhere, the surprising discovery of an older man who proceeds to take care of the heroine, solving all her troubles in an uncanny way, has more in common textually with the maternal memory than with the encountering of a father figure, as an interpretation based on an overly religious adherence to psychoanalysis might conclude.[10]

In fact, as I have already suggested, what Rodoreda does is to (con)fuse both narratives, the maternal and the paternal, the Oedipal and the pre-Oedipal, always intertwined in the dialogical structures of her texts. In the context of my study, therefore, the neurosis of the Rodoredian characters must be seen as inscribed in a compensatory impulse. Most of her characters appear to be orphans in search of an original bond with the (M)Other. My contention concerning *Isabel i Maria* is that this posthumous novel marks the preeminence of the maternal in Rodoreda's textual body. That is why I will refer to that novel as the embryo or the matrix of the Rodoredian canon. *Isabel i Maria* becomes, ultimately, the most significant example of Rodoreda's ability to undermine Freud's family romance from within. Indeed, this novel is about the search for the father, but it is also, and even especially, about the pain of maternal loss and about the extraordinary struggle to (re)cover it by means of a textual supplement. It is precisely in her relentless gesture of giving voice to the absent mother where one should find Rodoreda's uncompromising commitment to a feminist aesthetic.

Isabel i Maria or the Importance of the Maternal Metaphor in Rodoreda

> To return to the plot of *Isabel i Maria,* Rodoreda uses narrative material that is totally melodramatic, a kind of soap opera. . . . If we follow the story line, we find two neighboring gardens and the childish complicity of the two brothers, Joaquim and Lluís, with Isabel. This complicity is obviously broken with the coming of age and amorous choice. Isabel marries Joaquim and the triangle explodes when Lluís returns to live with them. Maria, the daughter, is born without a clear father figure. The fact of her diffused paternity, a paternity that remains unclear throughout the text, prompts Joaquim to take her away from the family household. The girl grows up with "the two uncles," far from Isabel, who lives among dreams. Joaquim's death brings about the end of Isabel's childhood and the beginning of a new life with Isabel, *"the unknown mother."*[11]

> The projected angry mother of the psychoanalytic narrative, then, would react to the child's so-called inevitable hostility with anger of her own, would feel wronged when, after years of nurturing and care, she is left behind. Should she rebel, however, should she express her own feelings about an enforced and inevitable separation, she would cease to be maternal. For the essence of the maternal in psychoanalytic writing lies in the service to the interests of the child. And to be angry is to assert one's own self, not to subordinate it to the development of another's self. A mother cannot ar-

> ticulate anger *as a mother;* to do so she must step out of a culturally circumscribed role which commands mothers to be caring, and nurturing to others, even at the expense of themselves.[12]

In 1991, eight years after Rodoreda's death, *Isabel i Maria* was published. It was the second posthumous novel to emerge from the unfinished literary works that Rodoreda bequeathed to the Institut d'Estudis Catalans [Catalan Studies Institute]. The first, *La mort i la primavera* [Death and Spring], an impressive tale of a rural society where desire is suppressed by means of ritualized violence, appeared in 1986.[13] Unlike *La mort i la primavera,* which pushes Rodorda's "fantastic" mode to an expressive climax, *Isabel i Maria* sends the reader back to the very origins of Rodoreda's entire creative project. It is, as I have stated above, this function of narrative matrix that I want to explore here. *Isabel i Maria* is, in fact, a double matrix. On the one hand, as has been established by Carme Arnau, who took charge of organizing and editing the unfinished text, this novel clearly becomes an "embryo" of Rodoreda's best fiction.[14] On the other hand, and this will be the basis of my argument here, it shows the importance of the maternal metaphor in Rodoreda's work. Motherhood, in this unfinished novel, is represented as a patriarchal imposition and a process of self-loss while emerging, at the same time, as the ultimate binding force that allows this *unknown mother* to reclaim the bond with her daughter beyond all social prohibitions. As Marianne Hirsch tells us, the history of the mother, her own story, has always been silenced in the name of an essentialist notion of motherhood. Patriarchal western societies have sanctioned motherhood as the primordial feminine function. Any woman who rejects maternity or who assumes it from the perspective of self-affirmation becomes a threat to the precarious balance of the dominant social model. That explains, in my view, why Rodoreda has chosen the narrative path of the conventional melodrama, of the Freudian family romance, to inscribe her subtle deconstruction of the traditional (male) desiring subject. And, in so doing, she has managed to articulate her own outrage and her own desire, both as a woman and as a mother for whom the social imposition of motherhood appears to be the true monstrosity. It is important to consider also how Rodoreda manages to avoid the pitfalls of an essentialist position by means of a consistent historicity that springs from her lifelong commitment to Catalonia and to the Catalan language. This position, according to some critics, has been betrayed by most feminist approaches. Joan Ramon Resina exemplifies that critical warning:

> Attention to Rodoreda's work has come almost exclusively from feminist criticism, for reasons that have little to do with a genuine interest in the position of her work within the culture that produced it. By appropriating it as an illustration of feminist tenets, such critics have in fact substituted one hegemonic ground for another, displacing the work from its geopolitical and historical coordinates to engraft it into a heterogeneous cultural and social movement that poses as universal.[15]

Although Resina's cautionary remarks are not without merit, I think his position tends to obviate the fact that most ideological, and patriarchal, interpretations of Rodoreda have superimposed their own master narratives onto her stories. A paradigmatic case may be found in Francesc Betriu's filmic version of Rodoreda's *La plaça del Diamant.*[16] Elizabeth Scarlett, while stressing the value of Rodoreda's testimonial work, takes on Resina's argument when she writes:

> His [Resina's] linking of these texts with the concept of a minor literature that evokes a certain oppressed socio-historical community through the very use of its language (Catalan) in recreating colloquial speech and in naming places and things, underlines the testimonial quality. However, Resina is perhaps understandably disquieted by what he deems a "deterritorialization" of the author—a slighting of the importance of her attachment to the Catalan community—perpetrated by American feminist critics practicing hermeneutic readings. Resina does make some concessions to the importance of gender in Rodoredian writings, but he groups the body in the same category as "things" that are named and used to indicate the passage of time (236). An either/or phallacy plagues his dismissal of feminist scholarship on Rodoreda, for the resulting exclusion, while perhaps effecting a "reterritorialization," would impoverish any reading: the spirit of place that is evoked is often directly related to the protagonist's inhabiting of a female body, in addition to a geographic location. Cultural specificity alone might make her work a major one for Catalan readers only. The territory Rodoreda reclaims in her novels is also that of a female body inextricably linked to a particular woman's consciousness, universalizing her work.[17]

Trying to avoid that "either/or phallacy," I would like to add that Rodoreda's nationalism does not contradict her textual commitment to create a "maternal supplement" that becomes a true historical document of the silenced voice of many middle- and lower-class Catalan mothers who resisted Spain's Civil War. In the context of my essay, therefore, the significance of *Isabel i Maria* must be understood precisely as residing in its documental value. It constitutes an impressive document about Rodoreda's own alienated motherhood, which haunted her throughout her life. Beyond the question of its literary value lies the fact that this novel forces us, as readers and critics, to effect a circular return and to re-evaluate Rodoreda's entire production. What was at the center of Rodoreda's imaginary? Which is the Ariadne-like thread that allowed Rodoreda to weave one of the most spectacular textual tapestries of Catalan literature? Questions that are impossible to answer univocally, of course. And yet, if one looks for the narrative link in the melodramatic plot of this novel, one finds that, at the beginning, in a quasi-replica of the childish game of *Fort* and *Da* that helped Freud conceptualize his theory of human libido, there appears here a similar game, albeit a more pathetic one.[18] It is the maid Crisantema who tells us about Isabel's reenacting the loss of her daughter:

> Es clar que d'ençà que la Maria va marxar, la senyora Isabel em fa una mica de pena; però és molt de la comèdia, ella. Quan vaig explicar la història del fil a la meva cunyada, no se la volia creure. "Però el treu i el posa, el fil?" "Si—li vaig dir—.El treu i el posa." Ho fa mig d'amagat, però a mi no se m'escapa res: és un fil blanc de l'útima enfilada d'agulla que la seva filla va enfilar per cosir-se el tirant de la combinació que se li va descosir despenjant roba de l'armari per posar-la a la maleta. Aquest bocí de fil va quedar enganxat en un cantell del sofà. . . . Quan hi he de fer dissabte, el fil desapareix; quan he acabat de fer dissabte, el fil hi torna a ser, i sempre caragolat de la mateixa manera i amb un cap penjant avall que, amb l'aire que un fa entrant i sortint, es gronxa. (39)

> [It's true that since Maria left, I feel a bit sorry for Senyora Isabel, although she's a bit of an actress. When I told my sister-in-law the story of the thread, she could not believe it. "But she takes it out and puts it back, the thread?" "Yes," I told her, "She takes it out and puts it back." She does it half on the sly, but I don't miss a thing: it's a white thread from the last time that her daughter threaded the needle to sew the strap of her slip, which had torn while she was taking her clothes out of the closet to put them in her suitcase. This piece of thread got stuck on the edge of the couch. . . . Whenever I come to clean, the thread disappears; when

I've finished cleaning, the thread is back, and it is always hanging in the same way, with one end twisting downwards and, with the breeze you make as you come and go, it swings back and forth.]

This passage, which may count among Rodoreda's best, contains one of those moving poetic miniatures that characterize Rodoreda's best style. The daughter's loss is figuratively inscribed in the precarious presence of this white thread, which symbolically links mother with daughter. Metonymically, while alluding to the broken umbilical cord, it reminds us—thanks to the reference to "fer-ho d'amagat" (doing it in hiding)—that it was Isabel herself who wanted to break that cord since she, in fact, dared ask doctor Riera to perform an abortion on her. ("No podria, vostè . . .?) [Could you . . .?] (88). And it was also Isabel who, in her previous pregnancy, managed to avoid having Lluís's son. All the novel revolves around this narrative element; what Rodoreda had previously represented only tangentially becomes the thematic center: motherhood lived as self-loss and social imposition and, at the same time, the notion of the impossible and ardently desired union between mother and daughter, beyond all the institutional prohibitions erected by the law of the father. The significance of *Isabel i Maria* lies precisely in the clarity with which Rodoreda inscribed these basic concerns. This early novel illustrates a series of narrative structures revolving around feminine and maternal desire which will later be elaborated and transformed with the superimposition of Oedipal narratives and, especially, with Rodoreda's artistic use of her dialogical poetics.

Elsewhere,[19] I have characterized Rodoreda's modernity from the perspective of the impact that Virginia Woolf, Franz Kafka and James Joyce had on her work. To the "neurotic, mythical and parodic" tryptic of qualifiers used then, I would like to add here another three that re-define that very modernity: post-Joycean, feminist, and semiotic. If, for instance, we read *Isabel i Maria* from the Joycean intertext, we can see its parallel use of an endogamic family that strongly resembles the one that occupies the melodramatic center of Joyce's *Finnegan's Wake,* in which the brothers Shem and Shaun are always fighting to achieve their sister Issy's attentions. To the central position of the cainite theme, one should add the importance given to the theme of paternity as a legal fiction, a topic favored by Stephen Dedalus in his sermon during the visit to the hospital where Mrs. Purefoy is in labor in *Ulysses*. Needless to say, Joyce's parody of the legal and psychological notion of paternity was embedded in a series of personal ghosts which he tried somehow to exorcize in the Circe chapter. The haunting presence of personal ghosts is another link between Joyce and Rodoreda. It is, in fact, one of the universalizing aspects of many great novelists, as Carme Arnau reminds us in her prologue to *Isabel i Maria:*

> These words remind us of those written by the British novelist Iris Murdoch who stated, quite similarly, that art "is a fight against obsessive and unconscious forces." . . . In Rodoreda's case, at least in the beginning and despite having lived through two wars and an exile, these demons are not those major dramatic events, but another kind of wars, more personal ones: those wars in the center of which we find an outraged and closed-in family world.[20]

From a compositional viewpoint, moreover, *Isabel i Maria* constitutes quite clearly one of the initial moments in Rodoreda's narrative spiral. Like Joyce, the Catalan novelist will return over and over to the same images and motifs. To mention only a few of the most important, I want to call attention to the image of the scales, a crucial one in *La plaça del Diamant*, which appears here without its complex dialogical sense, but merely indicating the injustice of the situation:

> I el dia que vaig saber que els famosos diumenges que en Lluís passava fora de casa, els passava a casa del seu germà, em va semblar que em tornava boja. Un dia vaig veure la nena. Estava asseguda als graons de l'entrada i jugava amb unes balances a pesar palets. Quan es va adonar que la mirava va agafar les balances i va entrar a la casa. (134)

> [And the day that I learned that on those famous Sundays that Lluís spent away from home he was at his brother's home, I thought I'd go crazy. One day I saw the girl. She was sitting on the staircase at the entrance playing at weighing sticks on a scale. When she noticed that I was staring at her, she picked up the scale and went into the house.]

Isabel, to whom any contact with her daughter Maria has been forbidden, transgresses this prohibition only once and is happy with this longing look that will be met by the indifference, almost the cruelty, of the girl who "es va girar i em va fer llengotes" (134) [who turned only to make ugly faces at me]. The second most important symbolic image in the poetic dialogism of *La plaça del Diamant,* the pigeon-dove, is also incorporated without complexity in this novel:

> Cada diumenge menjàvem colomins i a mi, només de pensar-hi, em venia mareig. Cuits i tot, sempre sentia aquella pudor de febre i de colomasa. . . . Vaig ficar la mà sota d'un colom, vaig agafar els ous i els vaig començar a sacsejar amb fúria. . . . Vaig esguerrar totes les cries. Aviat no vam menjar més colomins. El meu oncle va acabar venent tots els coloms. (172–3)

> [Every Sunday we ate little pigeons and it made me sick just to think of it. Even cooked, I always noticed their strong, feverish pigeon smell. (One day) I stuck my hand under a pigeon, I grabbed the eggs, and I started shaking them furiously. . . . I spoiled the whole breed. Soon, we stopped eating little pigeons and my uncle finally sold all the pigeons.]

Like Natàlia, Maria also hates the pigeons that appear to her as an imposition that unsettles her life. Her anti-maternal gesture becomes, as in *La plaça del Diamant,* the desperate beginning of her own self-affirmation, the first revolt against her own domestication. The list of basic symbols should include also the heart of diamonds that Joaquim gives to Isabel as a present and that will find its counterpart in that cross of diamonds that Maria Cinta used to wear and that fascinated Cecília Ce in *El carrer de les Camèlies;* or, even more, uncle Joaquim's watch with the tiny diamonds that Maria will take with her when she leaves for France, thus starting uncle Lluís' last emotional breakdown. Without insisting here on the allegorical importance of the watch motif,[21] what Rodoreda already achieves in this novel is to dialogically inscribe the watch both as a patriarchal fetish, marking uncle Lluís' anger for having been deprived of its possession, and also as an emblem of the impossible transgression:

> I el tic-tac del rellotge dintre el calaix de la tauleta de nit, com una companyia i com una amenaça. Totes les rodetes que no cessaven de girar, d'anar i venir endavant i endarrera, els robins com minúscules gotes de sang: tot allò tan polit amidava la claror i la fosca. . . . I aquests copets dels segons són el temps que passa, i que passa així: quiet i segur; i quan un mot t'atura de viure o quan sents un mal més violent que el mal d'aleshores al genoll, voldries que el temps es precipités i fugís; el temps, el temps és

> aquí, dintre d'aquesta capsa d'or rodona i vella i robada, i no canvia . . . (240)
>
> [And the tick-tock of the watch in the drawer of the nightstand was both company and a threat. All those little wheels that never stopped turning, coming and going backwards and forwards, the rubies like tiny drops of blood: all of that neat, polished stuff measuring light and dark. . . . And those little knocks of the seconds are time passing, and it passes like this: quiet and sure; and when a word keeps you from living or when you feel a pain, more violent than that pain in your knee, you'd like for time to rush forward and flee; time is here, time within this old, round and stolen gold box, and it never changes . . .]

The "temps robat" (stolen time) is that of the impossible transgression. The golden box, like memory, may contain time but it may not stop it from passing. This obsessive Rodoredian motif receives, therefore, its entire dialogical power from the very first turns in the narrative spiral, in the textual wheel of Rodoreda's historical time which constitutes *Isabel i Maria.*

Earlier in this essay, I suggested that this embryonic novel contained already the three major characteristics of Rodoreda's entire narrative project and that it is a post-Joycean, a feminist and a semiotic text. I will conclude with a passage that condenses these last three aspects. I am referring to the almost autonomous section in which we witness Maria's unbelievable walk, when she goes out to buy bread and is followed by the dog that becomes her shadow:

> El sol ens ve de cara i em giro i em veig l'ombra llarga: la meva ombra em sembla tan llarga com la d'una persona gran; i el gos s'atura, i la seva ombra em fa una mica de por. Sentim el ball de les campanetes i com que no passa ningú començo a ballar damunt de la meva ombra, que em fa por, i trepitjo amb fúria el ventre de la meva ombra, fort, fort, i em vull trepitjar el pit, però quan estic a punt de trepitjar-lo, fuig lluny i no hi arribo. Alço el cap i d'una paret alta surten uns arbres de fulla molt fina, tots desmaiats i de color de cendra, i l'ombra de les branques es mou per terra i fa molt bonic. (198)
>
> [The sun shines in our faces and I turn around and see my own long shadow: my shadow seems as long as that of an older person; and the dog stops, and its shadow scares me a little. We hear the dance of the bells and since nobody is coming I start dancing on my own shadow, it scares me and I stomp on the belly of my own

shadow good and hard, and I want to stomp on my chest but when I'm about to get there, it goes far away and I can't reach it. I raise my head and from a high wall emerge some trees with very thin leaves, all droopy and ash-colored, and the shadow of their branches moves on the ground and it is very pretty.]

The semiotic quality of Rodoreda's dialogical poetics is already quite impressive in moments like this one where her narrative powers are at their best. This new epiphanic miniature sheds light into the innermost drama that is in store for Maria: that of the woman-girl who is left alone and who becomes fascinated and entrapped in the limited space marked by the projection of her own shadow. Like the beautiful moment in which Natàlia's shadow merges itself with the shadow of Rita, her daughter, in *La plaça del Diamant,* as if forming a time see-saw that could project her onwards,[22] here we see how Maria's shadow merges with that of an older person. And yet it is a dog that follows her, both company and a threat. This loneliness that is both tended to and threatened by the street dog takes us back to the very first moments in the narrative of *El carrer de les Camèlies,* when Cecília Ce is found by the night watchman who saves her from the dog which was already smelling her. Cecília will indeed be the woman who is condemned to live in the shadows of her own imprisoned feminine condition. Maria, however, starts dancing in this "ball robat" (stolen dance) since nobody—no male—is staring at her with desire. She dances with her own shadow until that moment of narcissistic self-satisfaction is interrupted by her own fury, a fury already addressed in a strikingly revealing semiotic gesture towards her own belly. Thus, this first unconscious rejection of motherhood becomes inscribed in a self-aggressive gesture that betrays the interiorization of a guilty conscience, a process of self-aggression that will recur throughout Rodoreda's work,[23] and that here is seen in the double condemnation of Isabel's culpability, carried out ex-aequo by the two brothers, Joaquim and Lluís: "En realitat, era la seva mare qui tenia la culpa de tot." (100) [In fact, it was her mother who was responsible for it all.] And this guilty feeling will be interiorized by Maria, the forbidden daughter. The emblematic scene quoted in the previous passage ends with a sense of restored peacefulness that is achieved through the contemplation of the ash-colored leaves and the movement made by the shadows of the tree branches. In this merging of life and death imagery,

Rodoreda anticipates the essential symbolic landscape of her *La mort i la primavera,* while presenting yet another beautiful example of the passage of time and of its permanence. It should not surprise us, therefore, that in her last self-representation Maria, already alone in Bordeaux as an old woman, will recapture that image of herself as the girl with the dog in order to use it as a new time see-saw that allows her finally to realize her intimate union with her *unknown mother:* "I aleshores vaig endevinar-ho tot. Sóc la meva mare. La meva mare he estat jo." (255) [And then I saw everything. I am my mother. My mother has been me.] This circularity of the mother's return or the return to the mother marks the end of *Isabel i Maria* while inaugurating the impressive maternal supplement which is Mercè Rodoreda's narrative work.

Notes

This essay is part of a longer study titled "Mercè Rodoreda's Dialogical Poetics" that rereads Rodoreda's maternal metaphor while suggesting an interpretation that subverts the Oedipal readings that have dominated Rodoreda's canonical criticism.

1. See, for instance: Kathleen McNerney and Nancy Vosburg, eds., *The Garden Across the Border: Mercè Rodoreda's Fiction* (Selinsgrove, Pa.: Susquehanna University Press, 1994); Jaume Martí-Olivella, ed., *Homage to Mercè Rodoreda. Catalan Review* 2, no. 2 (December 1987) or Elizabeth A. Scarlett's *Under Construction: The Body in Spanish Novels* (Charlottesville: University Press of Virginia, 1994).

2. Quotations in this essay in the original Catalan (with page references in parentheses) are from Mercè Rodoreda, *Isabel i Maria* (Valencia: Eliseu Climent, 1991). The English translations, in brackets, are all mine. I want to thank my colleague and friend Mary Ann Newman for her assistance with the translations.

3. See Dolors Oller and Carme Arnau's "Entrevista amb Mercè Rodoreda" in *La Vanguardia* (Barcelona), (2 July 1991), 6 and Anne Charlon's *La condició de la dona en la narrativa catalana* (Barcelona: Edicions 62, 1990), 110.

4. For a detailed account of Rodoreda's lifelong relationship with the Catalan writer Joan Prat, who used the pseudonym Armand Obiols, see Montserrat Casals i Couturier's biography, *Mercè Rodoreda: Contra la vida, la literatura* (Barcelona: Edicions 62, 1991).

5. I formulated this concept of double articulation as a simultaneous presence and absence of mother figures in Rodorda's narrative in the essay "The Witches' Touch: Towards a Poetics of Double Articulation in Rodoreda," *Homage to Mercè Rodoreda. Catalan Review* 2, no. 2 (1987): 159–69.

6. Carme Arnau, *Introducció a la narrativa de Mercè Rodoreda: El mite de la infantesa* (Barcelona: Edicions 62, 1979), 183. My translation.

7. Hélène Cixous and Catherine Clément: *The Newly Born Woman,* trans. Betsy Wing (Minneapolis: University of Minnesota Press, 1986), 26.

8. Joaquim Poch and Conxa Planas, *Dona i psicoanàlisi a l'obra de Mercè Rodoreda* (Barcelona: Promociones Publicaciones Universitarias, 1987), 89. My translation.

9. This alternative to the Freudian and Lacanian models was first formulated by Julia Kristeva in *La révolution du langage poétique* (Paris: Seuil, 1974). See also the pioneering work done by Hélène Cixous and Luce Irigaray in this respect.

10. Mercè Rodoreda," chapter 3 in Elizabeth Ann Scarlett, "Spanish Women Writers and the Reconquest of Inner Space: Gender, the Body, and Sexuality in Novels by Emilia Pardo Bazán, Rosa Chacel, and Mercè Rodoreda," (Ph.D diss., Harvard University, 1991), 126–44. I thank the author for having sent me the unpublished manuscript.

11. Montserrat Palau, "La matriu de la narrativa de Mercè Rodoreda," *Avui* (Barcelona), 21 December 1991, Cultura section, 9. Emphasis and translation are mine.

12. Marianne Hirsch, *The Mother/Daughter Plot. Narrative, Psychoanalysis, Feminism* (Bloomington: Indiana University Press, 1989), 170. In the following passage, Hirsch elaborates on Kristeva's fundamental work on this subject: "In the theoretical discourse of Julia Kristeva, for example, the maternal occupies a central space: . . . The mother as split subject, as locus of the semiotic, as both phallic and castrated, present and absent, omnipotent and powerless, the body before language, unrepresentable, inexpressible, unsettling, has become the privileged metaphor for a subversive femininity." (171)

13. Mercè Rodoreda, *La mort i la primavera.* (Barcelona: Club, 1986).

14. See Carme Arnau, "Pròleg" to *Isabel i Maria* (Valencia: Eliseu Climent, 1991), 11–31.

15. Joan Ramon Resina, "The Link in Consciousness: Time and Community in Rodoreda's *La placa del Diamant,* in Jaume Martí-Olivella, ed., *Homage to Mercè Rodoreda, Catalan Review* 2, no. 2 (1987): 226.

16. For an extended discussion of how the female subject is both silenced and essentialized to become a national metaphor in Betriu's film, see, among others: Leah Ball: "El lenguaje de la división y el silencio en Rodoreda," in George Cabello-Castellet, Jaume Martí-Olivella and Guy Wood, eds., *Cine-Lit: Essays on Peninsular Film and Fiction* (Corvallis: Oregon State Press, 1992), 92–99 and María Pilar Rodríguez, "Experiencias, literatura y cine: Traducciones y traiciones en *La plaza del Diamante," Anuario de cine y literatura en español,* 1 (1995): 111–20.

17. Elizabeth A. Scarlett, "Spanish Women Writers," 130.

18. For a detailed description, see Sigmund Freud: *Beyond the Pleasure Principle* (New York: Norton, 1989). Especially relevant to my discussion is the following passage: "At the same time, he was greatly attached to his mother, who had not only fed him herself but had also looked after him without any outside help. This little boy, however, had an occasional disturbing habit of taking any small objects he could get hold of and throwing them away from him into a corner, under the bed, and so on, so that hunting for his toys and picking them up was often quite a business. As he did this he gave vent to a loud, long-drawn-out "o-o-o-o," accompanied by an expression of interest and satisfaction. His mother and the writer of the present account were agreed in thinking that this was not a mere interjection but represented the German word "fort" (gone). . . . The child had a wooden reel

with a piece of string tied round it. It never occurred to him to pull it along the floor behind him, for instance, and play at its being a carriage. What he did was to hold the reel by the string and very skillfully throw it over the edge of his curtained cot, so that it disappeared into it, at the same time uttering his expressive "o-o-o-o." He then pulled the reel out of the cot again by the string and hailed its reappearance with a joyful "da" (there). This, then, was the complete game—disappearance and return. . . . The interpretation of the game then became obvious. It was related to the child's great cultural achievement—the instinctual renunciation (that is, the renunciation of instinctual satisfaction) which he had made in allowing his mother to go away without protesting. He compensated himself for this, as it were, by himself staging the disappearance and return of the objects within reach." (13–14).

19. See my essay, "Rodoreda o la força bruixològica," in Philip D. Rasico and Curt J. Wittlin, eds., *Actes del Cinquè Col.loqui d'Estudis Catalans a Nord-Amèrica* (Montserrat: l'Abadia, 1988), 283–300.

20. Carme Arnau. "Pròleg" (prologue) to *Isabel i Maria,* 17.

21. The metonymic representation of Quimet's haunting ghost in *La plaça del Diamant* will have his watch as signifier. Natàlia is given the watch as a memento of Quimet's death on the front. His ghostly reappearances in Natàlia's mind will exemplify Rodoreda's conflation of a cronological time with a more personal sense of inner time which cannot be measured by (patriarchal) watches.

22. I am referring to the following passage in *La plaça del Diamant:* "El peu anava d'un costat a l'altre i anava fent ratlla i tot d'una em vaig adonar que jo estava damunt de l'ombra del cap de la Rita; més ben dit, l'ombra del cap de la Rita em pujava una mica damunt dels peus, però així i tot, el que em va semblar, va ser que l'ombra de la Rita, a terra, era una palanca, i que a qualsevol moment jo podria anar enlaire perquè feien més pes el sol i la Rita a fora que l'ombra i jo a dintre. I vaig sentir d'una manera molt forta el pas del temps." (Barcelona: Club, 27th printing, 1983), 234. [Her foot went from side to side drawing the line, and all of a sudden I realized I was standing on Rita's shadow's head; or more precisely the shadow of her head fell a little above my feet, but even so I felt like Rita's shadow on the floor was a see-saw and I could go flying through the air any minute because Rita and the sun outside were heavier than me and the shadow inside. And I got a strong feeling of the passage of time.] *The Time of the Doves,* trans. David Rosenthal (New York: Taplinger, 1980), 183.

23. For a detailed analysis of this guilty conscience in *La plaça del Diamant,* see Loreto Busquets, "El mite de la culpa a *La plaça del Diamant*" in Nathaniel Smith, et al., eds., *Actes del IV Col.loqui d'Estudis Catalans a Nordamèrica* (Montserrat: l'Abadia, 1985), 306–19.

Mercè Rodoreda and the Criticism of her Work: Analysis and Selected Bibliography

María Isidra Mencos

In 1976, Carme Arnau wrote in her prologue of the first volume of Mercè Rodoreda's *Obres completes:*

> The bibliography with respect to this author amounts to no more than a few interesting interviews, and some penetrating essays—which, however, are too brief and condensed—and, finally, numerous trivial articles, which are the fulfillment of a necessary obligation rather than the result of voluntary interest (the majority of them, newspaper reviews). (5)

Twenty years later, the situation has radically changed. Mercè Rodoreda's work is not only successful with the public, as it has been since the publication of *La plaça del Diamant,* but it is also gradually acquiring a privileged place in the world of academic criticism. The articles and books that have been published about Rodoreda's work have increased dramatically in number. Moreover, this criticism is no longer dominated by brief works, reviews, and newspaper articles. There now exist essays with substantial critical-theoretical underpinnings, which examine in detail the stories and novels of this talented writer. If in the years from 1963 to 1978 we find only thirteen publications with these characteristics, in the last twelve years (1984–96), the number has increased to over ninety.

In this article, I present a study of the evolution of criticism on Mercè Rodoreda's work. Moreover, I indicate which themes and works have been thoroughly studied by critics, and I go on to suggest possibilities for future research.

The bibliography following this study includes critical works published between 1963 and 1996. I have selected those works containing interpretations that have facilitated subsequent readings of Rodoreda's work.

It is necessary to indicate that many of the articles excluded from this bibliography were published in newspapers (for example, *La Vanguardia, Avui,* etc.). These generally consist of reviews that describe the plot of a given work and offer a brief commentary, or they contain news items giving facts about the author's life or the publication of her work; for example, the awarding of a prize, the printing of a new edition, etc. In other cases, some of the articles published in magazines discuss five or six different works in a few pages. This results in a superficial treatment of the works, typical of this kind of brief essay. In some cases, an article focuses on a single work, but from a descriptive angle, or else it relies on intepretations made in previous studies that are well known, and without adding any kind of original or personalized analysis.[1]

Those who are familiar with Rodoreda criticism may be surprised not to find included here certain critical works which are repeatedly found in other bibliographies. Upon consulting these works, I have found them to be extremely brief. The facts and ideas that they contain can also be found in later articles, where they are elaborated in more detail.[2]

I have not listed reviews, nor the prologues to the various editions and translations of Rodoreda's work. Although these pieces are often written with intelligence and sensitivity, they do not tend to contribute new and/or detailed critical perspectives.

In the case where a single study exists in several different versions, such as a translation, selection or summary appearing in various publications, I cite either the original study or the most complete version, and I mention the others in a note.

The Evolution of Rodoreda Criticism

As various critics have indicated, Mercè Rodoreda was marginalized as an author in various respects.[3] First, because of her political position as a *catalanista* and a supporter of the Republic, she was forced into exile after the Spanish Civil War. Second, her way of life, atypical with respect to the social norms of the period—specifically, her relationship with a married man, the writer Armand Obiols—produced feelings of hostility in a certain sector of the Catalan intelligentsia.[4] And finally, as a woman who, moreover, belonged to a minority culture, her literary efforts were condemned to being undervalued. This is revealed in histories of contemporary Spanish literature: these concede far less importance to Rodoreda than to her male contemporaries, whose works entered the canon much earlier, although they are neither superior in quality, nor as well received by the reading public.[5]

Undoubtedly, these marginalizing factors, in conjunction with Rodoreda's well-known natural reserve and the semi-isolation in which she lived during the greater part of her life, contributed to the lack of critical interest in her work, a situation that has only begun to change in recent years.

In effect, until 1979, the year in which Carme Arnau published her first book about Rodoreda's work (entry 4), only thirteen articles or studies had been published in Catalonia.[6] After this date, specialized criticism increased, although not greatly. Each year one or two works were published, except in 1987 and 1988, when five publications came out in each year. I should indicate, however, that approximately one-third of all that was published was the work of a single researcher, Carme Arnau.

Publications in the United States, the other major source of Rodoreda criticism, began to appear later. Although there were notable indications of interest in Rodoreda's work dating from the beginning of the 1980s, clearly the year that signalled a breakthrough in criticism was 1987.[7] That year, an issue of the *Catalan Review* was dedicated to Mercè Rodoreda, and it contained sixteen articles, four of them by researchers based in Catalonia. Every year since that issue appeared, something has been published in the United States about Rodoreda's work. In 1994, with the publication of *The Garden Across the Border,* yet another milestone was achieved in Rodoreda criticism: this collection contains fifteen articles, many of them of profound interest.

The pace of publishing criticism about Rodoreda has been much slower in other countries. In this bibliography, I include seventeen articles or books originally published in Italy, England, France, Germany, Puerto Rico, Canada and Australia. In several cases, the authors are Catalan researchers who are living and working in these countries.

An examination of the criticism of Rodoreda's work enables us to identify different theoretical perspectives, although, in many cases, several are combined within a single study. The perspectives most frequently utilized are the following:

—thematic or symbolic analysis, which associates the work of Rodoreda with her biography
—feminist analysis
—psychoanalysis
—historical analysis
—linguistic analysis
—formalist analysis, structuralist analysis, narratological analysis, etc.

This last type of analysis does not usually occur by itself, but rather as an aid to another method of approach.

There are also notable differences between the criticism in Catalonia and other parts of Europe, and criticism in the United States.

One difference, perhaps the most obvious, is that in Catalonia, more of the books published are monographs. Examples of this are: Arnau's three studies—two discuss Rodoreda's entire literary *oeuvre* (entries 4 and 11), and the third is a biography (entry 139); the psychoanalytical study by Poch i Bullich and Planas, which analyzes feminine characters in four novels (entry 100); the symbolic study of the last two novels, by Cortés i Orts (entry 39); the studies on *Mirall trencat,* one by Campillo and Gustà (entry 31), and another by Oriol i Giralt (entry 91); and the study of *La plaça del Diamant,* by Carbonell (entry 33).[8] To these we should add two other biographies, one by Casals i Couturier (entry 140), and the other by Ibarz (entry 142). In contrast with these nine monographic studies, only one complete book about Rodoreda has been published in the United States, the above-mentioned *The Garden Across the Border,* a collection of fifteen articles by different researchers.

Some of the books cited above are written for a nonspecialized public. For example, the biographies by Ibarz and by Casals i Couturier are written in a journalistic style and moreover, the latter work is somewhat sensationalistic. As Nichols has observed, the lack of footnotes in these works, as well as their ambiguity with respect to sources of information, result from the authors' intention of reaching a large reading public. However, this does not diminish the potential interest which these data may have to the serious researcher.[9]

We must keep in mind that Rodoreda's work is taught as part of the curriculum in Catalonia beginning at the high-school level. Moreover, her work attracts a wide reading public, which is not limited to members of academia. This explains the publication of books intended for the general public, such as those cited above, as well as books intended for use in teaching, such as the one by Oriol i Giralt.

In contrast, the tendency in the United States is to choose one aspect or one specific theme from one or several works, and to analyze it in detail. Such analysis tends to be guided by a strong and explicit theoretical foundation, as well as a clearly elaborated critical thesis. Scholars in the United States value the kind of study that, rather than include and describe a broad sampling of Rodoreda's work, dissects and problematizes one of its particular facets.

Moreover, we can observe differences in the theoretical perspectives utilized to approach Rodoreda's work. In the United States, there is a marked tendency to work on thematic aspects related to the concerns of postmodernism. That is, there is a consistent attempt to bring to light the marginal aspects of Rodoreda's work, as well as a to enact a playful reading of those aspects of the text which were previously considered peripheral issues. It is, above all, the feminist perspective that has been most often utilized in recent years to reveal those aspects of Rodoreda's works scarcely analyzed by previous critics. Martí-Olivella, the editor of the commemorative edition of the *Catalan Review* published in 1987, indicates in his prologue that "it was through the scholarly attention of American researchers that a feminist reappraisal of her fiction was first attempted." (11) And Elizabeth Rhodes affirms in 1994 that "the majority of Rodoreda's gardeners now tending the field are women, or feminist critics of either gender." (162).

Researchers in the United States doing feminist analysis most often base their studies on the theories of Julia Kristeva, although they also use Sandra M. Gilbert and Susan Gubar, Nancy Miller, Nancy Chodorow, Luce Irigaray, and Alice Jardine, among others.[10] Some of the themes that have been treated are the contrasting of semiotic and symbolic impulses (Kristeva), and the existence of a double discourse in the texts of Rodoreda (Gilbert and Gubar).

In Catalonia, there have also been some attempts at feminist criticism, but they lack the above-mentioned theoretical foundation, and almost always occur in very brief articles. When a study does contain a feminist approach, it is developed from a thematic-biographical angle, as Arnau and Pessarrodona do, for example (entries 10 and 99, respectively). This does not prevent Rodoreda critics, who may be using a different approach, such as the analysis of symbols, from commenting on images and symbols concerned with the repression and liberation of feminine figures in Rodoreda's work.

The psychoanalytic perspective has had many skilled adherents in all parts of the world. In Catalonia, such studies tend to be based on Freud and Jung.[11] In contrast, in the United States, Lacan reigns supreme. Consequently, studies published in Europe tend to treat themes such as guilt, repression of the erotic impulse, narcissism, and the reenacting of childhood traumas in adult life—that is, the set of symptoms associated with the theories of Freud. In contrast, in the United States, this type of study tends to focus on the conflict between the semiotic and the symbolic, and on the patriarchal repression of the pre-oedipal phase. Therefore, psychoanalytic analysis in the United States tends to be allied with a strong feminist tendency, which is typical of one of the theorists most frequently cited, Kristeva, whose own theories were, in turn, influenced by Lacan.

The analyses based on a linguistic approach are few in number but interesting, since their authors bring to bear concrete proofs that sustain their hypotheses in a convincing manner.[12] These authors tend to treat the theme of orality, as well as the feminist thematic.

The perspective that perhaps has the most adherents in Catalonia is that which is based on thematic and symbolic analysis, and which is closely linked to Rodoreda's biography. It was Arnau who initiated this line of criticism, which, because she was the first researcher to do a study of Rodoreda's entire oeuvre, has become an obligatory point of reference for subsequent criticism.[13]

There are researchers in many places who have based all or part of their studies on symbolic analysis. Bachelard is the theorist most often cited (Arnau herself mentions him, as do Varderi and Martí-Olivella, among others). There are many articles, however, that are based directly on Rodoreda's work, and that accomplish a contextual analysis of its symbols.[14] Many of these articles combine symbolic and thematic analysis with other types, and they reveal a certain bias—feminist, narratological and/or psychoanalytic—but without explicitly aligning themselves with a specific theory. We should include in this category of symbolic analysis the studies of archetypes, which link Rodoreda's work to rites of initiation and the trajectory of the hero; such studies are often made with respect to *Quanta, quanta guerra. . . .*[15] Another example of this, although somewhat different, is the study of the symbols in *La mort i la primavera,* carried out from an anthropological perspective.[16]

Comparative analysis also has various facets. On the one hand, Rodoreda's work is compared with that of other female writers, in the attempt to establish parallelisms and contrasts related to their situation as women authors.[17] There are also those who find connections between Rodoreda's work and a certain literary tradition—for example the picaresque, the Gothic novel, the detective story—or who study the intertextuality and influences of other writers' work on her oeuvre.[18] Third, scholars tend to study how Rodoreda rewrites canonical texts, such as the Bible and fairy tales.[19] Another tendency is to compare Rodoreda's works among themselves, for example, the two versions of *Aloma,* or earlier with later works, in order to discover developmental trends in her writing.[20] A final aspect of this type of analysis is the comparison of Rodoreda's written work to its cinematic adaptation by Francesc Betriu.[21]

Finally, we must also consider the historicist perspective, which attempts to link Rodoreda's work to the temporal and spatial circumstances in which she lived. The articles published in Spanish journals tend to take a comparative approach in developing this theme (for example, studying Rodoreda's work in parallel with the work of other writers who were also affected by the war).[22] In Catalonia, brief studies have been published that show the mythologizing of history and the presence of the city in her work.[23] The latter theme is beginning to receive more attention in the United States.[24] But the majority of scholars, especially those based in the United States, has tended to emphasize the allegorical representation of exile and of the marginalization of Catalan culture in her works. This theme has been developed in two principal ways: on the one hand, it is linked with feminine figures, who are victims of the oppression inherent in a patriarchal regime. And on the other hand, scholars interpret the metamorphosis, the solitariness and the isolation of Rodoreda's protagonists as metaphors of exile, and/or as metaphors of the marginalization suffered by those who do not conform to the conservative and rigid laws of the society in which they live.[25]

To conclude this brief overview, I would point out that it does not seem productive to transform the field of Rodoreda criticism into a battlefield of valid or invalid perspectives, for example, between those that defend or attack the feminist viewpoint. In this respect, I echo the words of Elizabeth Rhodes:

> I would suggest that gender, configured in a specific way, is a primary issue in the interpretation of Rodoreda's works, and that other matters, such as politics and language, are divorced from the topic of feminine experience at the peril of those very texts we are seeking to illuminate. That is, it is not a question of thematic or formal dominion, or of presence and absence, rather of interdependence and coexistence of themes and forms. (163)

Possible Approaches for Research into Rodoreda's Work

As one can gather from reading the titles included in this bibliography, some of Rodoreda's works have been analyzed and interpreted exhaustively. Of course, there is always room for a reinterpretation that might bring to bear a new way of seeing a particular work, or that might touch on an aspect of a work that has been previously ignored.[26] But there are certain interpretations that it is unnecessary to reelaborate, since they have not only been made on repeated occasions, but they have also led to coherent and persuasive conclusions. I do not think it is worthwhile to list here all of the themes that have been overly analyzed. I will, however, mention a few examples. These include: feminist and psychoanalytic interpretation of *La plaça del Diamant;* metamorphosis as an allegory of the marginalization of the feminine and/or as an allegory of exile (in stories from the collection *La meva Cristina i altres contes*); the archetypal interpretation of *Quanta, quanta guerra . . .* ; structuralist analysis of *Mirall trencat* (and especially with respect to its points of view); and the orality of Rodoreda's style. To elaborate these themes once again with respect to these specific works, if it is not with the intention of refuting the conclusions reached by existing studies, or else as a starting point or as supporting material for an article focused on other areas, seems to contribute little to the existing body of criticism. In any case, research on the above-mentioned themes must begin by reading what has already been published, in order to assure oneself of the originality of one's contribution.

There remains, however, much to be done with the work of Mercè Rodoreda on the level of criticism, as is always the case when we confront literary texts of high quality and great complexity. In the first place, it is clear that we can direct our attention toward those works which remain largely unstudied. A glimpse at the bibliography's final index, which groups the entries according to the work they cover, clearly indicates those works which have been marginalized by critics. This is the case of collections of stories such as *Viatges i flors,* to which only one article is wholly dedicated.[27] From the other collections of stories, critics consistently select the same stories and the same themes, ignoring wonderful stories that could yield up much for interpretation.[28] This is also the case of a fascinating and complex work such as *La mort i la primavera,* of which I am sure much will be written about in the future, especially when we have access to a good critical edition of this posthumous novel. And, of course, this kind of marginalization occurs with respect to works that are difficult to obtain, remain unpublished, or have only been published recently. This is the case with works such as: Rodoreda's first four novels, which she later disowned; the stories written before 1939, which were published only in magazines or in anthologies of multiple authors; and finally, the author's plays and poems. Rodoreda's abundant and interesting private correspondence deserves special mention, especially her correspondence with Armand Obiols, but also with her editor, Joan Sales, with members of her family, and with other writers.[29] Fortunately, the Fundació Mercè Rodoreda has among its objectives the publication of this material, the republication of works that are out of print, and a critical edition of the posthumous works. Any one of these texts, which have been studied only cursorily, will benefit from the application of the theoretical perspectives mentioned in the previous section, or from other types of analysis.

Secondly, there are certain aspects of Rodoreda's work, including those already receiving much critical attention, which, in my opinion, require more elaboration. I cannot, of course, even attempt to give an exhaustive list of the many possibilities for investigation. I would, however, like to offer a small sampling. For example, the presence of urban space, especially in the works up to *Mirall trencat,* is one aspect that has been somewhat neglected, especially when compared to the consistent attention devoted to representation of the garden and the plant world.[30] In addition, analyses about the use of contemporary history in the work of Rodoreda could be developed, as long as they do not limit themselves to either echoing the author herself, who affirms that history does not play an important role in her works, or to identifying the metaphor of exile—this is a valid interpretation, but one that has already been done.[31] Critics could also focus more on the representation of the body in Rodoreda's work.[32] Another interesting topic, which has only recently opened up for critics, is the influence of the detective novel, a genre favored by Rodoreda.[33] Moreover, we need to analyze other influences recognized by the author herself—such as certain movies, the work of Katherine Mansfield, etc. And to finish this list, which necessarily remains incomplete, I will mention comparative analysis. Not only can this type of analysis continue to yield interpretations of great interest, but it can also contribute toward integrating Rodoreda into the canon of twentieth-century Spanish literature.

Works of Mercè Rodoreda

Books

Aloma. Barcelona: Institució de les Lletres Catalanes, 1938; rev. ed., Barcelona: Edicions 62, 1969.

Una campana de vidre: antologia de contes. Edited by Carme Arnau. Barcelona: Destino, 1984.

El carrer de les Camèlies. Barcelona: Club, 1966.

Cartes a l'Anna Murià, 1939–1956. Edited by Isabel Segura i Soriano. Barcelona: La Sal, 1985.

Del que hom no pot fugir. Barcelona: Clarisme, 1934.

Un dia en la vida d'un home. Badalona: Proa, 1934.

Isabel i Maria. Valencia: Climent, 1991.

Jardí vora el mar. Barcelona: Club, 1967.

La meva Cristina i altres contes. Barcelona: Club, 1967.

Mirall trencat. Barcelona: Club, 1967.

La mort i la primavera. Barcelona: Club, 1986.

Obres completes. 3 vols. Barcelona: Edicions 62, 1976–1984.

La plaça del Diamant. Barcelona: Club, 1962.

Polèmica. With Delfí Dalmau. Barcelona: Clarisme, 1934.

Quanta, quanta guerra . . . . Barcelona: Club, 1980.

Semblava de seda i altres contes. Barcelona: Edicions 62, 1978.

Sóc una dona honrada? Barcelona: Llibreria Catalònia, 1932.

El torrent de les flors. Valencia: Climent, 1993. Includes the following plays: *La senyora Florentina i el seu amor Homer; La casa dels gladiols* (a second version of the first few pages of *La senyora Florentina . . .); Maniquí 1, Maniquí 2; L'hostal de les tres camèlies* and *Un dia*.

Tots els contes. Barcelona: Edicions 62, 1979.

Viatges i flors. Barcelona: Edicions 62, 1980.

Vint-i-dos contes. Barcelona: Selecta, 1958.

Works Published in Books, Newspapers and Magazines

Contes de guerra i revolució. Edited by Maria Campillo. Barcelona: Laia, 1981. Volume 1 contains: "Camí de la guerra," "L'hora més silenciosa en el diari d'un soldat," and "Sònia." Volume 2 contains: "Tres cartes," "Trossos de cartes," "Carta d'una promesa de guerra," "Els carrers blaus," and "Uns quants mots a una rosa."

"Entrevistes de Mercè Rodoreda a *Clarisme*." *Llengua i Literatura* 5 (1992–93): 495–573. Edited by Teresa Muñoz Lloret.

Joc d'asos. Edited by Alex Broch. Barcelona: Magrana, 1981. Contains "Aquella paret, aquella mimosa."

Els marges 30 (1984): 55–71. Contains "Obra poètica."

El pont 35 (1969): 33–35. Contains "Flors de debò."

Revista de Girona 157 (March-April 1993): 188–91. Contains poetry, "Bestioles."

Serra d'Or 270 and 273 (March and June 1982): 29–30 and 31–34. Contains "Imatges d'infantesa" in two parts.

Els set pecats capitals vistos per vint-i-un contistes, en homenatge a Víctor Català. Barcelona: Selecta, 1960. Contains "Rom negrita."

English Translations

Camellia Street [El carrer de les Camèlies]. Translated by David H. Rosenthal. St. Paul, Minn: Graywolf Press, 1993.

My Christina and Other Stories [La meva Cristina i altres contes]. Translated by David H. Rosenthal. Port Townsend, Wash.: Graywolf Press, 1984.

"The Nursemaid" [La mainadera]. In *Two Tales*. Translated by David H. Rosenthal. New York: Red Ozier, 1983.

The Pigeon Girl [La plaça del Diamant]. Translated by Eda O'Shiel. London: Deutsch, 1967.

"The Salamander" [La salamandra]. In *Two Tales*, translated by David H. Rosenthal. New York: Red Ozier, 1983. Also appears in *Catalan Review* 2, no. 2 (1987): 49–59.

"Summer" [Estiu]. In *Catalonia: A Self-Portrait*, translated by Josep Miquel Sobrer. Bloomington and Indianapolis: Indiana University Press, 1972: 72–76.

The Time of the Doves [La plaça del Diamant]. Translated by David H. Rosenthal. New York: Taplinger, 1980; St. Paul, Minn.: Graywolf Press, 1986.

"That Wall, that Mimosa" [Aquella paret, aquella mimosa]. In *Catalonia: A Self-Portrait.* translated by Josep Miquel Sobrer. Bloomington and Indianapolis: Indiana University Press, 1972: 76–80.

Spanish Translations

Aloma [Aloma]. Translated by J. F. Vidal. Madrid: Al-Borak, 1971.

La calle de las camelias [El carrer de les Camèlies]. Translated by José Batlló. Barcelona: Planeta, 1970.

Cuanta, cuanta guerra . . . [Quanta, quanta guerra . . .]. Translated by Ana Maria Moix. Barcelona: Edhasa, 1982.

Espejo roto [Mirall trencat]. Translated by Pere Gimferrer. Barcelona: Seix Barral, 1978.

Golpe de luna y otros relatos [Cop de lluna]. Translated by Angelina Gatell Comas. Madrid: Aguilar, 1995. Also contains "Carnaval" and "La sangre."

Jardín junto al mar [Jardí vora el mar]. Translated by J. F. Vidal. Barcelona: Edhasa, 1983.

Mi Cristina y otros cuentos [La meva Cristina i altres contes]. Translated by José Batlló. Madrid: Alianza, 1982.

La muerte y la primavera [La mort i la primavera]. Translated by Enrique Sordo. Barcelona: Seix Barral, 1986.

Parecía de seda y otras narraciones [Semblava de seda i altres contes]. Translated by Clara Janés. Barcelona: Edhasa, 1981.

La plaza del Diamante [La plaça del Diamant]. Translated by Enrique Sordo. Madrid: Edhasa, 1965.

Veintidós cuentos [Vint-i-dos contes]. Translated by Ana Maria Moix. Madrid: Mondadori, 1988.

Viajes y flores [Viatges i flors]. Translated by Clara Janés. Barcelona: Edhasa, 1981.

Movies

Betriu, Francesc. *La plaça del Diamant.* Barcelona, 1982.

Critical Bibliography on Mercè Rodoreda

1. Albrecht, Jane W. and Patricia V. Lunn. "*La plaça del Diamant* i la narració de la consciència." In *Homenatge a Josep Roca-Pons,* edited by Jane W. Albrecht, Janet DeCesaris, Patricia V. Lunn and Josep Miquel Sobrer, 9–22. Montserrat: l'Abadia 1991.[34]
2. Altisent, Marta E. "Intertextualidad y fetichismo en un relato de Mercè Rodoreda." *Revista Hispánica Moderna* 43, no. 1 (1990): 58–67.
3. Aritzeta, Margarida. "Mercè Rodoreda, el mirall i el miratge." *Serra d'Or* 337 (1987): 47–51.
4. Arnau, Carme. *Introducció a la narrativa de Mercè Rodoreda: el mite de l'infantesa.* Barcelona: Edicions 62, 1979.[35]
5. ———. "La narrativa de Mercè Rodoreda. 'Treball, silenci, astúcia.'" *Saber* 4 (1980): 4–5.

6. ———. "Premi d'Honor de les Lletres Catalanes 1980. De la plaça del Diamant a la plaça de tothom. *Viatges i flors* de Mercè Rodoreda." *Serra d'Or* 250–51 (1980): 512–14.
7. ———. "Vegetació i mort en la narrativa de Mercè Rodoreda." *Revista de Catalunya* 22 (1988): 124–33.
8. ———. "Mercè Rodoreda o la força de l'escriptura." *Literatura de dones: una visió del món.* Barcelona: La Sal, 1988: 81–96.
9. ———. "Mort et métamorphose: *La meva Cristina i altres contes* de Mercè Rodoreda." *Revue des Langues Romanes* 93 (1989): 51–60.
10. ———. "Mercè Rodoreda; la mujer marginada." *Destino* 14, no. 2065 (5–11 May 1977): 46.
11. ———. *Miralls màgics. Aproximació a l'última narrativa de Mercè Rodoreda.* Barcelona: Edicions 62, 1990.[36]
12. ———. "*Isabel i Maria* o l'infern familiar." *Revista de Catalunya* 65 (1992): 148–60.[37]
13. Ball, Leah. "El lenguaje de la división y el silencio en Rodoreda." *Cine-Lit: Essays on Peninsular Film and Fiction,* edited by George Cabello-Castellet, Jaume Martí-Olivella and Guy H. Wood, 92–99. Corvallis: Oregon State University Press, 1992.
14. Berbis, Neus and Maria Josep Simó. "Berenguel i Rodoreda: la concreció de la novel.la psicològica a Catalunya." *Revista de Catalunya,* 99 (1995): 105–15.
15. Bergmann, Emilie L.[38] "Reshaping the Canon: Intertextuality in Spanish Novels of Female Development." *Anales de la literatura española contemporánea* 12, no. 1–2 (1987): 141–57.
16. ———. "Flowers at the North Pole: Mercè Rodoreda and the Female Imagination in Exile." *Catalan Review* 2, no. 2 (1987): 83–99.
17. ———. "Letters and Diaries as Narrative Strategies in Contemporary Catalan Women's Writing." In *Critical Essays on the Literatures of Spain and Spanish America,* edited by Luis T. González del Valle and Julio Baena, 19–28. Boulder, Colo.: Society of Spanish & Spanish-American Studies, 1991.
18. ———. "Fragments of Letters: Mercè's Rodoreda's Wartime Fiction." In *The Garden,* 223–39.[39]
19. Bertrand, Louise. "*La Plaça del Diamant* de Mercè Rodoreda. Propositions pour une lecture." *Annales de la Faculté des Lettres et Sciences Humaines de Nice* 23 (1975): 259–76.
20. Bieder, Maryellen. "The Woman in the Garden: The Problem of Identity in the Novels of Mercè Rodoreda." In *Actes del Segon Col.loqui d'Estudis Catalans a Nord-Amèrica,* edited by Manuel Duran, Albert Porqueras-Mayo and Josep Roca-Pons, 353–64. Montserrat: l'Abadia, 1982.
21. ———. "Cataclysm and Rebirth: Journey to the Edge of the Maelstrom: Mercè Rodoreda's *Quanta, quanta guerra . . . .*" In *Actes del Tercer Col.loqui d'Estudis Catalans a Nord-Amèrica,* edited by Patricia Boehne, Josep Massot i Muntaner and Nathaniel B. Smith, 227–37. Montserrat: l'Abadia, 1983.
22. ———. "La mujer invisible: lenguaje y silencio en dos cuentos de Mercè Rodoreda." In *Homenatge a Josep Roca-Pons,* edited by Jane W. Albrecht, Janet DeCesaris, Patricia V. Lunn and Josep Miquel Sobrer, 93–110. Montserrat: l'Abadia, 1991.

23. Bou, Enric. "Exile in the City: Mercè Rodoreda's *La plaça del Diamant.*" In *The Garden*, 31–41.
24. Busquets, Loreto. "Vers una lectura psicoanalítica de *La plaça del Diamant.*" *Quaderni di letterature iberiche e iberoamericane* 2 (1984): 74–96.
25. ———. "El mito de la culpa en *La plaça del Diamant.*" *Cuadernos Hispanoamericanos: Revista Mensual de Cultura Hispánica* 420 (1985): 117–40.[40]
26. ———. "The Unconscious in the Novels of Mercè Rodoreda." *Catalan Review* 2, no. 2 (1987): 101–17.[41]
27. ———. "*Quanta, quanta guerra* . . . o el procés d'individuació." *Estudis de llengua i literatura catalanes* 20 (1988): 213–36.
28. Cabré i Monné, Rosa. "Apocalipsi i edat d'or en *Quanta, quanta guerra* . . . ." *Antipodas* 5 (1993): 185–202.[42]
29. Callejo, Alfonso. "Corporeidad y escaparates en *La plaça del Diamant* de Mercè Rodoreda." *Butlletí de la North American Catalan Society* 16 (1983): 14–17.
30. Campillo, Maria. "Mercè Rodoreda: la realitat i els miralls." *Els Marges* 21 (1981): 129–30.
31. ———. and Marina Gustà. *"Mirall trencat" de Mercè Rodoreda.* Barcelona: Les Naus d'Empúries, 1985.
32. Capmany, Maria Aurèlia. "Mercè Rodoreda o les coses de la vida." *Serra d'Or* 104 (1968): 415–17.
33. Carbonell, Neus.[43] *"La plaça del Diamant" de Mercè Rodoreda.* Barcelona: Les Naus d'Empúries, 1994.
34. ———. "In the Name of the Mother and the Daughter: The Discourse of Love and Sorrow in Mercè Rodoreda's *La plaça del Diamant.*" In *The Garden*, 7–30.
35. Casals i Couturier, Montserrat. "La ciutat, una casa, un trencaclosques." *El Temps* 586 (1995): 1–8.
36. Clarasó, Mercè. "The Angle of Vision in the Novels of Mercè Rodoreda." *Bulletin of Hispanic Studies* 57 (1980): 143–52.
37. ———. "The Two Worlds of Mercè Rodoreda." *Women Writers in Twentieth-Century Spain and Spanish-America*, edited by Catherine Davies, 43–52. Lewiston, Me.: Mellen Press, 1993.
38. Cortés i Orts, Carles. "El simbolisme en la narrativa de Mercè Rodoreda." *Revista de Catalunya* 96 (1995): 97–104.
39. ———. *Els protagonistes i el medi en la narrativa de Mercè Rodoreda.* Alacant: Institut de Cultura "Juan Gil-Albert", 1996.[44]
40. Encinar, Angeles. "Mercè Rodoreda: hacia una fantasía liberadora." *Revista Canadiense de Estudios Hispánicos* 11 (1986): 1–10.
41. Esteban, Manuel A. "*Quanta, quanta guerra* . . . *:* De la teoría a la práctica." In *Actes del Cinquè Col.loqui d'Estudis Catalans a Nord Amèrica*, edited by Philip D. Rasico and Curt J. Wittlin, 301–12. Montserrat: l'Abadia, 1988.
42. Faulí, Josep. "*La plaça del Diamant:* mite i història." *Butlletí Interior Informatiu: Omnium Cultural* 33 (1980): 6–8.
43. Fayad, Mona. "The Process of Becoming: Engendering the Subject in Mercè Rodoreda and Virginia Woolf." *Catalan Review* 2, no. 2 (1987): 119–29.
44. Forrest, Gene S. "El diálogo circunstancial en *La plaza del Diamante.*" *Revista de Estudios Hispánicos* 12 (1978): 15–24.

45. ———. "Myth and Antimyth in Mercè Rodoreda's *Quanta, quanta guerra . . .*" In *German and International Perspectives on the Spanish Civil War: The Aesthetics of Partisanship,* edited by Luis Costa, Richard Critchfield, Richard Golsan and Wulf Koepke, 367–75. Columbia, S.C.: Camden House, 1992.
46. Gamisans, Pere. "La il.lusió referencial a la novel.la de Mercè Rodoreda *Jardí vora el mar.*" In *Estudis de llengua i literatura catalanes.* Vol. 9, edited by Rolf Eberenz, Joseph H. Gulsoy, Josep Massot i Muntaner, Joan M. Pujals, Joaquim Rafel, Nic Stolp, Giuseppe Tavani, Arthur Terry and Alan Yates. Montserrat: l'Abadia, 1984.
47. ———. "Intriga i narració a la novel.la de Mercè Rodoreda: el cas de *Jardí vora el mar.*" In *Estudis de llengua i literatura catalanes.* Vol. 19, edited by Rafael Alemany, Kálmán Faluba, Antoni Ferrando, Josep Massot i Muntaner, Joaquim Rafel, Josep Roca-Pons, Nic Stolp, Giuseppe Tavani and Joan Veny. Montserraat: l' Abadia, 1988.
48. Glenn, Kathleen M. "*La plaza del Diamante:* The Other Side of the Story." *Letras Femeninas* 12, no. 1–2 (1986): 60–68.
49. ———. "Muted Voices in Mercè Rodoreda's *La meva Cristina i altres contes.*" *Catalan Review* 2, no. 2 (1987): 131–42.
50. ———. "The Autobiography of a Nobody: Mercè Rodoreda's *El carrer de les Camèlies.*" In *The Garden,* 110–18.
51. ———. "Rare Birds and Hardy Flowers: Mercè Rodoreda's *La senyora Florentina i el seu amor Homer.*" *Catalan Review* 8, no. 1–2 (1994): 193–201.
52. González, Josefina. "Mirall trencat: Un umbral autobiográfico en la obra de Mercè Rodoreda." *Revista de Estudios Hispánicos* 30, no. 1 (1996): 103–19.
53. ———. "La mímesis en un cuento de Mercè Rodoreda: 'Aquella paret, aquella mimosa.'" *Romance Notes* 36, no. 1 (1995): 93–99.
54. González-Castro, Francisco. "Tanatocracia y sociedad en *La muerte y la primavera.*" *RLA* 3 (1991): 465–68.
55. Grilli, Giuseppe. "Estructures narratives a l'obra de Mercè Rodoreda." *Serra d'Or* 155 (1972): 39–40.
56. ———. "A partir d'*Aloma.*" *Catalan Review* 2, no. 2 (1987): 143–58.
57. Hart, Stephen M. "Mercè Rodoreda: *La plaça del Diamant.*" In *White Ink: Essays on Twentieth-Century Feminine Fiction in Spain and Latin America.* London: Tamesis Books, 1993.
58. Hart, Patricia. "More Heaven and Less Mud: The Precedence of Catalan Unity over Feminism in Francesc Betriu's Filmic Version of Mercè Rodoreda's *La plaça del Diamant.*" In *The Garden,* 42–60.
59. Hess, Josefina A. "La subjetividad femenina en *Aloma, La calle de las camelias* y *La plaza del diamante* de Mercè Rodoreda." *Alba de América* 11, no. 20–21 (1993): 281–90.
60. Krogstad, Jineen. "*El jardí vora el mar:* vida, mort, innocència i Deu." In *Actes del Segon coloqui d'Estudis Catalans a Nord-Amèrica,* edited by Manuel Duran, Albert Porqueras-Mayo and Josep Roca-Pons, 377–82. Montserrat: l'Abadia, 1982.
61. Kutlin, Katalin. "A Diamant ter." *Filologiai Kozlony* 26 (1980): 78–84.
62. Lucarda, Mario. "Mercè Rodoreda y el buen salvaje." *Quimera* 62 (1987): 34–39.

63. Lucio, Francisco. "La soledad, tema central en los últimos relatos de Mercè Rodoreda." *Cuadernos Hispanoamericanos: Revista Mensual de Cultura Hispánica* 242 (1970): 455–68.
64. Marco, Joaquim. "Humiliats i ofesos: *El carrer de les Camèlies.*" In *Sobre literatura catalana i altres assaigs.* Barcelona: Llibres de Sinera, 1968.
65. Martí, Sadurní. "Història de dues novel.les." *Revista de Girona* 157 (1993): 180–86.
66. Martí-Olivella, Jaume.[45] "The Witches' Touch: Towards a Poetic of Double Articulation in Rodoreda." *Catalan Review* 2, no. 2 (1987): 159–69.
67. ———. "Rodoreda o la força bruixològica." In *Actes del Cinquè Col.loqui d'Estudis Catalans a Nord Amèrica,* edited by Philip D. Rasico and Curt J. Wittlin, 283–300. Montserrat: l'Abadia, 1988.
68. ———. "Bachelardian Myth in Rodoreda's Construction of Identity." In *Imagination, Emblems and Expressions: Essays on Latin American, Caribbean and Continental Culture and Identity,* edited by Helen Ryan-Ramson, 315–28. Bowling Green, Ohio: Popular, 1993.
69. ———."Death and Spring or Mercè Rodoreda's Semiotic Chora." *Romance Quarterly.* 42 (1995): 154–62.
70. Martín, Salustiano. "La lúcida mirada de Mercè Rodoreda." *Reseña de literatura, arte y espectáculos* 176 (1987): 2–6.
71. Martínez Romero, Carmen. "Relaciones textuales en la novela femenina de la subjetividad: Gaite, Rodoreda y Riera." In *Ensayos de literatura europea e hispanoamericana,* edited by Félix Menchacatorre, 293–97. San Sebastian: Universidad del País Vasco, 1990.
72. Martínez Ruiz, Florencio. "Mercè Rodoreda: anatomía de la burguesía catalana." *La Estafeta Literaria* 581 (1976): 2358–59.
73. McGiboney, Donna Janine.[46] "Rituals and Sacrificial Rites in Mercè Rodoreda's *La mort i la primavera.*" In *The Garden,* 61–72.
74. McNerney, Kathleen.[47] "La identitat a *La plaça del Diamant:* supressió i recerca." *Actes del Quart Col.loqui d'Estudis Catalans a Nord Amèrica.* Edited by Nathaniel B. Smith, Josep M. Solà-Solé, Mercè Vidal-Tibbits and Josep M. Massot i Muntaner. Montserrat: l'Abadia, 1985: 297–302.
75. ———. "Masks and Metamorphoses, Dreams and Illusions in Mercè Rodoreda's *Carnaval.*" *Catalan Review* 7, no. 1 (1993): 71–77.
76. ———, and Nancy Vosburg, eds. *The Garden Across the Border: Mercè Rodoreda's Fiction.* Selinsgrove: Susquehanna University Press, 1994.
77. Mees, Inge and Uta Winsheimer. "'Un roman c'est un miroir qu'on promène le long du chemin': Rodoredas *Mirall trencat* und die 'gebrochene Spiegel'-perspektive." *Zeitschrift fur Katalanistik* 1 (1988): 62–72.
78. Mencos, María Isidra. "Mercè Rodoreda: la mirada transgresora en *La meva Cristina i altres contes.*" *Actes del Setè Col.loqui d'Estudis Catalans a Nord-Amèrica, Berkeley 1993,* edited by August Bover-Font, Jaume Martí-Olivella and Mary Ann Newman, 167–74. Montserrat: l'Abadia, 1996.
79. Molas, Joaquim. "Mercè Rodoreda i la novel.la psicològica." *El Pont* 31 (1969): 12–17.
80. Möller-Soler, Lourdes. "El impacto de la guerra civil en la vida y obra de tres novelistas catalanas: Aurora Bertrana, Teresa Pàmies y Mercè Rodoreda." *Letras Femeninas* 12, no. 1–2 (1986): 34–44.
81. Montagut, Maria Cinta. "Una vida y una obra: Mercè Rodoreda." *La Bañera* 1 (1979): 12–15.

82. Nance, Kimberly A. "Things Fall Apart: Images of Disintegration in Mercè Rodoreda's *La plaça del Diamant.*" *Hispanófila* 34, no. 2 (1991): 67–76.
83. Navajas, Gonzalo. "La microhistoria y Cataluña en *El carrer de les camèlies* de Mercè Rodoreda." *Hispania* 74, no. 4 (1991): 848–59.
84. ———. "Normative Order and the Catalan *Heimat* in Mercè Rodoreda's *Mirall trencat.*" In *The Garden,* 98–109.
85. Navarro, Josep. "Ruptura i linealitat temporal als contes de Mercè Rodoreda." In *Actes del Tercer Col.loqui Internacional de Lengua i Literatura Catalanes,* edited by R. B. Tate and Alan Yates, 301–309. Oxford: Dolphin, 1976.
86. Nichols, Geraldine Cleary. "Exile, Gender, and Mercè Rodoreda." *MLN* 101 (1986): 405–17.[48]
87.———. "Sex, the Single Girl, and Other Mésalliances in Rodoreda and Laforet." *Anales de la Literatura Española Contemporánea* 12, no. 1–2 (1987): 123–40.[49]
88.———. "Writers, Wantons, Witches: Woman and the Expression of Desire in Rodoreda." *Catalan Review* 2, no. 2 (1987): 171–80.
89. ———. "'Mitja poma, mitja taronja': génesis y destino literarios de la catalana contemporánea." In *Literatura de dones: una visió del món,* 121–55. Barcelona: La Sal, 1988.[50]
90. ———. Stranger than Fiction: Fantasy in Short Stories by Matute, Rodoreda, Riera." *Monographic Review* 4 (1988): 33–42.[51]
91. Oriol i Giralt, Joan. *"Mirall trencat" de Mercè Rodoreda.* Barcelona: Andros, 1988.
92. Ortega, José. "Mujer, guerra y neurosis en dos relatos de Mercè Rodoreda. (*La plaza del Diamante* y *La calle de las Camelias*)." *Cuadernos Hispanoamericanos: Revista Mensual de Cultura Hispánica* 339 (1978): 503–12.[52]
93. Pavía-Sesma, Elena. "No-aceptación y búsqueda de identidad en *La plaza del Diamante* o 'quien no me acepta me duplica.'" *Cine-Lit: Essays on Peninsular Film and Fiction,* edited by George Cabello-Catellet, Jaume Martí-Olivella and Guy H. Wood, 108–11. Corvallis: Oregon State University, 1992.
94. Pérez, Janet. "Metamorphosis as a Protest Device in Catalan Feminist Writing: Rodoreda and Oliver." *Catalan Review* 2, no. 2 (1987): 181–98.
95. ———. "The Most Significant Writer in Catalan." In *Contemporary Women Writers of Spain.* Boston: Twayne Publishers, 1988.
96. ———. "Time and Symbol, Life and Death, Decay and Regeneration: Vital Cycles and the Round of Seasons in Mercè Rodoreda's *La mort i la primavera.*" *Catalan Review* 5, no. 1 (1991): 179–96.
97. ———. "Presence of the Picaresque and the Quest-Romance in Mercè Rodoreda's *Quanta, quanta guerra . . . .*" *Hispania* 76, no. 3 (1993): 428–38.
98. ———. "Gothic Spaces, Transgressions and Apparitions in *Mirall trencat:* Rodoreda's Adaptation of the Paradigm." In *The Garden,* 85–97.
99. Pessarrodona, Marta.[53] "Les dones a l'obra de Mercè Rodoreda." *Serra d'Or* 290 (1983): 17–19.
100. Poch i Bullich, Joaquim and Conxa Planas i Planas. *Dona i psicoanàlisi a l'obra de Mercè Rodoreda: un estudi del narcissisme femení.* Barcelona: Promociones Publicaciones Universitarias, 1987.

101. ———. "El fet femení en els textos de Mercè Rodoreda (una reflexió des de la psicoanàlisi)." *Catalan Review* 2, no. 2 (1987): 199–224.
102. Pope, Randolph D. "Mercè Rodoreda's Subtle Greatness." In *Women Writers of Contemporary Spain: Exiles in the Homeland,* edited by Joan L. Brown, 116–35. Newark: University of Delaware Press, 1991.
103. ———. "*Aloma*'s Two Faces and the Character of Her True Nature." In *The Garden.* 135–47.
104. Porrúa, María del Carmen. "Tres novelas de la guerra civil." *Cuadernos Hispanoamericanos: Revista Mensual de Cultura Hispánica* 474 (1989): 45–57.
105. ———. "La configuración espacial en discursos femeninos: Pardo Bazán, Martín Gaite, Rodoreda." *Filologia* 26, no. 1–2 (1993): 291–99.
106. Quintana, Angel and Imma Merino. "Dues propostes cinematogràfiques sobre la mirada de Mercè Rodoreda." *Revista de Girona* 157 (1993): 192–99.
107. Resina, Joan Ramon. "The Link in Consciousness: Time and Community in Rodoreda's *La plaça del Diamant.*" *Catalan Review* 2, no. 2 (1987): 225–46.
108. ———. "Detective Formula and Parodic Reflexivity: *Crim.*" In *The Garden,* 119–34.
109. Rhodes, Elizabeth. "The Salamander and the Butterfly." In *The Garden,* 162–187.
110. Roca Mussons, Maria A. *Construzioni simboliche nel romanzo di Mercè Rodoreda 'La plaça del Diamant'*. Sassari: Centro Stampa, 1986.[54]
111.———. "La colomba nera: dall vermouth all'acido muriatico." *Codici del Gusto,* edited by Maria Grazia Profeti, 314–44. Milano: Franco Argelino, 1992.
112. ———. "Novalis e M. Rodoreda: Il Fiore Azurro." In *La Cultura Catalana tra l'Umanesimo e il Barocco,* edited by Carlos Romero and Rosend Arquès. Padua: Editoriale Programma, 1994. 495–98.
113. Rodríguez, María Pilar. "Experiencias, literatura y cine. Traducciones y traiciones en *La plaça del Diamant.*" *Anuario de cine y literatura en español* 1 (1996): 118–32.
114. Roselló Bover, Pere. "Mercè Rodoreda i *El manuscrit trobat a Saragossa.*" *Revista de Catalunya* 108 (1996): 118–32.
115. Rueda, Ana. "Mercè Rodoreda: From Traditional Tales to Modern Fantasy." In *The Garden,* 201–22.
116. Saludes i Amat, Anna Maria.[55] "Suggestioni Lulliane in Mercè Rodoreda: 'Aloma' in *Aloma.*" *Annali Instituto Universitario Orientale* 34, no. 1 (1992): 433–43.
117. ———. "Una passió secreta de Mercè Rodoreda: el teatre." *Revista de Catalunya,* 76 (1993): 121–29.
118.———."Teatre i narració: possibles interrelacions en l'obra de Mercè Rodoreda." In *La Cultura Catalana tra l'Umanesimo e il Barocco.* Edited by Carlos Romero and Rosend Arquès. Padua: Editoriale Programma, 1994. 495–98.
119. Sanders-Terhorst, Christa. "Mercè Rodoreda, *La plaza del Diamante.*" *Hispanorama* 58 (1991): 77–80.
120. Scarlett, Elizabeth A.[56] "Mercè Rodoreda." In *Under Construction: The Body in Spanish Novels.* Charlottesville and London: University Press of Virginia, 1994.

121. ———. "'Vinculada a les flors': Flowers and the Body in *Jardí vora el mar* and *Mirall trencat*." In *The Garden*, 73–84.
122. Sobrer, Josep Miquel. "L'artifici de *La plaça del Diamant*, un estudi linguistic." In *In memoriam Carles Riba*. Edited by Institut d'Estudis Hel.lènics, Departament de Filologia Catalana, 363–75. Esplugues de Llobregat: Ariel, 1973.
123. ———. "Gender and Personality in Rodoreda's Short Fiction." In *The Garden*, 188–200.
124. Solé i Oltra, Xavier and Rosé Tintó i Gimbernat. "Els símbols en l'obra de Mercè Rodoreda: el ganivet i les estrelles." *Antipodas* 5 (1993): 203–21.
125. Soler i Marcet, Maria Lourdes. "Mercè Rodoreda: Eine Schriftstellerin im Exil." *Die horen* 35 (1990): 157–61.
126. Triadú, Joan. "Una novel.la excepcional: *La plaça del Diamant* de Mercè Rodoreda." In *Llegir com viure*. Barcelona: Fontanella, 1963.[57]
127. ———. "Panorama de la novel.la catalana" *Serra d'Or* 120 (1969): 63–65.
128. ———. "Aparició de *La plaça del Diamant*." In *La novel.la catalana de postguerra*. Barcelona: Edicions 62, 1982.
129. ———. "El com i el què de *La plaça del Diamant*." In *La novel.la catalana de postguerra*. Barcelona: Edicions 62, 1982.
130. ———. "*La plaça del Diamant* en l'excepcionalitat." In *La novel.la catalana de postguerra*. Barcelona: Edicions 62, 1982.
131. ———. "Mercè Rodoreda després de *La plaça del Diamant*." In *La novel.la catalana de postguerra*. Barcelona: Edicions 62, 1982.
132. Varderi, Alejandro. "Mercè Rodoreda: més enllà del jardí." *Catalan Review* 2, no. 2 (1987): 263–71.
133. Vives, Lluïsa. "*La meva Cristina i altres contes* dins l'obra de Mercè Rodoreda." *Nous Horitzons* 14 (1968): 45–48.
134. Vosburg, Nancy.[58] "The Roots of Alienation: Rodoreda's *Viatges i flors*." In *The Garden*, 148–61.
135. ———, and Kathleen McNerney, eds. *The Garden Across the Border: Mercè Rodoreda's Fiction*. Selinsgrove: Susquehanna University Press, 1994.
136. Waldman, Gloria F. "Vindicación feminista: Lidia Falcón, Esther Tusquets y Mercè Rodoreda." *La Torre* 115 (1982): 177–85.
137. Wyers, Frances. "A Woman's Voices: Mercè Rodoreda's *La plaça del Diamant*." In *Actes del Segon Col.loqui d'Estudis Catalans a Nord-Amèrica*, edited by Manuel Duran, Albert Porqueras-Mayo and Josep Roca-Pons, 365–75. Montserrat: l'Abadia, 1982.[59]
138. Zimmerman, Marie-Claire. "La reconstruction romanesque du lien familiel dans *La plaça del Diamant* de Mercè Rodoreda." *Iberica*, n. s. 1 (1992): 187–98.

Biographies and Interviews

139. Arnau, Carme. *Mercè Rodoreda*. Barcelona: Edicions 62, 1992.
140. Casals i Couturier, Montserrat. *Mercè Rodoreda: contra la vida, la literatura*. Barcelona: Edicions 62, 1991.[60]
141. Castellet, Josep Maria. "Mercè Rodoreda." In *Els escenaris de la memòria*. Barcelona: Edicions 62, 1988.
142. Ibarz, Mercè. *Mercè Rodoreda*. Barcelona: Empúries, 1991.

143. Murià, Anna. "Mercè o la vida dolorosa." *Catalan Review* 2, no. 2 (1987): 17–26.[61]
144. Oller, Dolors and Carme Arnau. "L'entrevista que mai no va sortir." Suplemento "Cultura y arte." *La Vanguardia,* 2 July 1991, 4–6.
145. Porcel, Baltasar. "Mercè Rodoreda o la força lírica." In *Grans catalans d'ara.* Barcelona: Destino, 1972.[62]
146. Roig, Montserrat. "L'alè poètic de Mercè Rodoreda." In *Retrats Paral.lels.* Vol. 2, 163–77. Montserrat: l'Abadia, 1976.[63]

Index of Works by Mercè Rodoreda and Their Criticism

This index lists all the criticism discussing each of Rodoreda's works. Each critical work is identified by its entry number in the bibliography. In some cases, if an article mentions a work only briefly, without analyzing it, that article does not appear in the list corresponding to that work.

(Un dia): Entry 106
Viatges i flors: Entries 6, 11, 16, 95, 102, 112, 134.
Vint-i-dos contes: Entries 4, 14, 37, 56, 75, 85, 86, 88, 95, 102, 123, 124, 125.

NOTES

This study and the bibliography that follows are part of a larger and more comprehensive study, *La crítica frente a la obra de Mercè Rodoreda: Bibliografía selecta y comentada,* which received the 1996 Premi Mercè Rodoreda. This work will soon be published by the Fundació Mercè Rodoreda. In this complete version of the bibliography, I comment on 148 critical works, including six doctoral dissertations. I also indicate research currently in progress on Rodoreda's work.

In the present bibliography, four dissertations, whose authors have published other studies on Rodoreda, are cited in a subsequent note. Two other dissertations do not appear in any subsequent notes, and thus I cite them here: Isabel Guerra McSpaden, "Dos voces femeninas desde el exilio" (Ph.D. diss., Texas Tech University, 1991); María del Mar Martínez Rodríguez, "El lenguaje del autodescubrimiento en la narrativa de Mercè Rodoreda y Carmen Martín Gaite" (Ph.D. diss., University of Wisconsin-Madison, 1988).

The present bibliography has been translated from Spanish by Patricia A. Heid, University of California at Berkeley.

1. In the case of Catalonia, where many brief articles have been published in general-interest magazines and newspapers, writers tend to paraphrase the studies of Carme Arnau, and usually, though not always, explicitly cite her as a source.

2. This is the case of brief newspaper reviews, such as Stephen Wall, "Lost for Words: *The Pigeon Girl,*" review of *La plaça del Diamant, The Observer,* 2 July 1967, 21 and Giuseppe Tavani, "*Piazza del Diamante:* un romanzo che 'cattura' al lettore," *Paese sera,* 25 May 1970; or articles such as Joan Triadú, "Marits i amants en termes literaris," *Serra d'Or* 123 (1969): 86, in which Rodoreda is mentioned in the space of only a few sentences. My exclusion of these articles does not imply any kind of disagreement with their content, but rather a preference for other, more lengthy and analytical studies, which have developed the same ideas in more detail.

3. See the articles by Bergmann (entry 16), Martí-Olivella (entry 68), and Nichols (entry 86), among others.

4. See Anna Murià, *Mercè Rodoreda: cartes a Anna Murià, 1939–1956* (Barcelona: l'Eixample, 1991), 26–28.

5. A flagrant example of this occurs in the widely consulted history of literature published by Ariel. In the volume dedicated to twentieth-century literature, Mercè Rodoreda is not even mentioned. See Santos Sanz Villanueva, *Historia de la literatura española, 6/2,* 4th ed. (Barcelona: Ariel, 1991).

6. I am referring only to those articles with the specific characteristics I have cited, and which are thus included in this project. Among the thirteen I mention here, two are by Carme Arnau herself. These consist of the introduction to the first volume of the *Obres completes* and "Una segona edició en veu baixa" (see note 36). It is somewhat surprising that only two of these thirteen works focus exclusively on *La plaça del Diamant* (entries 122 and 126). The others either have as their focus stories from the various collections (entries 63 and 133), *El carrer de les camèlies* (entry 64), and *Jardí vora el mar*

(entry 72), or they provide a brief review of various works (entries 32, 55, 79, 92 and 127).

7. In the second, third and fourth annual meetings of the North American Catalan Society, researchers such as Bieder, Krogstad, and McNerney presented papers about Rodoreda, which were published in the *Actes* (Proceedings) of the 1982, 1983 and 1985 annual meetings. Two other important researchers specializing in Rodoreda, Nichols and Glenn, began to publish articles on her work in 1986. One isolated and earlier case is Forrest's first article, published in 1978 (entry 44).

8. I should point out that although Carbonell published this book in Catalonia, she obtained her doctorate at the University of Indiana, where she wrote her doctoral dissertation on Mercè Rodoreda.

9. See the reviews by Nichols of the following works: *Mercè Rodoreda: contra la vida, la literatura,* by Montserrat Casals i Couturier, and *Mercè Rodoreda,* by Mercè Ibarz, in *Hispania* 75, no. 5 (1992): 1183–84.

10. To cite only a few examples, Kristeva's influence is evident in the articles by Bergmann, Carbonell, McGiboney, Martí-Olivella (who also uses Irigaray, Dale, and Jardine), and Scarlett, among others. The influence of Gilbert and Gubar and/or Miller is seen in the articles by Glenn, Nichols, and Wyers. Bergmann also utilizes Chodorow. Other researchers clearly use a feminist perspective to approach Rodoreda's work, although they do not explicitly align themselves with a particular theory. This is the case of Bieder, Stephen M. Hart, Hess, and McNerney.

11. For example, the study by Arnau, and that by Poch and Planas, although the latter authors also base their study on Klein and Groddeck. Busquets, who has published articles in several countries, also uses Freud and Jung as a starting point for analysis.

12. The studies by Albrecht and Lunn (entry 1), Gamisans (entry 46), and Sobrer (entry 122) are examples of this type of approach.

13. The reception of Arnau's criticism by other critics has been somewhat polemical. Initially it was considered to be indisputable, an opinion which continues to prevail among the majority of critics in Catalonia, where Arnau is frequently quoted and paraphrased. Over time, however, as critics have developed various theoretical perspectives, they have refuted some of Arnau's hypotheses, especially those concerned with Rodoreda's last two novels, *Quanta, quanta guerra . . .* and *La mort i la primavera*. Arnau bases her analysis of these works on Rodoreda's attraction to the occult, especially alchemy and the Rosicrucian sect, and she interprets Rodoreda's symbols in accordance with this premise. Recent criticism, however, has either conceded far less importance to these influences, or has completely ignored them, proposing instead archetypal, feminist, and/or comparative interpretations (see the articles by Bieder, Cabré i Monné, Esteban, Forrest, and Pérez, among others, entries 21, 28, 41, 45, and 97, respectively). Another assumption being debated by critics is the division of Rodoreda's oeuvre into two distinctive stages, a realist stage, and another dominated by fantasy. In addition, Arnau has been accused of having an excessively Freudian perspective (Rhodes, 162) and attempting to establish "universal criteria that eliminate . . . the contradictions and shades of difference from the discourse" of Rodoreda (Carbonell, *La plaça del Diamant,* (8). Arnau's pioneering work is, nevertheless, very valuable, and is recognized as such by all Rodoreda scholars. We must keep in mind that Rodoreda was familiar with Arnau's

work, and held it in high esteem. On the other hand, it is logical that the diverse methods of criticism now in existence would cause scholars to take issue with many of her interpretations, and propose interesting alternatives. In my opinion, the possiblity for divergent approaches and even for conflict between different critical perspectives is not only unavoidable, but it enriches our academic dialogue. For example, one can observe yet another case of mutually contradictory conclusions in the articles by Esteban and Forrest on *Quanta, quanta guerra . . .* (entries cited above).

14. Scholars such as Bertrand, Bieder, Campillo y Gustà, Forrest, Lucio, McNerney, Roca, Scarlett, Solé i Tintó, etc., have pursued this line of criticism.

15. Examples are found in Arnau, Esteban, and Forrest, among others.

16. See González-Castro (entry 54) and McGiboney (entry 73).

17. The articles by Bergmann (15, 16, 17), Fayad (43), Martínez Romero (71), Nichols (87, 89 and 90), Pérez (94), Porrúa (104) and Waldmann (136) follow this line of criticism.

18. The picaresque: Glenn (50), Marco (64) and Pérez (97); the Gothic novel: Pérez (98); the detective novel: Gamisans (47) and Resina (108); Ramon Llull: Saludes i Amat (116); *Bearn,* by Villalonga: Altisent (2); contemporary Catalan literature: Triadú (128) and Berenguel (14); *A Midsummer Night's Dream,* by Shakespeare: McNerney (75).

19. The Bible: Cabré i Monné (28), Martí-Olivella (67), Nichols (89) and Rueda (115); fairytales: Bergmann (15), Martí-Olivella (67), and Rueda (115).

20. For example, in the articles by Bergmann (17), Grilli (56), Pope (103) and Triadú (127).

21. See the articles by Ball (13), Patricia Hart (58), Quintana and Merino (106) and Rodríguez (113).

22. Examples of this type of study are Möller-Soler (80), Ortega (92), and Porrúa (104).

23. See Faulí (42), Marco (64) and Triadú (131).

24. See, for example, the article by Bou, (entry 23).

25. Examples of these kinds of interpretative approaches are found in the articles by Bergmann (16), Lucarda (62), Navajas (83), Nichols (86), Resina (107) and Vosburg (134), among others.

26. This is the case with respect to *La plaça del Diamant,* the work of Rodoreda most often discussed by critics. Several articles analyzing aspects of this novel that had previously not received much critical attention or elaboration were published in 1994. Notable examples are the works of Patricia Hart (58) and Quintana and Merino (106), which discuss in detail the cinematographic adaptation. Another example of a reinterpretation is the article by Rhodes about the story "La salamandra," in which she reconsiders the question of genre in Rodoreda—a question that has been treated extensively, but that in this case results in an original approach (109).

27. I am referring to the valuable article by Vosburg, entry 134. Of course, other critics, such as Arnau, Bergmann, and Soler i Marcet, have discussed *Viatges i flors,* but without making it the sole focus of an article or book.

28. From *La meva Cristina i altres contes,* critics tend to privilege those stories related to the theme of metamorphosis, neglecting other excellent stories, such as "Un ramat de bens de tots colors," and "Aquella paret, aquella mimosa." From *Semblava de seda,* critics show a marked preference

for "Paràlisi." From *Vint-i-dos contes,* in contrast, critics tend to treat a variety of stories.

29. The Fundació Mercè Rodoreda generously made this correspondence available to me during the summer of 1994. I hope that it will soon undertake the publication of this correspondence, since it is truly fascinating—not only does it better acquaint us with the author, but it also allows us to observe the development of her literary style. I believe that it was in these letters, and not only in the stories she had written before 1962, in which Rodoreda gradually forged the literary voice, which would come to fruition in *La plaça del Diamant.* Her passion for detail, the meticulous description of objects, the visual and tactile sensitivity so characteristic of her style, are already evident in these letters. Moreover, the description of her life in isolation and her reserve as a person is comparable to that of some of her characters.

30. As I have already mentioned, Bou has written an article about the representation of space in *La plaça del Diamant,* and other critics have also treated this theme with respect to other works, but there is still much to be said concerning it.

31. Examples of this line of criticism, which problematizes the use of history in Rodoreda, are the articles by Navajas, entries 83 and 84.

32. Much attention has been devoted to this theme by Scarlett in a long and interesting analysis that discusses four of Rodoreda's novels (entry 120). There remain, however, other works and other aspects of this theme to discuss. One, suggested by Arnau but not discussed in detail, is the role of food and nourishment. Roca Mussons has an interesting yet brief analysis of this topic with respect to *La plaça del Diamant* (entry 111). With respect to this work and others, new readings relating to this theme could be done.

33. As I have already indicated, Gamisans and Resina study this topic with respect to two novels, *Jardí vora el mar* and *Crim* respectively (entries 46 and 108). In my opinion, these articles signal a promising approach for future critical studies.

34. A previous version of this article, shorter in length, is contained in Jane W. Albrecht and Patricia V. Lunn, "A note on the language of *La plaça del Diamant,*" *Catalan Review* 2, no. 2 (1987): 59–64. An almost literal translation is also available in Patricia V. Lunn and Jane W. Albrecht, "*La plaça del Diamant:* Linguistic Causes and Literary Effect," *Hispania* 75, no. 3 (1992): 492–99.

35. This book developed from Carme Arnau's doctoral dissertation. As is normal practice among literary scholars, Arnau published several articles and introductions while this book was being prepared for publication, and even after it was published. These shorter works summarize or transcribe portions of the book, and I list them here. However, I highly recommend this book, as well as the book listed in entry 11, for a more comprehensive understanding of Arnau's perspective on Rodoreda's work.

Other versions of this work published by Arnau: "Nota introductòria," in *Obres completes* (Barcelona: Edicions 62, 1984, first edition, 1976), 1:5–46, is a shortened version; "La obra de Mercè Rodoreda," *Cuadernos Hispanoamericanos: Revista Mensual de Cultura Hispánica* 383 (1983): 239–58 is a shortened version, which also includes the analysis of *Viatges i flors* and *Quanta, quanta guerra* . . . contained in the book listed in entry 11 of this bibliography; "Una segona edició 'en veu baixa': *Vint-i-dos contes* de Mercè Rodoreda," *Els Marges* 1–2, no. 2 (1974): 105–14; "El temps i el record a *Mirall trencat,*" *Els Marges* 6 (1976): 124–28.

36. Other publications that reproduce or summarize parts of this book are "L'àngel a les novel.les de Mercè Rodoreda," *Serra d'Or* 290 (1983): 20–23; "El viatge iniciàtic: *Quanta, quanta guerra* . . . de Mercè Rodoreda," *Catalan Review* 2, no. 2 (1987): 65–82.

37. A shorter version of this article can be found in "*Isabel i Maria* o la novel.la com alquímia." In *La Cultura Catalana tra l'Umanesimo e il Barroco,* ed. Carlos Romero and Rosend Arquès (Padua: Editoriale Programma, 1994), 475–79.

38. Bergmann has also written the entry for Mercè Rodoreda in Kathleen McNerney and Cristina Enríquez de Salamanca, eds., *Double Minorities of Spain: A Bio-Bibliographical Guide to Women Writers of the Catalan, Galician and Basque Countries* (New York: Modern Language Association, 1994), 324–30.

39. This abbreviation refers to Kathleen McNerney and Nancy Vosburg, eds., *The Garden Across the Border: Mercè Rodoreda's Fiction,* (Selinsgrove, Pa.: Susquehanna University Press, 1994).

40. This also appears in the Nathaniel B. Smith, Josep M. Solà-Solé, Mercè Vidal-Tibbits, and Josep Massot i Muntaner, eds., *Actes del Quart Col.loqui d'Estudis Catalans a Nord Amèrica* (Montserrat: l'Abadia, 1985), 303–19.

41. This also appears in Philip D. Rasico and Curt J. Wittlin, eds., *Actes del Cinquè Col.loqui d'Estudis Catalans a Nord Amèrica,* (Montserrat: l'Abadia, 1988), 267–82. The article "*La mort i la primavera* de Mercè Rodoreda" (*Cuadernos Hispanoamericanos: Revista Mensual de Cultura Hispánica* 467 (1989): 117–22) is an English translation of the sections in the article cited in this and the subsequent entry (entries 26 and 27) that discuss this particular novel.

42. This article also appears in Carlos Romero and Rosend Arquès, eds. *La Cultura Catalana tra l'Umanesimo e il Barroco* (Padua: Editoriale Programma, 1994), 481–90.

43. Carbonell wrote her doctoral dissertation on Mercè Rodoreda: "Beyond the Anxiety of Patriarchy: Language, Identity and Otherness in Mercè Rodoreda's Fiction" (Ph.D. diss., Indiana University, 1993).

44. Another book on Rodoreda's work by Carles Cortés is forthcoming.

45. Martí-Olivella is the editor of this issue of the *Catalan Review,* which is wholly dedicated to Mercè Rodoreda, as well as the author of the prologue on pages 9 to 15. His doctoral dissertation was on the work of Rodoreda and Cabrera Infante: "Estructuras joyceanas en la narrativa catalana y latinoamericana contemporánea" (Ph.D. diss., University of Illinois at Urbana-Champaign, 1989).

46. McGiboney wrote her doctoral dissertation on Mercè Rodoreda, as well as other female authors: "Language, Sexuality, and Subjectivity in Selected Works by Ana María Matute, Carmen Laforet and Mercè Rodoreda" (Ph.D. diss., State University of New York, Stony Brook, 1994).

47. McNerney writes the introduction of *The Garden* on pages 7 to 12. She also lists and briefly summarizes Rodoreda's published works in "Mercè Rodoreda," in *Women Writers of Spain: An Annotated Bio-Bibliographical Guide,* ed. Carolyn L. Galerstein and Kathleen McNerney (Westport, Conn.: Greenwood Press, 1986), 273–75. The article listed in this entry is also found integrated into another article, of broader scope, which discusses the works

of Montserrat Roig, Maria Antònia Oliver, Carme Riera and Helena Valentí. See "A Feminist Literary Renaissance in Catalonia," in *Feminine Concerns in Contemporary Spanish Fiction by Women*, ed. Roberto C. Manteiga, Carolyn Galerstein and Kathleen McNerney (Potomac, Md.: Scripta Humanistica, 1988), 124–33.

48. Shorter versions of this article are found in: *Monographic Review* 2 (1986): 189–97; "El exilio y el género en Mercè Rodoreda," in *Des/cifrar la diferencia: narrativa femenina de la España contemporánea* (Madrid: Siglo XXI, 1992), 114–32.

49. Also published as "Sexo, mujer soltera, mésalliances en Rodoreda y Laforet," in *Des/cifrar la diferencia: narrativa femenina de la España contemporánea* (Madrid: Siglo XXI, 1992), 133–51.

50. Also appears in *Anthropos* 60–61 (1986): 118–25.

51. This article, with a more extensive introduction, can also be found in "Limits Unlimited: The Strategic Use of Fantasy in Contemporary Women's Fiction of Spain," in *Cultural and Historical Grounding for Hispanic and Luso-Brazilian Feminist Literary Criticism*, ed. Hernán Vidal (Minneapolis: Institute for the Study of Ideologies and Literatures, 1989), 107–28. The introductory section emphasizes the importance of the socio-cultural background of Barcelona for all of these female writers, and explains the feminist theoretical base used by the author of this study.

52. This also appears in Janet W. Pérez, ed., *Novelistas femeninas de la posguerra española*, (Madrid: José Porrúa Turranzas, 1983), 71–83.

53. Pessarrodona has published a brief commentary about *Mirall trencat* in "Recompongamos los fragmentos: the last novel of Mercè Rodoreda," *La Bañera* 1 (1979): 17.

54. An abbreviated version of this book is found in "Aspectes del sistema simbòlic a *La plaça del Diamant*," *Catalan Review* 2, no. 2 (1987): 247–61.

55. With regard to Mercè Rodoreda's collaborations in *Clarisme* in 1933–34, see "Mercè Rodoreda, periodista," *Revista del Centro de Lectura de Reus* 241 (1972): 1324–26.

56. Scarlett wrote her doctoral dissertation on Mercè Rodoreda, Emilia Pardo Bazán, and Rosa Chacel: "Spanish Woman Writers and the Reconquest of Inner Space: Gender, the Body and Sexuality in Novels by Emilia Pardo Bazán, Rosa Chacel and Mercè Rodoreda" (Ph.D. diss., Harvard University, 1992).

57. This also appears in "La plaça del Diamant de Mercè Rodoreda," *Guia de literatura catalana contemporània*, Ed. Jordi Castellanos (Barcelona: Edicions 62, 1973), 401–407.

58. Nancy Vosburg is the author of a bio-bibliographic study on Rodoreda: "Mercè Rodoreda," in *Spanish Woman Writers: A Bio-Bibliographical Source Book*, ed. Linda Gould Levine, Ellen Engelson Marson and Gloria Feiman Waldman (Westport, Conn.: Greenwood Press, 1993), 415–28.

59. This also appears in *Kentucky Romance Quarterly* 30, no. 3 (1983): 301–309.

60. A previous version, in briefly summarized form, is found in "El 'Rosebud' de Mercè Rodoreda," *Catalan Review* 2, no. 2 (1987): 27–47.

61. This brief article is extracted from the prologue to *Mercè Rodoreda: cartes a Anna Murià, 1939–1956* (Barcelona: L'Eixample, 1991).

62. This also appears in *Serra d'Or* (1966): 231–35.

63. A shorter version of this interview appears in "El aliento poético de Mercè Rodoreda," *Triunfo* 573 (1973): 35–39.

Works Cited

Note: For works by or about Rodoreda, see Mencos. This bibliography lists other works cited in the articles, and works about Rodoreda only if they are not covered by Mencos. (KM)

Armstrong, Nancy. "A Language of One's Own: Communication-Modeling Systems in *Mrs. Dalloway*." *Language and Style* 16 (1983): 343–60.

Bachelard, Gaston. *El aire y los sueños.* México: Fondo de cultura económica, 1986.

———. *The Poetics of Space.* New York: Orion Press, 1964. Originally published as *La Poétique de l'espace.* Paris: Presses Universitaires de France, 1957.

Baker, Mona. "Corpus Linguistics and Translation Studies. Implications and Applications." In *Text and Technology,* edited by Mona Baker, Gill Francis, and Elena Tognini-Bonelli, 233–252. Amsterdam and Philadelphia: John Benjamins, 1993.

Bakhtin, Mikhail M. "Discourse in the Novel." In *The Dialogic Imagination: Four Essays by M. M. Bakhtin,* edited by Michael Holquist, translated by Caryl Emerson and Michael Holquist, 259–422. Austin: University of Texas Press, 1981.

Ball, Leah. "El lenguaje de la división y el silencio en Rodoreda." In *Cine-Lit: Essays on Peninsular Film and Fiction,* edited by George Cabello-Castellet, Jaume Martí-Olivella, and Guy Wood, 92–99. Corvallis: Oregon State University Press, 1992.

Barthes, Roland. *The Fashion System.* Translated by Matthew Ward and Richard Howard. New York: Hill and Wang, 1983.

Busquets i Grabulosa, Lluís. "Mercè Rodoreda, passió eterna i fràgil." *Plomes catalanes contemporànies,* 57–64. Barcelona: Mall, 1980.

Broeck, Raymond van den. "The Limits of Translatability Exemplified by Metaphor Translation." *Poetics Today* 2, no. 4 (1981): 73–87.

Calzada Pérez, María. "Trusting the Translator." *Babel* 39, no. 3 (1993): 158-74.

Charlon, Anne. *La condició de la dona en la narrativa catalana.* Barcelona: Edicions 62, 1990.

Chevalier, J., and A. Gheerbrant. *Diccionario de los símbolos.* 1969; translation, Barcelona: Herder, 1991.

Cixous, Hélène. "The Laugh of the Medusa." In *New French Feminisms,* edited by Elaine Marks and Isabelle de Courtivron, 245–265. Amherst: University of Massachusetts Press, 1980.

———. and Catherine Clément. *The Newly Born Woman.* Translated by Betsy Wing. Minneapolis: University of Minnesota Press, 1986.

Clarasó, Mercè. "The Two Worlds of Mercè Rodoreda." In *Women Writers in Twentieth-Century Spain and Spanish America,* edited by Catherine Davies, 43–52. Lewiston, Me.: Mellen Press, 1993.

Cohn, Dorrit. *Transparent Minds: Narrative Modes for Presenting Consciousness in Fiction.* Princeton N.J.: Princeton University Press, 1978.

Compton's Interactive Encyclopedia. 1994.

Cukor, George. *The Women.* Film. Metro-Goldwyn-Mayer, 1939. Starring Norma Shearer, Joan Crawford, Rosaline Russell, Joan Fontaine, and Paulette Goddard.

Davis, Robert Con, and Ronald Shleifer. *Contemporary Literary Criticism: Literature and Cultural Studies.* New York: Longman, 1994.

De Lauretis, Teresa. *Technologies of Gender: Essays on Theory, Film, and Fiction.* Bloomington: Indiana University Press, 1987.

Deleuze, Gilles, and Félix Guattari. *A Thousand Plateaus: Capitalism and Schizophrenia.* Translated by Brian Massumi. Minneapolis: University of Minnesota Press, 1987.

D'Hulst, Lieven. "Les variantes textuelles des traductions litteraires." *Poetics Today* 2, no. 4 (1981): 133–141.

Duch, Lluís. *Mircea Eliade: El retorn d'Ulisses a Itaca.* Montserrat: l'Abadia, 1983.

Duchêne, Roger. *L'impossible Marcel Proust.* Paris: Robert Lafont, 1994.

Eliade, Mircea. *Imágenes y símbolos.* Madrid: Taurus, 1955. Reprint 1983.

———. *Mito y realidad.* Barcelona: Labor, 1963. Reprint 1991.

———. *Le mythe de l'éternel retour.* Paris: Gallimard, 1949. Reprint 1969.

———. *Occultisme, sorcellerie et modes culturelles.* Paris: Gallimard, 1976.

———. *Lo sagrado y lo profano.* Barcelona: Labor, 1957. Reprint 1988.

Even-Zohar, Itamar. "Translation Theory Today: A Call for Transfer Theory." *Poetics Today* 2, no. 4 (1981): 1–7.

Flaubert, Gustave. *Madame Bovary.* Paris: Garnier, 1961.

Freud, Sigmund. *Beyond the Pleasure Principle.* New York: Norton, 1989.

Fried, Debra. "The Men in *The Women.*" In *Women and Film,* edited by Janet Todd, 43–68. New York and London: Holmes and Meier, 1988.

Fromm, Erich. *El lenguaje olvidado: Introducción a la comprensión de los sueños, mitos y cuentos de hadas.* Buenos Aires: Hachette, 1972 [1951].

Gennette, Gerard. *Figures III.* Paris: Seuil, 1972.

———. *Figures of Literary Discourse.* New York: Columbia University Press, 1986.

Gilbert, Sandra, and Susan Gubar. *The Madwoman in the Attic.* New Haven, Conn.: Yale University Press, 1979.

———. *No Man's Land: The Place of the Woman Writer in the Twentieth Century.* New Haven: Yale University Press, 1988.

Gilligan, Carol. *In a Different Voice: Psychological Theory and Women's Development.* Cambridge: Harvard University Press, 1982.

Grosz, Elizabeth. *Space, Time and Perversion: Essays on the Politics of Bodies.* New York: Routledge, 1995.

Has, Wojciech J. *Rekopis Znaleziony w Saragossie.* Film. Zespoly Filmwe, 1965. Starring Zbigniew Cybulski, Iga Cembrzynska, Joanna Jedryka, and Kazimierz Opalinski.

Heilbrun, Carolyn G. *Writing a Woman's Life.* New York: Ballantine, 1988.

Hermans, Theo, ed. *The Manipulation of Literature: Studies in Literary Translation.* New York: St. Martin's Press, 1985.

Hickey, Leo, Rosa Lorés, Hilaria Loya Gómez, and Antonio Gil de Carrasco. "A Pragmalinguistic Aspect of Literary Translation." *Babel* 39.2 (1993): 77–88.

Hirsch, Marianne. *The Mother/Daughter Plot: Narrative, Psychoanalysis, Feminism.* Bloomington: Indiana University Press, 1989.

Hollander, Anne. *Seeing through Clothes.* Berkeley: University of California Press, 1975. Reprint, 1993.

Homer. *The Odyssey.* Garden City, NY: Doubleday Anchor Books, 1963.

Irigaray, Luce. *This Sex Which Is Not One.* Translated by Catherine Porter. Ithaca: Cornell University Press, 1985.

———. *Speculum of the Other Woman.* Translated by Gillian Gill. Ithaca: Cornell University Press, 1985.

Jones, Margaret E. W. "Las novelistas españolas contemporáneas ante la crítica." *Letras femeninas* 9, no. 1 (1983): 22–34.

Jung, Carl G. *Símbolos de transformación.* Barcelona: Paidós, 1952. Reprint, 1982.

Klee, Paul. *On Modern Art.* London: Faber and Faber, 1948. Reprint, 1974.

Kloepfer, Rolf. "Intra- and Intercultural Translation." *Poetics Today* 2, no. 4 (1981): 29–37.

Kristeva, Julia. *La révolution du langage poétique.* Paris: Seuil, 1974.

———. *Le temps sensible: Proust et l'expérience littéraire.* Paris: Gallimard, 1994.

La Belle, Jenijoy. *Herself Beheld: The Literature of the Looking Glass.* Ithaca and London: Cornell University Press, 1988.

Lindenfeld, Jacqueline. "The Cross-Cultural Translation of Linguistic Routines." *Babel.* 39, no. 3 (1993): 151–57.

Lomholt, Karsten. "Problems of Intercultural Translation." *Babel* 37.1 (1991):28–35.

Manteiga, Roberto, Kathleen McNerney and Carolyn Galerstein, eds. *Feminine Concerns in Contemporary Spanish Fiction by Women.* Potomac, Md.: Scripta Humanistica, 1988.

Martín Gaite, Carmen. *La búsqueda de interlocutor y otras búsquedas.* Barcelona: Destino, 1982.

———. "El huerto cercado de Mercè Rodoreda," *Agua Pasada: Artículos, prólogos y discursos.* Barcelona: Anagrama, 1993.

Martí-Olivella, Jaume. "Paseo crítico e intertextual por el jardín edípico del cine español." *Letras peninsulares* (Spring 1994): 93-118.

Michaux, Henri. *Le jardin exalté.* Paris: Fata Morgana, 1983.

Miller, Jane. *Women Writing about Men.* New York: Pantheon, 1986.

Mitchell, W. J. T. "Against Comparison: Teaching Literature and the Visual Arts." In *Teaching Literature and Other Arts,* edited by Jean-Pierre Barricelli, Joseph Gibaldi, and Estella Lauter, 30–37. New York: Modern Language Association, 1990.

———. *Picture Theory.* Chicago: University of Chicago Press, 1994.

Monjo, Joan M. *Ducat d'ombres.* Valencia: Eliseu Climent, 1982.

Nida, Eugene A. "Science of Translation." *Language* 45 (1969): 483–498.

———. *Toward a Science of Translating, with Special Reference to Principles and Procedures Involved in Bible Translating.* Leiden: E. J. Brill, 1964.

Owens, Craig. "The Discourse of Others: Feminists and Postmodernism." In *The Anti-Aesthetic: Essays on Postmodern Culture,* edited by Hal Foster, 57–82. Seattle, WA: Bay Press, 1983.

Painter, George D. *Marcel Proust: A Biography.* 2 vols. New York: Random House, 1987.

Palau, Montserrat. "La matriu de la narrativa de Mercè Rodoreda." *Avui* (Barcelona) 21 December 1991, "Cultura," 19.

Paz, Octavio. *The Labyrinth of Solitude: Life and Thought in Mexico.* Translated by Helen R. Lane. New York: Grove Press, 1961.

Pérez, Janet. *Contemporary Women Writers of Spain.* Boston: G. K. Hall, 1988.

Pierce, James S. *Paul Klee and Primitive Art.* New York: Garland, 1976.

Porcel, Baltasar. "La dama entre las flores." *Destino* no. 1964 (22–28 May 1975): 47.

———. "Mercè Rodoreda, frente a los árboles." *Destino* no. 1689 (14 February 1970): 15.

Pratt, Annis. *Archetypal Patterns in Women's Fiction.* Bloomington: Indiana University Press, 1981.

Proust, Marcel. *In Search of Time Lost. Swann's Way.* Vol 1. Translated by C. K. Scott Moncrieff and Terence Kilmartin, revised by D. J. Enright. New York: Random House, 1992.

———. *Remembrance of Things Past.* Vol. 3. Translated by C. K. Scott Moncrieff, Terence Kilmartin, and Andreas Mayor. New York: Random House, 1981.

Rodríguez, María Pilar. "Experiencias, literatura y cine: Traducciones y traiciones en *La plaça del Diamant.*" *Anuario de cine y literatura en español.* Vol. I (1995): 111–20.

Rosenberg, Harold. *The De-Definition of Art.* Chicago: University of Chicago Press, 1972. Reprinted 1983.

Rubin, Gayle. "The Traffic in Women: Notes on the 'Political Economy' of Sex." In *Toward an Anthopology of Women,* Edited by Rayna Reiter, 157–210. New York: Monthly Review, 1975.

Saludes, Isabel. "Mercè Rodoreda, un ram de flors transparents." *Serra d'Or* no. 376 (April 1991): 43–48.

Seaton, Beverly. *The Language of Flowers: A History.* Charlottesville and London: University Press of Virginia, 1995.

Sempronio [pseud]. "Cuatro cuartillas: mis mujeres." *Tele/expres* (Barcelona) 10 October 1970, 6.

Shen, Dan. "Literalism: NON-Formal-Equivalence." *Babel* 35, no. 4 (1989): 219-235.

Showalter, Elaine. "Towards a Feminist Poetics." In *The New Feminist Criticism: Essays on Women, Literature, Theory,* 125–143. NewYork: Pantheon, 1985.

Smith, Johanna M. "Cooped up: Feminine Domesticity in Frankenstein." In *"Frankenstein" by Mary Shelley: Case Studies in Contemporary Criticism,* edited by Ross C. Murfin, 270–97. Boston: St. Martin's Press, 1992.

Steiner, George. *After Babel: Aspects of Language and Translation.* London: Oxford University Press, 1975.

Sternberg, Meir. "Polylingualism as Reality and Translation as Mimesis." *Poetics Today* 2.4 (1981): 221–239.

Tazi, Nadia. "Celestial Bodies: A Few Stops on the Way to Heaven." In *Fragments for a History of the Human Body: Part Two,* edited by Michel Feher, Ramona Naddaff, and Nadia Tazi, 518–552. New York: Zone, 1989.

Todorov, Tzvetan. *Genres in Discourse.* New York: Cambridge University Press, 1990.

———. *The Fantastic.* Ithaca: Cornell University Press, 1975.

Toury, Gideon. *Descriptive Translation Studies.* Amsterdam and Philadelphia: John Benjamins, 1995.

———. "Translated Literature: System, Norm, Performance: Towards a TT-Oriented Approach to Literary Translation." *Poetics Today* 2, no. 4 (1981): 9–27.

———. "Translation-Specific Lexical Items and Their Representation in the Dictionary." In *Meaning and Lexicography,* edited by Jerzy Tomaszczyk and Barbara Lewandowska-Tomaszczyk, 287–300. Amsterdam and Philadelphia: John Benjamins, 1990.

Ugarte, Michael. *Shifting Ground: Spanish Civil War Exile Literature.* Durham, N.C., and London: Duke University Press, 1989.

Van Buren, Jane Silverman. *The Modernist Madonna: Semiotics of the Maternal Metaphor.* Bloomington: Indiana University Press, 1989.

Varderi, Alejandro. *Anotaciones sobre el amor y el deseo.* Caracas: Academia Nacional de la Historia, 1986. See especially "Los dos caminos de Marcel," 15–21.

Warhol, Robyn R., and Diane Price Herndl, eds. *Feminisms: An Anthology of Literary Theory and Criticism.* New Brunswick, N.J.: Rutgers University Press, 1991.

Wittig, Monique. *The Straight Mind and Other Essays.* Boston: Beacon Press, 1992.

Wolfe, Tom. *The Painted Word.* New York: Bantam, 1976.

Woolf, Virginia. *A Room of One's Own.* New York: Harcourt Brace Jovanovich, 1929. Reprinted 1957.

List of Contributors

MICHELE ANDERSON is Assistant Professor of Modern Languages at Franklin College in Franklin, Indiana. Anderson discovered Mercè Rodoreda while studying Women's Literature under Dr. Frances Wyers at Indiana University. Dr. Wyers is also responsible for Anderson's interest in the "double self" and its relation to female identity. In addition to teaching French Language and Literature, Anderson teaches a comparative course on Canadian Women Writers, for which she recently received a research grant from the Canadian Embassy.

J.-VICENTE ANDREU-BESÓ is Professor of English and Translation in the Department of English and German Philology at the University of Valencia. His professional interests include comparative studies on translation and discourse analysis with emphasis on cultural and pragmalinguistic aspects of the language. He is co-editor of *English in Specific Settings* and *Lingüística aplicada en su contexto académico*.

MÓNICA AYALA is from Barranquilla, Columbia and received bachelor's degrees there in philosophy and literature in 1988 and in psychology in 1989. She earned a master's in Spanish at West Virginia University and a Ph.D. at the University of Miami with a dissertation on "El Espacio Hecho Palabra (Imágenes del sertão brasilero en Da Cunha, Guimarães Rosa and Vargas Llosa)." She has published several articles on Latin American Literature.

MARYELLEN BIEDER is Professor of Spanish and Adjunct Professor of Comparative Literture at Indiana Universty, Bloomington, where she teaches 19th- and 20th-century Spanish literature and European Realism and Naturalism. She writes on questions of gender, language, and body in Emilia Pardo Bazán, Carmen de Burgos, Mercè Rodoreda, and contemporary women authors from Spain. Her articles and chapters have appeared in numerous journals and books. She has edited a volume on Spanish women writers, "Writing Against the Current," for the *Indiana Journal of Hispanic Literatures* and written *Narrative Perspective in the Post-Civil War Novels of Francisco Ayala*. Her most recent work centers on Emilia Pardo Bazán.

NANCY L. BUNDY is a former Associate Professor of Spanish and French whose research focuses on the poetry of contemporary Spanish women. She has written on Ana María Fagundo and Ana Rossetti as well as on female poets who write in Catalan.

CARLES CORTÉS I ORTS was born in Alcoi and holds a degree in Catalan philology from the University of Alacant, where he now teaches. He is also the Linguistics Specialist for the Program of Linguistic Normalization at that university. He earned his *licenciatura* with a study of Mercè Rodoreda which was published as *Els protagonistes i el medi en la narrativa de Mercè Rodoreda* (Valencia, 1995). His doctoral thesis addresses Rodoreda's novels published previous to the Spanish Civil War.

JOSEFINA GONZÁLEZ is Assistant Professor at Agnes Scott College, and received her Ph.D. in Spanish Literature from New York University after working as a graphic artist in New York City for ten years. Previously, she was a studio artist and exhibited her work in several galleries. She received a master of fine arts in printmaking from Wayne State University, and most of her articles deal with issues relating the arts and literature.

JAUME MARTÍ-OLIVELLA holds degrees in English philology and Catalan literature from the University of Barcelona and in comparative literature from the University of Illinois. He is a founding member of the North American Catalan Society. Currently an Associate Professor of Spanish at Allegheny College, Martí-Olivella has published extensively on Catalan narrative, peninsular film, and literary theory. He has edited two special issues of the *Catalan Review:* "Homage to Mercè Rodoreda" (Barcelona, 1987) and "Women, History and Nation in the Fiction of Maria Aurèlia Capmany and Montserrat Roig" (Barcelona, 1993). He has also co-organized *CINE-LIT I, II* and *III* (First, Second and Third International Conference on Hispanic Film and Fiction, Portland, 1991, 1994, and 1997).

KATHLEEN MCNERNEY is Professor of Spanish and Benedum Distinguished Scholar at West Virginia University. Her publications include Latin American and Castilian literature, but most focus on Catalan women writers. She received her degrees at the University of New Mexico and studied in Barcelona and Girona. In 1990, she was awarded the Catalonia Prize for dissemination of Catalan culture. With Nancy Vosburg, she coedited *The Garden Across the Border: Mercè Rodoreda's Fiction* (1994) and with Cristina Enríquez de Salamanca, *Double Minorities of Spain: A Bio-Bibliographic Guide to Women Writers of the Catalan, Galician, and Basque Countries* (1994).

María Isidra Mencos was born in Barcelona, where she earned a B.A. at the University of Barcelona. Since 1992 she has studied at the University of California at Berkeley, where currently she is preparing her dissertation on the sublime and the carnivalesque in Spanish Romanticism. She won the Premi Mercè Rodoreda (1996) for her *La crítica frente a la obra de Mercè Rodoreda: Bibliografía selecta y comentada* and published the essay "Mercè Rodoreda: la mirada transgresora (en *La meva Cristina i altres contes*)" in the *Actes del Setè Col.loqui de la NACS* (1993).

Adela Robles Sáez was born in Alcoi and studied *filologia anglesa i italiana* at the University of Valencia. In 1995, she obtained her M.A. in comparative literature at West Virginia University, writing her thesis on the structural changes from novel to film in Rodoreda's *La plaça del Diamant.* She is currently working towards her Ph.D. at the University of California at Berkeley in romance languages and literatures. She is particularly interested in the interaction between linguistics and the literary text, and to that end she has contributed to DISE, a publication of the University of Valencia.

Alejandro Varderi is Assistant Professor of Spanish at Borough of Manhattan Community College of the City University of New York. His books of criticism include *Severo Sarduy y Pedro Almodóvar: del barroco al kitsch en la narrativa y el cine postmodernos, Anatomía de una seducción: reescrituras de lo femenino,* and *Anotaciones sobre el amor y el deseo.* His novels include *Para repetir una mujer* and *Amantes y reverentes.* He is currently working on a novel called *Origen final,* as well as on a book dealing with uses of popular culture and film in Spanish and Latin American fiction.

LISA VOLLENDORF is Visiting Assistant Professor of Spanish at Miami University of Ohio. She specializes in Golden Age literature and is working on a feminist study of bodily discourse in María de Zayas's *novelas.* She has published articles on María de Zayas and contemporary author Ramón Hernández.

NANCY VOSBURG is Associate Professor of Foreign Languages at Stetson University, where she teaches courses in peninsular literature and culture and the Women and Gender Studies Program. She has published several articles on various Spanish women writers in exile and coedited with Kathleen McNerney *The Garden Across the Border: Mercè Rodoreda's Fiction.* Other scholarly interests include contemporary Spanish women writers and women's erotic literature.

Index

99~~5~~ yrs.

95 yrs.

Ground rent & maintenance.

700 pa.